SO-AWF-558

ADVENTURING
WITH CHILDREN

AN INSPIRATIONAL GUIDE TO
WORLD TRAVEL & THE OUTDOORS

While there is time,
let's go out and feel everything...
Steve Winwood, The Finer Things

ADVENTURING WITH CHILDREN

AN INSPIRATIONAL GUIDE TO WORLD TRAVEL & THE OUTDOORS

by Nan Jeffrey

AVALON HOUSE
PUBLISHING
family • *adventure* • *travel*

distributed to the book trade by
Menasha Ridge Press

Avalon House Publishing
All text and photographs are copyright © 1990, 1992, 1996 by Nan
Jeffrey unless otherwise noted.

All rights are reserved. No part of this book may be transmitted in any
form by any means without permission in writing from the publisher.

Travel and outdoor recreation entails an element of risk. The author,
publisher and distributor of this work assume no liability for personal
injury or loss from using information contained in this book.

Printed in the United States Of America
10 9 8 7 6 5 4 3 2

Jeffrey, Nan, 1949—
        Adventuring with children: an inspirational guide to world
        travel and the outdoors / Nan Jeffrey
            p. cm.
        ISBN 0-9627562-4-5 (pbk.)
        1. Family travel
        2. Outdoor recreation—camping, hiking, bicycling, sailing,
            canoeing.
        910.202—dc20   LC 94-074025

distributed by:
Menasha Ridge Press
700 South 28th Street, Suite 206
Birmingham, AL 35233 USA
Orders: 1-800-247-9437
Fax: 1-205-326-1012

specialty orders & editorial requests:
Avalon House, c/o HFCO
P.O. Box 126
Ashland, MA 01721 USA
Tel: 1-508-881-4602
Fax: 1-508-881-3846

Contents

Acknowledgments

We would like to thank everyone who made this third edition of *Adventuring With Children* possible, including the thousands of families striving for an independent life-style and the many wonderful people we have met on our travels. We extend a special thanks to Cannondale, LaFuma and Merrell for their help with outdoor gear, and to Mike Jones, Katie Whychok and the staff at Menasha Ridge Press for their support.

Author's Note

In an attempt to simplify matters, and at the risk of seeming biased, we always refer to one child as "he" in this book. As parents of boys and a girl ourselves, the choice was simply a matter of convenience and is not intended to imply that boys are more adept at adventuring than girls.

Prologue

Qualifying Adventure

We were traveling deck class on the ferry from Crete to Rhodes when we met another family adventuring with children. Like us, they were executing a series of lingering steps across the southern Greek Isles to the coast of Turkey. Our two sons and their two daughters, ranging in age from six to ten, immediately struck up the quick friendship of traveling children and set off to explore the extensive craft. Settling amidst the backpacking youths and Greeks scattered across the deck, we parents rushed headlong into the rapid exchange of thoughts and ideas and personal anecdotes that so characterizes friendships made while traveling.

They were from Washington D.C., we were from Massachusetts, both of us dedicated to periodic departures from our more accepted ways of life. Sitting together on the windswept deck as the ferry labored towards distant Rhodes, we spoke a common language—that of homeschooling and one-burner meals, of family cohesion and a sense of achievement, of sleeping in strange places and absorbing alien cultures, of raising our children in a neighborhood that encompassed the world. It was the language of an adventuring family.

Months later, long after we returned home, people continued to ask questions about our travels, most of them simple, basic probes into the mechanics of adventuring with children. How did we decide where to go? What clothes did we take? Where did we sleep? What did we eat? Were the children ever bored or sick or lonely or afraid? The questions came with such frequency, genuine interest and a hint of longing that we recognized the need to show just how possible it really is for a family to go adventuring.

How does one qualify adventure? One person's adventure might be another person's nightmare, for that which constitutes "an adventure" is as personalized and intangible as that which triggers moments of joy or flashes of fear. Some defining factors can be isolated. Adventure forces you to confront situations outside the established, secure, familiar structure of your life. For us, family adventure is a combination of two things, outdoor activities and travel. Travel takes you away from your familiar surroundings while outdoor activities challenge you and give you an exposure to an area unattainable from more conventional means of travel. The length of time you travel, where you go, or how physically demanding the outdoor activity is are unimportant provided you as a family feel challenged. By demanding much of you, an adventure generates feelings of sheer pleasure and aware-ness and a new sense of your ability to survive and excel and rise above. It develops not only yourselves as a family, but your understanding of the rest of the world. Ultimately, it is a reward-ing, enriching experience.

A child is never too young to start adventuring.

More importantly, it doesn't take long to grasp that family adventuring is much more than taking a highly stimulating trip. It's time apart, a chance to discover and reflect, to explore and grow. Pursued on one's own terms and level of expertise, it brings together a host of desirable qualities, activities and behavioral patterns missing from modern life. Regardless of destination or mode of travel, the benefits of this temporary life-style are many: living simply, becoming self-sufficient, experiencing new cultures and ideas, challenging your mind and body, being in harmony with the natural world, learning to have patience and tolerance and be content, and developing an unassailable *joie de vivre*. Best of all it fosters an interdependence within the family, one that encompasses all ages as you work towards a common goal.

Successful family adventuring has more to do with the success of the family itself than with being well-versed in the mechanics of travel. While the mechanics supply the basic vehicle to making a trip work, a cohesive family is both the prime tool and the final result of any successful adventure. Taking an occasional trip is not only fun and exciting, but highly therapeutic as well, for it encourages a quality of existence sustained long after the trip is over.

Bicycling through Morocco, realizing you are doing something you never thought you would.

Travel helps clarify what is meaningful in life , focusing our view of the world and our proper place in it. For families, adventure travel offers the opportunity to break with convention and develop an inner strength at odds with today's social trends. Freed from the constraints of peer pressure and jobs, daily routines and social pressures, children and parents alike can follow their own instincts, developing a personal and joint fortitude.

Although adventure can begin in your own back yard, for the purposes of this book we have defined weekend outdoor activities and travel as part of the training period. While these can be initially adventurous, their intent is to prepare you for longer trips that take you farther afield.

Adventuring With Children is an outdoor guide for travelers and a travel guide for outdoor enthusiasts. While it's not possible within the scope of this book to cover all the potentially adventurous places in the world or all the challenging ways a family can experience them, we have chosen from among the most popular outdoor activities and suggested a number of destinations both within and beyond North America appropriate for family adventure travel. All levels of family adventuring have been included, thus allowing each family to naturally gravitate to its own level of competence. Because a family's view of what constitutes an adventure will continually change with time, the book has provided a format for continuing up the adventure ladder. When our twin sons were only six months old, camping in Florida was the most adventurous thing we could conceive of. Yet twelve years later, after gradually increasing our family's scope, bicycling in Guatemala and Costa Rica seemed a natural thing to do.

Adventure travel is best suited to families, for a family traveling modestly and under its own steam receives the warmest welcome around the world. Even if you have never contemplated foreign travel, *Adventuring With Children* outlines for you the basics in adventurous outdoor activities and shows what it would be like to travel in this style to other cultures. Beginning with the first stage of making the initial decision, the book shows you that any family can make a success of adventure. Family adventuring should not be missed. The experience will last a lifetime.

PART I

LAYING THE GROUNDWORK

Children make friends easily around the world.

Chapter

1

Preparation For Adventure

Kevin and I have been adventuring with our children for many years, yet each new time still involves the same series of preparatory steps: making the decision to undertake a certain type of adventure, assessing our needs and abilities, and laying some groundwork in appropriate expertise. No matter how experienced we become or how ambitious our trips, each time we return to these three basic issues that lie at the core of all adventure preparation.

This type of travel is different from other types of activities. The more intimately you experience a place, the more adventurous it becomes. Touring Nova Scotia by car is a trip. Traveling by bicycle or canoe is an adventure. Booking into an hotel in London is conventional travel. Camping in Marrakesh is adventure travel. This level of intimacy also means that you will be experiencing many things out of the ordinary and coping with a number of unknowns in your day to day living, things that can be quickly adapted to, given proper preparation.

An adventure should be fun and exciting for the whole family. Even unpleasant things take on an aura of excitement, making almost anything that happens a lively experience. The key to enjoying your trip is to a large degree dependent on how prepared you are before you even leave. There are a number of areas of acquired knowledge, expertise, and attitude common to all forms of adventure travel. Even if you don't initially use them they will stand you in good stead on other, more ambitious trips. An adventurer gradually acquires the ability to cope with a wider and wider range of situations, thus increasing his self-reliance and degree of self-sufficiency. A family does the same. In a world where success is often equated with the accumulation of material wealth, adventure travel presents a whole new criteria for achievement, one that originates at home even before the trip begins.

Making The Decision

If you've picked up this book, the chances are you want to go on an adventure with your children. As we all know, wanting and doing something are two separate things. Nothing causes more doubt, anxiety, and stress than deciding to go. The trip itself is easy in comparison to the mental confusion experienced by many first-time travelers. Making the decision to go traveling together as a family is a matter of having faith—in the success of your trip, in your children's capabilities, in the wisdom of your chosen destination and type of adventure. Like any major decision, whether it's choosing a mate, buying a house, accepting a job or having children, once the commitment is made, the fun begins.

One of the hardest things to deal with when getting up the resolution to go is the often negative reaction of well-meaning friends and relatives. People who may once have blithely waved you off for trekking in Nepal or biking through France will suddenly react with horror at the mention of children accompanying you on such a trip. The more exotic the trip, the more ominous will become the warnings. Others will assure you the trip will be much more enjoyable without the children. As one acquaintance informed us, "There are two kinds of vacations; the one you take with your kids and the one you enjoy". That's become a favorite quote in our family and the brunt of many a joke as we have yet, in sixteen years of parenting, to take a vacation without ours.

Children Are Natural Adventurers

The ultimate irony is that children, the cause of all this indecision and mental agony, are the most underestimated asset to adventure travel. Children are inherently adventurous, adaptable, open-minded, enthusiastic and energetic. Given the opportunity, most children will exhibit an aptitude for adventure that surpasses your own. The younger the child, the easier the transition from home to travel. Recognizing your children's needs, tapping their resources, and tailoring your trip to their capabilities will contribute much towards a successful family adventure.

In addition to their innate strengths, children are of immeasurable value when it comes to foreign travel. For someone who has never experienced a foreign culture, the prospect can be a daunting one. While conventional travel insulates you from foreign cultures, adventure travel subjects you to them. Some countries are poor and entrenched in a deeply rooted cultural background that affects all aspects of their life-style, making them sometimes seem strange, uncomfortable, and even fearful.

Adventuring brings families together.

The presence of children will do much towards bridging the cultural gap, for children represent the ultimate peace offering the world over. Most of the world dotes on their young and will welcome yours with open arms. Your children will elicit a hospitality and generate a warmth denied most tourists, resulting in a more meaningful, enjoyable experience.

Teenagers

Older teenagers need some special consideration of their own, for unlike younger children, the parental groundwork has already been laid and their pattern of behavior within the family established. Basically, teenagers can make or break a family adventure. They can be the most enthusiastic or the most disdainful, the most helpful or the most disruptive. There should be no element of surprise here, only an honest assessment of the situation. If your teenager is excited, eager and interested at the prospect of a family adventure, you have nothing to worry about. If not, then leave him behind or postpone your plans for another year. Unenthusiastic teenagers do not become overnight converts just because you remove them from the influences of home.

If your family is a close-knit one, teenagers will delight in adventure travel, seeing it as the ultimate escape from the social confines that they unconsciously rebel against. It's hard to complain or feel frustrated or resentful when everyone is doing something exciting and challenging. Adventure travel is ideally suited to the needs of teenagers, to satisfying their desire to have a focus and acquire a more adult role in life. No longer little children, they want to lead rather than follow. A family adventure provides all the opportunity in the world for teenagers to develop a sense of self-worth and pride within, instead of outside of, the family unit. Before long you'll find them eagerly building fires, carrying canoes, planning routes, and livening up your trip with a dose of teenage *joie de vivre*.

Children are the world's best ambassadors.

Assessing Your Needs And Abilities

You've made the decision to go, now it's time to assess your needs and abilities before choosing an appropriate trip. First, any number of questions should be asked. Does your family enjoy outdoor, adventure-type activities like hiking, camping or bicycling? Is one parent more experienced or enthusiastic or committed than the other? How physically fit is your family? Have you ever worn a backpack, cooked on a campstove, or slept in a tent? Does a certain country or part of the world or outdoor activity appeal to you more than another? If you have teenagers, are they independent and eager to travel? If your children are young, are they imaginative, do they play well together, are they used to exercise? If you have a baby, have you ever carried it in a backpack or used cloth diapers?

Learning Together

If no one in your family has ever traveled, hiked, backpacked, camped, or done anything of an adventuresome nature, all is not lost. It's never too late to introduce a family to adventure travel and acquiring the necessary skills to set off the first time can be an enjoyable family activity. In some ways this is the easiest situation. With each member of the family as green as the next, there's no one to pontificate, lose patience, and give orders. More than one potential adventure has met its demise when the husband, an experienced adventurer, began barking commands and generally cowing his novice wife. Learning together allows the whole family to maintain an equilibrium of expertise. If one member of the family does have previous experience, it's important that he or she recognize the others' inexperience for what it is—just inexperience, not inability.

While certainly not always true, we have found throughout our travels that more often than not the man is the avid adventurer and the woman a tentative participant. As a woman myself, I have often asked myself why so many women are reluctant to undertake an adventure. The reason seems to be a combination of basic needs, upbringing, and role playing. Women, I have found, are usually more fearful, security-conscious, domesticated, and sensitive to physical discomfort than men. As children, females are rarely taught the practical skills needed to inspire a sense of independence and self-sufficiency. Traditional female roles, such as cooking, cleaning, home-making, and child rearing, have historically had little place or value in adventure. Items such as camping equipment, outdoor clothing, eighteen-speed bicycles, and boat interiors were all originally developed primarily for men. It's only recently that women's physical and inherent differences have been given consideration.

Women often perceive adventure as an extension of the "weekend-trip" nightmare. How many wives have slaved all day to shop, plan meals, pack food, clothing and essentials, organize children, and attend to home needs, only to have the husband return from work, throw a few belongings into a bag, announce it's time to leave, and ask incredulously why she still isn't ready?

Adventuring with children offers women with little or no previous experience a nice introduction to adventure travel. Aspects of travel that are of minimum importance when traveling alone, concerns that cause many women to balk at the idea of adventure travel, become major issues when children are included: regular meals, decent nutrition, cleanliness, acceptable sleeping quarters, sufficient sleep, a relaxed travel pace, a sense of security. The presence of children can act as an anchor, linking you to those qualities of homelife that you value without inhibiting your exposure to adventure. With children your home, in a sense, goes with you.

Family Adventuring Skills

One important area of assessment is determining what aspects of adventuring your family needs to become familiar with. A number of skills apply to many types of family adventure. By familiarizing your family with them through a training period you can give yourself a head start in ease of travel.

The following is a list of skills fundamental to most forms of family adventure:

—Living together in small areas (tent, boat, camper, hotel room, etc.)

—Reducing your needs to the size of a backpack, tent, canoe, car, etc.

—Carrying your belongings in a backpack

—Walking good distances

—Handwashing laundry

—Cooking on a one or two burner stove

—Fixing things by hand

—Knowing basic first aid skills

—Speaking one or more foreign languages

—Entertaining yourselves away from television, toys, friends, and so on

These are basic challenges to the uninitiated that, given practice, can become accepted ways of life. All can play a large part in a family adventure, be practiced prior to departure, and become permanently integrated into your life-style. Even an adventure that involves minimal mobility, such as renting in a foreign country, will draw on a number of those skills. When we lived in a village in Greece, for instance, I cooked on a two-burner hot plate and washed laundry in the bidet. Our apartment on the island of Madeira, a comparative luxury abode complete with washing machine and hot water heater, presented a challenge of a different sort. In this case the adventure lay in getting the things to work.

Some of the skills require a certain level of physical fitness. The more physically fit you are the easier it will be. This applies equally to children as well as parents and is another area that can be improved on prior to departure. Physical fitness will evolve naturally through the labor-intensive life-style generated by most adventuring, but a number of initial aches and pains can be avoided through proper preparation.

The ages of your children will play a part in determining what types of skills each member of the family will need. Infants, while undemanding and adaptable, will need to be carried, diapered, and fed. Young children beyond the backpack age are capable of more physical output than most people realize provided they have acquired sufficient training at a pace they can enjoy. Children of all ages will need the ability to entertain themselves and play well together. Teenagers should develop all the necessary adult skills.

Depending on the type of adventure that appeals to you, certain skills will be needed more than others. Camping through Mexico would require a different set of criteria from bicycling around Prince Edward Island. Any family adventure, however, will benefit from a basic preparation of the skills and inner resources that are inherent in adventuring of all kinds.

By now you should have a grasp of what areas your family can work at before embarking on an adventure. As you train, not only will abilities develop and improve, but the family as a whole will enjoy working together towards a common goal. This is the first step on the way to successful family adventuring, a cohesive family unit with a shared sense of commitment.

The Training Period

Pre-adventure training not only lays a secure groundwork for future travels, but can become an adventure in itself. Some skills can be acquired right in your backyard, others practised on short ventures away from home. Whatever method you choose, training should be kept fun and exciting.

Throughout the training period a few perspectives should be kept in mind. Training, while enjoyable, is never as thrilling as the real adventure. Washing laundry in a bucket in your backyard can not compare with doing it alongside native women in a mountain stream. The simplest meals will taste ambrosial in a foreign setting or after a long hike. Don't lose faith if certain things seem tedious at this point. Within the context of an adventure the most mundane act can generate a memorable occasion.

With children, the training period is a means of defining ability and generating enthusiasm. Children already possess a formidable amount of energy, a love of the outdoors, and an immunity to physical discomfort, all tremendous assets on any adventure. What they don't have is an appreciation for the benefits of exercise or character-building tests of endurance. These will come naturally, so don't defuse your children's interest by concentrating on activities that are deliberately difficult. As a child's perspective is generally a reflection of his parents', his response to adventuring will correspond with yours. If you are excited and enthusiastic, he or she will be too.

Adventuring With An Infant

This requires some parental practice, much of which can be done at home. Get used to carrying your baby in some sort of backpack. Walk to town with him, wear him while you grocery shop or cook dinner or work. Wean yourself from a carriage, if that's what you're used to. Change his diapers on the floor, in the yard, at the mall. Learn to use cloth diapers, bathe a baby in a bucket or dishpan or sink, and breast-feed with a discretion that will keep everyone guessing. Sleep him in the living room surrounded by noise. Take him to a restaurant or movie theater or friend's party. This will teach you to cope in different surroundings and the baby to accept them. Infants used to sleeping in noisy, well-lit areas will do so happily. Worn on a parent's back or bedded down in a familiar blanket, a baby will accept any surroundings with equanimity.

Living In Small Spaces

Learning to live together in small spaces can be a challenging aspect of adventure travel to many families, accustomed as we often are to spacious accommodations. Today's homes are frequently designed with buffer zones to separate adults from children and siblings from each other. They encourage lack of both communication and tolerance between family members and the accumulation of material things. Adventuring does the opposite. During an adventure, living space and material possessions are reduced to a level that promotes qualities within a family often neglected by our modern life-style—not only communication and tolerance, but adaptability, ingenuity, self-sufficiency and conservation.

Camping

The easiest way to practice living with reduced space and possessions is to go camping. If you've never camped before, don't worry about the children. They'll love it. They even love it in the back yard. Pick a place to camp that holds some interest for you. Campgrounds are intimate places and sometimes hard to tolerate in an era when camping is equated more with RVs than tents. To help avoid the television-radio-motorbike crowd, pick a campground with a separate area for tents or no electric hook-ups. If it pours rain or some other equally untimely misfortune occurs, feel free to pack up and leave. That's what you'd do on an adventure if at all possible, so don't feel obligated to stick it out while training. Adventures have a way of raising the level of adrenaline at opportune moments, like athletes who perform way above average during competition. When it happens you'll find the whole family actually enjoying moments of discomfort, recognizing them as part of the challenge. The training period, however, is like a runner doing his daily laps. Keep the pace relaxed and comfortable and the family will come back for more.

There are other ways to familiarize the family with small spaces besides camping in one or two tents. Even if you've never sailed, but know someone willing to lend a boat, spend a few days just living on it without going anywhere. Try renting a small cabin or camping with a modest vehicle like a Volkswagon camper. All these offer more amenities than tenting, so the transition is an easier one while still familiarizing you with a reduced life-style.

Daily Jobs

A second area of training is in daily jobs; cooking, dishwashing, laundry, shopping, bathing, etc. Although parents with previous adventuring experience will already be familiar with these tasks, with children they can take on a whole new dimension. Cooking dinner for two on a one-burner stove with two small pots is not the same as producing a similar meal for a family with three hungry children. Children also get themselves and their clothes dirty faster, increasing the need for an efficient method of cleaning and bathing. Imagine life with no washing machine, dishwasher, oven, or hot running water. Think of producing meals with one bowl/cup/spoon per person, three pots, and a one-burner stove. What would it be like with only a few changes of clothes, a sleeping bag, and what fits into a back-pack? Now you are at the level that an adventuring family might be required to function at. This isn't to say you won't be able to find laundromats, sources of hot showers, more versatile cooking facilities, or beds with sheets, but on some adventures you can't depend on them.

If you've traveled before without children, you probably already have some system for dealing with these jobs on a lesser scale. If not, start practising until you find what works best for you. Try producing some meals for the family using just one burner and three cooking pots. Heat water on the stove for faces, dishes, laundry, and sponge baths. This may sound incredibly silly or simple, but it will always prove useful. In Chapter Three we give suggestions for methods that have worked well for us in dealing with these daily chores.

Notice how much food and essentials your family uses over a period of time. At home you're probably accustomed to a full refrigerator, food cupboard, and medicine cabinet. If you run out of something it's easy to hop in the car and go buy some more. Finding you miscalculated your supply of toothpaste or sugar while on a mountain trail, the high seas, or in some remote corner of the world will not be so easily remedied. Although many types of adventure don't require stockpiling essentials, others do, making it valuable information for future travels.

Improving Fitness

Improving the family's level of fitness, if necessary, should be done gradually and on a daily basis. Unless you're planning to hike the entire Appalachian Trail or canoe down the Mackenzie River, training can be an exercise in labor-intensive living rather than running laps or jumping rope. Most types of adventuring require that you periodically carry your home; on your back, in your boat, on your bicycle, in your car. Food and water might need to be fetched by hand, tents raised and lowered, sails handled, anchors hauled, stairs climbed, and streets, paths, and trails walked. Whenever possible, walk or bicycle instead of drive and rely on your hands instead of a machine to do a job. Encourage the children to participate as much as possible. Little ones usually want to do everything the parents are doing and older children will enjoy things like bicycling to school or carrying their own backpack. Fortunately, children need less training in this area than parents, provided they're used to performing some chores at home. The nature of children's play enables all but the most sedentary child to be physically fit. More important will be training them to rely on themselves and each other for entertainment.

Keeping Children Entertained

A mother told me one day that family adventure travel sounded like a great idea, but what she really needed was a book that told her what to do with the children once they were on a trip. Her concern was a valid one. It's all very well for me to say that adventuring is stimulating to children and entertainment a minor concern, but what of the child who has rarely experienced time alone or with siblings, whose environment up until now has been a far cry from that of adventure travel? This is one area where the training period is critical. Children accustomed to television, video games, a wealth of toys, and a neighborhood playgroup should experience time without them prior to an adventure.

Nowadays, siblings and children of different ages are often not expected to get along or play together, an attitude that traveling children can not afford. Give your children an opportunity to interact together without entertainment devices and discover what activities they prefer: playing games, reading, writing, drawing, make-believe, building, etc. Adapt the attitude that traveling with children needn't mean a re-enactment of a visit to Disney World. Given the opportunity, most children will exploit their vast imaginative powers and make do with anything at hand. For some specific ideas and tips on teaching your children to entertain themselves, see "Imaginative Play" in Chapter Thirteen.

Other Types Of Training

Other skills that can be learned at home include maintenance and repair, languages, and first aid. If one or more members of the family already has a background or aptitude in one of these areas, so much the better. There's nothing more reassuring than crossing an ocean with a doctor or nurse on board the boat, or traveling

Prepare your family well during the training period and you'll be surprised at what you can accomplish.

through Europe with a fluent linguist. Kevin happens to have good mechanical skills, which makes equipment crises infrequent and short-lived in our travels. Anyone, however, should know how to make simple repairs, do basic first aid, and have some knowledge of a language other than English. Children have a way of subjecting equipment to a fair amount of abuse, making repair a common occurrence. Be prepared to do things like patch shoes, mend clothes, repair a tent, fix a broken zipper, mend a backpack, or doctor a bicycle. Some knowledge of first aid is useful everywhere and imperative in remote circumstances like wilderness hiking, ocean sailing, and traveling to rural areas. Medical concerns, including training, common childhood complaints, and a first aid kit, will be dealt with in detail in Chapter Seven.

Outside English-speaking nations, the ability to speak another language will improve your chances of communicating with the local inhabitants. Except for tourist areas, English is often not understood and school children can be your best bet for finding a common language. The most widely used second languages, other than English, are French, Spanish, and German. A number of home courses are available that teach you the rudiments of a language in a short time. Our favorite is the Audio-Forum course designed to teach people in the diplomatic corps the language of the country they will be based in. The emphasis is on living in the country rather than learning phrases most relevant to tourists.

Training is a gradual process that should continue even as you choose and prepare for a specific adventure. Once the adventure and destination are selected, relevant areas of expertise will become evident that might warrant more training. On a boat you'll need to understand sailing, on a bicycle, bike repair. Remote areas will require more knowledge of first aid and an awareness of what necessities to take. Certain countries might require a particular language or an ability to cook with unfamiliar foods. While the learning and preparing process never really stops, acquiring some of the basic skills long before you leave will greatly ease your transition from living at home to a family adventure.

Making The Break

Once you've allayed your anxieties about taking the children along, fended off the pessimism of family and friends, and assessed your needs and abilities, you're ready to consider the practical angle. How can you find the time to travel, or the resources to pay for it? What about jobs and obligations back home, bills unpaid, and the demands of daily life? The one, two, or three week vacation is practically a cultural institution—longer breaks seem an impossibility, something to do while you're young, before parenting and career responsibilities tie you down.

Adventure travel knows no limitations. A week can be just as adventurous as a month, a month as rewarding as a year. The biggest role time will play is in how far you go and how much you can do. Flying halfway around the world for a week's trip is hardly practical, just as a month spent in a place will offer more scope than a few weeks. For the short term trip, it's best to plan modestly and limit travel time. The shorter the trip, the more important it becomes to chose somewhere you know you will like. Inclement weather also plays a greater role on short trips when a spell of rain can be a disaster to a planned holiday in the sun or when doing outdoor activities. We met one couple in Madeira who came for the hiking, spent a frustrated week of inactivity due to rain, and went home disappointed. On our two month visit, one bad week seemed hardly an imposition, allowing us to explore other areas of island life. Pick destinations with a high percentage of good weather, then still go prepared for the occasional bad day. Many international airlines give bargain rates for trips under three weeks, eliminating some of the main travel cost and making the short term trip as affordable as a long one.

Taking Time Off

Time and time again we hear the comment, "How can I take time off work?" Mired in career demands, they see little opportunity for long term travel. Sailing families are the first that spring to mind when contemplating long-term travel. The oceans, anchorages and foreign ports are filled with them, families that sold their homes to sail around the world, or took a one or two year leave of absence to go cruising. The most prevalent of adventuring families, they discovered long ago that schools, jobs, money and possessions can all be accommodated to permit an extended cruise. Secure in numbers, sailing families have no trouble convincing themselves that a year or more of travel is feasible, affordable, and even socially acceptable.

Land-based travelers have the disadvantage of being fewer in number, more individualized, and less a community effort. With the whole world to travel in a variety of ways, they find it hard to create the sense of camaraderie that strengthens the sailing scene. In addition, land-based adventure travel has traditionally been the dominion of the young and unwed, the backpacking crowd whose needs and desires bear little resemblance to those of a traveling family. The same society that tolerates the wanderings of youth looks askance at the adult who turns his back on a career, hauls the kids out of school, puts the house up for rent, and goes adventuring, yet why shouldn't he, or she, or the whole family? Given a moment of honesty, all those disapproving voices would own up to a burst of jealousy, a resentment that someone else was doing what they secretly longed to do.

If you want to go, you can. Given the proper determination, ways can be found to overcome most hurdles. The first is the job. Many families have the money for a trip, but only a two or three week vacation. Those with two working parents have the further complication of trying to synchronize time off. It's important that you treat your projected trip as a *fait accompli*, an unquestionable fact. Nothing paves the way to success faster than a positive attitude. Almost everyone recognizes the value of travel. Employers who have reacted negatively to tentative overtures of a projected trip might react favorably when told about it with confidence. Most will eventually see it as a character-building experience, something that will benefit the company when you return. Even if a trip means relinquishing a job or position, don't hesitate. It's amazing how fascinating you suddenly become to people, including prospective employers, after doing something adventurous. We know one government employee who actually travels every third year with his family for the entire year, returning each time to his same job. Yet the first time he left, he was told not to come back. Most two and three week vacations are also simply limited by a pay scale factor. Longer time off is possible, although without pay. No one is telling you you can't travel, just don't expect to draw a salary while you're away. It's amazing how few people contemplate taking time off without pay, yet this is one easy solution to the occasional long-term trip. Self-employed parents have the advantage of being their own bosses. The issue here is usually more one of money than time, for time off is up to their own discretion.

Affording The Trip

The nice thing about adventure travel is that it costs less than conventional travel. As my mother once remarked when seeing us off on one of our trips, the four of us were taking less money for three months in Europe than she and my father were taking for three weeks. The difference: they were staying in hotels, eating out, shopping and going skiing. We were backpacking, camping, hiking, and living like locals.

Even families with good resources, however, might feel the pinch when it comes to a long trip. How, they wonder, can they juggle trip costs on top of mortgage payments and car costs, insurance bills and savings plans? What it comes down to is priorities. Few families lack the financial resources to afford a trip. Too often, people in affluent countries have lost their perspective between what they actually need to live, and what they think they need. A comfortable life-style is possible with a lot less money than most people spend. Affording a family adventure means doing with less at home in order to save for a trip. Most salaries allow plenty of room for a savings plan. What might look like a small savings at the moment will all add up to an impressive travel fund, especially considering how far your money will go in many foreign countries. Even the most stringent budget plans will seem worthwhile when rewarded with adventure travel. We spent years living without owning things most Westerners take for granted (a house, second car, furniture, electronic equipment) in order to finance our travels, yet none of us has ever regretted it.

House and Home

If you own a house, consider renting it for six months or a year while you travel. If you live in a seasonably desirable spot, so much the better. Places by the seashore or in ski country can command high prices, as can many urban areas. Leave it in the hands of a Realtor so you don't have to deal with things like breakdowns or tardy rental payments on your trip. Although renting does have its drawbacks (people never seem to treat other people's possessions as carefully as their own), it will cover your home costs and probably contribute to the travel fund as well. Sailing families frequently do this, if they don't sell the home all together to buy a boat. Few families can carry the cost of both.

Work Opportunities

Long-term travel often presents opportunities for work that can supplement the travel kitty. Farm work is frequently available, especially in Europe. A few weeks spent working on a farm in Norway or a vineyard in France can be a fascinating experience for the whole family. Contact the various tourist boards to find out what's available. Other opportunities include temporary jobs in the medical field and teaching English to foreign students. Professional jobs like these are only practical if you plan to stay in one place for a while. We know one family that travels the world on a series of two-year teaching stints.

As mentioned earlier, taking work with you is sometimes practical, aided by the abundance of fax machines and computers that dominate the work force these days. Nearly all our long trips have involved some type of work, from designing houses and writing books, to installing solar systems and selling energy equipment. Although long-term cruising families, those who live aboard their boats, have found work opportunities abroad quite lucrative, it's best not to rely on them to finance your tip. Treat money earned while traveling more as a bonus than a necessity.

Travel Costs

When estimating how much a trip will cost, consider that your transportation will be your biggest expense, particularly getting to your destination. Beyond that, as a general rule of thumb your daily living costs will be the same as at home, although how you travel and where you stay will determine how much you pay. While car travel within North America is reasonable and the preferred choice, outside North America it is usually expensive. Much of the world outside North America depends on public transportation, which is wide-spread and relatively inexpensive. Accommodations vary from country to country and can range from luxurious to basic. As most families are budget-oriented, inexpensive travel is the preferred option and inherent to adventure travel. Traveling by foot, bicycle, boat or public transportation and either camping, renting, or staying in inexpensive lodgings, a family should rarely exceed their daily costs at home. A few areas like Scandinavia and Switzerland have the reputation for being expensive. They are compared to the rest of the world. But everywhere has its compensations. In Norway, for instance, you can camp anywhere for free. With bicycles and camping gear, a family could see the country on a shoe-string.

For more information on how to cut costs, see "Family Budget Travel Tips" in Chapter Fifteen.

The decision to go adventuring as a family is ultimately one of mind over matter. By accepting the premise that you can and will go, nothing should stop you. Any experienced adventurer will assure you that once away from home you will discover how easy it is to live in unknown surroundings. As parents who have traveled frequently with children since they were six months old, we can only add that there are always places to sleep, food to buy, things for your children to do, and ways to communicate. Having taken the plunge and embarked on a family adventure, you will soon look back and wonder what all the fuss was about.

Family adventuring is more obtainable than most people think. What the issue often comes down to is priorities; priorities of travel versus material things; of time off work versus money earned; of the experience gained versus things bought. Nothing and no one is stopping you other than yourself. Not family or friends, school or job, money or materials. Only motivation. If you want to take an adventurous trip with your family, you can.

Chapter
2
What To Take

The question I am asked most frequently by other mothers is what I take for the children on our family adventures. Nothing seems to perplex them more than the logistics of reducing their children's belongings to the mere contents of a child's backpack.

There's a popular maxim among travelers that after you have packed, take half of it out again and leave it behind. The theory is a valid one, particularly with adventure travel. There are no porters shuffling along behind you or taxis waiting at the door. Adventure isn't camping with your television or your microwave. It's meeting the world on its own terms, not yours.

What to take on a family adventure is determined by a number of things: what type of trip you plan, your destination, the ages of your children, the climate, the length of your trip, whether you will be traveling during the school year, your mode of transportation. This chapter deals with some of the common rules of thumb that govern all types of adventuring and helps determine what you should take when traveling with children.

Reduced Needs

It doesn't take much experience to discover how little your family needs to get by in life, and get by happily. Our ancestors once lived this way and much of the world still does. One of the lessons learned through adventure travel is that too much of something can be inhibiting, both towards your actions and your personal development. This concept of living with reduced needs is alien to modern trends. It refutes the popular conviction that increased wealth is synonymous with self-improvement.

Adventure travel will teach you to appreciate things more—your own abilities, your few possessions, your home when you return to it. The few toys you bring along for each child will be cherished more than a playroom full. Each new book will seem like a library's worth. A warm item of clothing on a cold day will be more welcome than a closet full of clothes. In the reduced life-style of adventure travel, nothing is taken for granted because there's nothing to replace it.

Children respond naturally to reduced needs. Given the choice, they would probably wear the same outfit every day. They're not fussy about where they sleep and rarely care about variety in meals. To them, fewer things mean less chores, a welcome situation in any child's opinion.

For parents the reduced needs means less work as well. At home I find there's always a sink full of dishes, laundry to be washed, a house to keep clean, and toys scattered everywhere. Yet none of us are better fed, better clothed, cleaner, or more enter-tained than while we are traveling. This reduction in household chores refutes the prevailing attitude that family adventuring must be a lot of work.

Keeping Mobile

Keeping mobile goes hand-in-hand with reduced needs, for the one determines the other. As travel implies mobility, keeping your possessions to a comfortable minimum is going to make life easier for you. No matter what type of adventure you have planned, ease of movement will enhance your trip.

With children the emphasis on ease of mobility is even more important. Children enjoy movement provided they don't associ-ate it with work. While a child will happily wear a backpack for hours, try getting him to carry a suitcase for a minute. If moving

Carrying everything in one load is the goal when packing for an adventure.

around involves a lot of tedious work, you're going to find the children in a state of rebellion halfway through your trip. Work to a child isn't an exciting activity like hiking or bicycling or setting up tents, but those boring jobs they associate with life at home.

Keeping children mobile doesn't have to mean traveling in a car. Granted, it's easy to heave everything in a vehicle when it's time to take off. But with a little planning and practice, packing up a backpack or a set of bicycle panniers can be just as simple. Because we all have a tendency to fill something to capacity, the smaller the load carrier the less there is to deal with.

With a baby, mobility will increase your enjoyment. Babies are really the easiest children to travel with because they can go anywhere in a backpack. Pushing a carriage or carrying a baby in your arms can be too restricting for this type of travel.

While deciding what to take, keep in mind this quest for mobility. Imagine catching a train or boarding a crowded bus or walking four kilometers to the nearest campground. Imagine shopping at a village market or sight-seeing or island hopping. Now imagine doing it with children. It's not what we do as a family that ties so many of us down, but how we do it. What we eat, where we sleep, what we wear, how we entertain ourselves can range from the very simple to the extremely complex. Children are not what slow us down, it's how we deal with them that does. Try to view life from a child's perspective and you'll discover that unhampered mobility is second nature to children.

Equipment

When faced with a household of possessions, it's hard to know what to take on your first family adventure. Subsequent trips will be simple because nearly all types of adventure travel require the same basic equipment, but that initial decision-making process can be overwhelming at first glance. A number of necessities immediately jump to mind. A family always needs clothing, food, first aid equipment, rain gear, reading material, a few toys, toiletries, laundry fixings. Added to that is the equipment necessary for specific types of adventures: sailing gear for a boat, camping gear, bicycle equipment, school or learning materials for long term trips, and so on. The list seems to grow alarmingly until you wonder how you will ever manage to fit it all in.

Basic Equipment List

No matter how long or short an adventure is, the basic equipment requirements stay the same. We've carried the same gear on a five-week trip to Newfoundland as on a five month trip through Greece and Turkey. The following list covers general recommended equipment for a family of four traveling with backpacks and is relevant for children of all ages and trips of any length or duration. Specific items pertinent to particular activities or remote destinations will be discussed in later chapters.

- camping gear
- cooking gear
- clothing
- 2 bath towels
- camera w/film
- notebooks, pens, pencils
- small clock and/or watch
- flashlight

- 1 hand towel
- 1 washcloth
- shampoo
- liquid handsoap
- tooth brushes & paste
- hairbrush and comb
- hair scissors
- laundry detergent
- clothespins & line
- toilet paper (2 rolls)
- 4 pillowcases
- 2 mopping-up cloths
- baggies (a few)

- first aid kit
- sewing kit
- Swiss army knife
- 4 water flasks
- paperback books
- safety pins
- drawing paper
- colored pencils
- stuffed animals
- plastic food containers
- picnic food
- small toys
- 1-2 net shopping bags

With a boat or vehicle you could expand the list as much as you felt comfortable with. Taking more, we have discovered, usually takes the form of more clothes, more books, more food, a larger tent, etc., as opposed to taking other types of equipment.

Daypacks

Bringing along one or two daypacks is always a good idea on any type of adventure. Whether you are traveling by car, boat, public transportation, bicycle, on foot, or even staying in one place, you'll have times you want to leave your belongings behind while your family goes on an outing. With a daypack or two you not only have room to carry your most important belongings with you, things like passports, traveler's checks, or a camera, but also those items that always seem to be in demand on an outing with children. Children are notorious for wanting something at the most inopportune moment—a drink when you're miles from water, a warmer shirt halfway up a mountain, a book in the middle of a bus ride, a snack when there's not a shop in sight. Daypacks are also useful for shopping at open-air markets in foreign countries. The type with straps on the bottom are the most efficient load-carriers. Bulky clothes can be rolled up and strapped underneath.

Children enjoy taking responsibility for their own things.

Extras

Toiletries for a family of four is mostly a matter of personal preference. We limit ourselves to toothbrushes, toothpaste, dental floss, fluoride pills, shampoo, and a razor with blades. I always carry extra supplies to eliminate the need to find more on our travels. Anywhere tourists frequent, however, will have all the usual necessities. The one exception is sunscreen. For some reason it's been difficult to find a good sunscreen rated #15 or higher outside the United States.

Small, plastic food containers are useful on any type of trip for carrying picnic foods like peanut butter, tunafish, jam, nuts and raisins, etc. On camping, hiking, or bicycling trips they're an absolute necessity.

For a sewing kit, make up your own or buy one of those small travel ones with a variety of threads, needles, pins, and a pair of small scissors. With so few clothes, some state of disrepair is inevitable. Include a spool of heavy-duty thread to cope with possible repairs to items like tents, sleeping bags, backpacks, or panniers. Net shopping bags are indispensable for shopping trips and for hanging food out of reach of animals and insects.

Clothes

Children of all ages require approximately the same clothing for any type of adventure. Faced with the amount of clothes your children run through in a week at home, you might wonder how you will cope on an adventure. The general maxim for everyday clothes is to take two of each item; two shorts, two long pants, two T-shirts, etc. This gives the child one to wear while the other is dirty, wet, or being laundered. Take enough underwear to last a week; enough socks to survive the usual wet feet scenarios; one of each other item of specialty clothing.

Children's Clothing List

All the children's clothing listed below was chosen with any type of adventure and destination in mind. It covers all items carried by us on adventures that ranged from backpacking to bicycling, from travel in North America to travel in North Africa, from trips that lasted three weeks to ones that lasted five months.

- 2 long pants
- 2 shorts
- 2 T-shirts
- 2 long-sleeved shirts
- 1 skirt or dress (for girls)
- 1 pajamas
- 1 sweatshirt with hood
- 1 woolen vest

- 1 rain jacket with hood
- 1 pair of gloves
- 8 pairs of underwear
- 4 pairs of socks
- 1 bathing suit
- 1 pair of sneakers
- 1 pair of sandals
- 1 pair of cotton tights

Try to choose clothes that combine well and serve a number of purposes. A button-down flannel shirt, for instance, can be worn over a turtleneck to create a sweater effect. With the addition of a T-shirt and windbreaker, it adds up to the equivalent of a heavy jacket. Cotton tights worn under long pants are a lightweight way to add warmth to an outfit. A hooded sweatshirt eliminates the need for a hat. Choose dark colors that hide the dirt, an obvious advantage with so few clothes. You're not going to feel like laundering a pair of pants or shirt every time your child plays in the dirt. Make sure you take items your child likes to wear. There's nothing sillier than going off on an adventure with two shirts and discovering your child hates one and always wears the other. Do the same for yourself. With only a few clothes you want to enjoy wearing all of them.

In tropical climates, choose clothes that are all cotton for comfort. These allow your body to "breathe" through the material. In cold or wet climates, wool is naturally water repellent and almost impervious to dirt.

For long pants, avoid blue jeans if possible, particularly if you know you will be hand-washing clothes. Jeans are bulky to pack, horrendous to hand-wash, and take forever to dry. The one exception is overalls like Osh-Kosh. These tend to be a softer material, comfortable for children when exercising and don't show up superficial dirt. With the help of the bib front, they also keep children looking neat and clean longer. Sweatpants should be included on any trip. They're comfortable, easy to wash, quick to dry, and popular with children.

Footgear can be limited to sneakers or trail shoes and sandals unless you plan some serious hiking. Sandals are useful on any

A sunhat and some lightweight cotton clothing is all little children need in a hot climate.

A warm pair of sweatpants and a good rain jacket are two indispensables for children.

trip, even ones to cool climates. Not only do they provide a lightweight change of footgear, but they are easy for children to take on and off when getting in or out of a tent, boat, or vehicle.

Entertainment

Keeping your children entertained is of minimal importance on a family adventure. The trip itself, the outdoor environment, the areas you visit will all provide ample entertainment. The growing emphasis on toys and other forms of child entertainment is the product of a confined, urban, affluent life-style. The less scope there is for outdoor, imaginative play, the more important become the supplementary tools for keeping a child entertained. The adventuring child uses the environment around him to create his own play things.

A few well-chosen items are always useful on any trip for those times when outdoor activities are curtailed or as a supplement to your child's usual play. Pick toys that are lightweight, versatile and imaginative. On a rainy day confined to a vehicle, tent, boat, or room, you're going to want something that won't bore your children in half an hour. Some sort of creative materials are a nice addition, plus one or two games for older children. When traveling to foreign countries, the presence of a few toys or a soccer ball to play with will do much towards breaking the ice between the local children and your own.

Suggested Toys

The following is a list of toys helpful on trips with children. With the exception of the soccer ball, all fit easily in a backpack. Most of them have been used by us in the course of our travels. We've found Legos to be the most versatile, creative toy invented and very appealing to local children as well as our own. Matchbox cars and small plastic figures are wonderful for playing in a pile of dirt, during a picnic break, or on a bus ride. Creative materials keep the children endlessly entertained on rainy days and have provided the decorations for a number of special events and holidays.

- Legos (Duplos for toddlers)
- Fisher Price "little people" sets (come with a farm, schoolhouse, etc.)
- soccer ball
- drawing paper, colored pencils
- scissors, scotch tape
- paper dolls
- dollhouse items
- matchbox cars
- stuffed animals
- playing cards
- small ball

The soccer ball was included on a lengthy trip of ours to Europe because of its popularity in that part of the world. Every time it put in an appearance, children would appear from all corners of the village or campground. Tristan and Colin played in one international game featuring children from five different countries, all speaking a different language. As a social ice-breaker, the only thing that proved as effective was the collection of Legos we carried.

Books

Books fall under a category of their own, for books are not only entertaining, but educational as well. Travel provides a wonderful opportunity to develop your children's reading skills. Divorced from the predominance of toys, television, and entertainment features that prevail in most homes, the adventuring child becomes the child that reads. Even toddlers will derive many hours of pleasure from looking at books or being read aloud to. A book can provide valuable entertainment at inactive times—on a long bus ride, waiting for a train, early in the morning, just before bed. Our children love to read at meal times and always have a book tucked into their packs on daily outings for reading at lunch break.

In addition, children derive much of their imaginative play from the books they read or have read to them. For some suggested authors and titles that lend themselves well to the adventuring child, refer to Chapter 11.

Finding English children's books is next to impossible in foreign-speaking countries, a situation we have coped with in a number of ways. Try to carry as many paperbacks as is reasonably

A couple of toys, some collected treasures and a good imagination will keep a child happily playing for hours.

possible. While toys can be fashioned from almost anything, books are impossible to reproduce and should take precedence when choosing what to take. If the trip is to be a long one, consider having someone send you a package of new books along your route. Trading with other English-speaking children met along the way is always a possibility. Ours made a welcome swap with a South African boy they befriended while we were all camped in Portugal. Check local bookstores for books intended for foreign students learning English. When desperation set in one year in Greece, we bought our children simplified versions of English classics used as text books.

In the absence of new material, your children will simply re-read what they have, so choose the books carefully. Young children will enjoy the "easy-to-read" books available in paperback form. Older children will average about five books on a three week trip. For teenagers who are voracious readers, include some classics by authors such as Robert Louis Stevenson, Louisa May Alcott or Charles Dickens, books destined to last many hours of reading.

PART II
OUTDOOR ACTIVITIES

Chapter

3

Camping

O ver the years we have camped in a variety of settings—the wilderness areas of Newfoundland, the moors of England, the Greek islands, the coast of Turkey, the mountains of Costa Rica. Accommodations varied widely, as did the size of the campgrounds, the company we kept and the cultures around us. Yet each place we camped, many of which we lingered at for days, weeks, or even a month, quickly became a home for our children, allowing us to adventure together as a family without stress.

The Advantages

Children of all ages usually love to camp, welcoming the freedom of the outdoors and the informality of life-style. The more basic the mode of camping, the more children like it. To a child camping means sleeping in a tent and eating outdoors. It conjures up visions of campfires at night and all of nature for a playground. Children who normally balk at the slightest household chore leap into action on a camping trip.

Camping can be incorporated into most family adventures, providing an enjoyable, affordable, adventurous means of accommodation. No skills are more frequently drawn upon or useful to an adventuring family than camping skills. If you've never camped together as a family, this is something that can be practised prior to your first real trip. Nearly everywhere in North

America has a campground in the vicinity, making it easy to gain some experience before venturing farther from home.

Even if you don't intend to camp all the time, carrying the necessary gear provides you with an added element of independence. With camping equipment you always have a place to stay, even if it's only a deserted field or someone's back yard. Places that might normally be prohibitive to budget minded families become affordable when camping.

As with everything else associated with adventuring, it's best to keep camping simple. Camping is possible in anything from small tents to large, well-equipped vehicles. It's worth remember-

A cold morning, a warm fire and breakfast: the simple pleasures of family camping.

ing that camping was originally designed as a means of enjoying the great outdoors with minimum human impact on the environment. Something all adventuring families share is an appreciation for nature and its fragile state. Camping in a simple, uncluttered way will not only increase your children's enjoyment, but help preserve the essence of camping as a gesture of goodwill towards the natural world around us.

Equipment

Basic camping gear is the same for any type of adventure and should always be combined with the equipment listed in Chapter Two. The amount has been kept to a minimum for the purposes of mobility. All the listed gear can be carried by a family traveling with backpacks, bicycles, canoe or car. The amounts are intended for a family of four with two small children and were used by us on trips of varying lengths, to a variety of destinations and carried either in backpacks or on bicycles. Children can be regarded as good load carriers by age six provided they are outfitted with a decent pack. Weight should be kept to about 20 pounds until they are older. A number of appropriate frame packs are covered in Chapter Four.

List of basic camping gear:

- 1-2 tents
- 4 sleeping bags
- 4 pads
- 1 3-pot cook set
- 1 camp stove
- 2 fuel containers
- 1 collapsible water jug
- 4 water flasks (1 qt each)
- 4 bowls
- 4 mugs
- 4 spoons/forks
- 1 blunt knife
- 1 sharp knife

- 1 spatula
- 1 hot mat
- 1 wooden spoon
- 1 dishbrush/rubber gloves
- dishsoap/dishrag
- 1 cutting board
- 1 carrot/potato peeler
- 1 can opener
- plastic food containers
- 4 linen napkins
- baggies w/ twisties
- 2 candle lanterns/candles
- basic cooking ingredients

Tents

A variety of lightweight tent options are available. We've tried the half-dome design and modified A-frame and find both are easy to pitch and roomy. The modified A-frame, such as the Eureka Alpine Meadows, has a center hoop that pulls the sides outward. The hoop gives much more interior room than a standard A-frame by eliminating sidewall sag. The modified A-frame is probably the easiest to set up, especially with the new clip-on connector systems, while the half-dome variety tends to keep its shape better in a wind. I highly recommend that you choose a tent that allows for the use of a vestibule, a lightweight, waterproof attachment that creates a protected area just outside the tent. This area is perfect for storing gear and taking off jackets and shoes in inclement weather.

With children you have a choice of all sharing one tent or having a separate one for adults. One deciding factor might be weight. Two lightweight, two-man half-dome tents weigh about 15 pounds, whereas one lightweight, four-man modified A-frame type is only 10-11 pounds, a significant difference if backpacking or bicycling. Although two tents gives you an obvious degree of privacy from each other, using one tent is convenient in rainy or cold weather or with small children you might want to keep an eye on. We shared a tent with our nine year old sons on a three month bicycle trip and found the arrangement worked fine. On the other hand, on a previous five-month trip to more tropical climates we enjoyed the privacy and spaciousness of two smaller backpacking tents. With one tent children simply learn to go to sleep with a lantern on or activity around them. By the time children are teenagers and able to carry their own tent, having more than one makes sense. If you are making a lengthy trip by vehicle, you might consider a tent large enough to stand up in, particularly when traveling somewhere with cold or rainy weather.

Campstoves

Campstoves come in the same wide variety as tents. The type that burns white gas is the most popular in North America where this type of stove fuel is widely available and usually sold at or near campgrounds. Outside the United States, Canada, and Australia, white gas is almost impossible to find. Most European countries use propane (or butane) campstoves fueled with small disposable cannisters. These are also available in North America, but only at specialty stores and for a fairly steep price compared to white gas. Other types of stoves run on kerosene, unleaded gasoline, alcohol, or some combination of these. Beyond North

When choosing a tent, pick one that's lightweight, easy to raise and well ventilated.

America and Europe, fuel sources become erratic and varied. We've found ourselves stranded a number of times with just the wrong type of stove. We took our white gas stove to Greece and had to buy a propane one instead. Then in Turkey we found they only used larger propane campstoves with bigger fuel tanks, often available for rent. Next we went to Madeira, confidently took our propane stove, and still couldn't find the proper fuel anywhere.

For world travel, a good solution to the campstove dilemma is a multifuel stove that burns kerosene in addition to white gas and unleaded gasoline. Kerosene can be found almost anywhere in the world. There are several good ones on the market, including the PEAK 1 *Apex*, the MSR *XGK-II*, and the MSR *Whisperlite Internationale.*. White gas burns the cleanest and most efficiently. Kerosene also works well, although a special kerosene fuel jet is usually required and the burner should be preheated with alcohol or burning paste when lighting. Gasoline clogs the stove more easily and tends to blacken the bottoms of pots, but it does work.

Although propane/butane type stoves are easier to light (no priming needed), the PEAK 1 and MSR stoves we use put out a formidable amount of heat and cook food quickly, always a nice bonus when trying to feed a ravenous family. In addition to the stove, carry two pint-size fuel containers. This will provide enough fuel to last about five to seven days of cooking.

Cook Sets

Most lightweight cooksets come with a small- and medium-size pot and a frying pan/lid. By adding another 6-quart pot and lid and a small tea kettle, you have a versatile set that's easy to carry and can cope with cooking for a family of four to six. I highly recommend the tea kettle if you don't want hot drinks tasting like last night's dinner. Stainless steel is healthier to use than aluminum due to the leaching of metals into the food.

Paper Products

Nearly all paper products can be eliminated from a camping trip. Not only is this more ecologically sound, but it cuts down on

Cooking gear for a family of four, easily carried in backpacks or bicycle panniers.

bulk as well. One dish towel, a hand towel, a couple of dish rags and one cloth napkin per person can take the place of any amount of paper towel and napkins. We always carry one or two old cloth diapers on any hike, trip, picnic, airplane ride or whatever for cleaning up spills, mopping up children and standing in for tissues. Only toilet paper is worth carrying on a regular basis for coping with those untimely childhood emergencies and rescuing you in areas of the world where toilet paper in public bathrooms is not standard issue.

Lighting

In addition to simple candle lanterns, which work well under most conditions, there are several alternatives to supplying lighting on a camping trip. Many flashlights are now available with efficient bulbs that produce high light levels and increase battery life. When used with built-in solar cells or rechargeable batteries that are powered by a lightweight solar charger you can have a continual supply of electricity from the sun. Another lightweight alternative is a small lantern that runs on propane. The disadvantages of this type of lantern are that it can't be used inside a tent and the propane cannisters are usually not recyclable.

Cooking

Cooking for a family on a camping trip can be a liberating experience for the cook. Anything that materializes out of those three pots is going to be treated like manna from heaven. The adventuring family, constantly outdoors and physically active, is among the least discriminating and most appreciative of diners.

Basic Ingredients To Carry

When cooking on a camping trip, a few basic foods will need to be carried at all times, preferably in small plastic containers. The following is a list of suggested provisions, most of which can be bought throughout the world.

- butter
- cooking oil
- mayonnaise
- vinegar
- jam
- sugar

- tea
- coffee
- Ovaltine (hot chocolate)
- bouillon
- peanut butter (if available)
- herbs and spices

Cooking Techniques & Suggestions

To cut down on cooking time and save fuel, organize what you plan to cook ahead of time. That way the stove can be lit once and things cooked in rapid succession, a definite fuel-saver and an advantage with stoves that require priming. One way to speed the cooking process and keep one pot from monopolizing the stove is to allow things to steam off the burner. When cooking rice, for instance, allow the rice to cook on the stove until the water is down below the level of the rice. Then press the lid on tightly, leave on the stove for about 10 seconds of high heat and remove. Do not lift the lid. Left to its own devices while you prepare the rest of the meal, the rice will continue to cook and soak up all the water. Fifteen minutes later, it will be perfect and ready to serve. This is also a good way to avoid burning foods, an easy thing to do on a one-burner stove where the heat is hard to regulate and concentrated in one small area of the pot. Vegetables and soups can be cooked this way as well.

All my campstove meals rely on this off-the-stove steaming process. Making a curry, for instance, I first get everything ready with tea water in the small pot, vegetables in the medium pot and rice water in the large one. Tea water goes on first, then rice, then another round of tea, then the vegetables, then dishwashing water while the rice and vegetables finish steaming.

A breakfast of hot cereal can be done quickly with the same juggling act. By removing it from the stove you also lessen the chances of scorching it, particularly when cooking the cereal in milk. This is a good way to improve both flavor and nutritional value. If your children aren't hot cereal fans you might find they like it more cooked this way. They will also enjoy adding things like nuts, fresh fruit or dried fruit. While the selection of cold cereals seems to diminish the further one gets from North America, hot cereals are available all over the world, making this a practical, low-cost, high-energy meal for families traveling abroad.

When cooking with a small campstove, it helps to deviate from the traditional meat-potato-vegetable type of meal with everything served separately on a plate. There's a reason stir-fries evolved in China and curries in India. Combining foods together with a variety of seasonings is the easiest, most practical, most efficient way to produce meals with limited facilities. Once, while staying on the island of Rhodes, I was cooking up one of our standard evening creations in the courtyard of our pension. A young Australian couple we'd met a number of times on our Greek island travels asked what it was that I managed to cook up night after night.

"We never know what to cook," they lamented, "yet every night your dinner always smells so good." Their mistake was trying to reproduce the typical meat-oriented meals they normally served at home where they had a variety of ingredients and an entire kitchen at their disposal. In contrast, those meals I cooked that "smelled so good" were the height of simplicity.

The trick to cooking on a campstove is to plan the meal around the carbohydrate, adding small amounts of meat, seafood, eggs, beans or cheese where needed to boost nutritional value and lend flavor. That's how most of the world eats and with good reason. It's quick, easy, inexpensive and interesting, welcome characteristics when feeding an active, hungry family. Most of my meals are based on rice or noodles in a variety of ethnic guises—curry spices for Indian, soy and ginger root for Chinese, soy and chilies for Indonesian, garlic, basil, oregano and parmesan for Italian.

If your children are the kind that shudder at the mere mention of garlic or pepper, leave the seasonings out when cooking and just add at the table. While not quite as tasty for spicy food lovers, this certainly beats trying to force feed your children an exotic dish. On the other hand, you may find your children become more daring gourmets on a camping trip, willing to try anything the parents are eating. All of our children became convinced at an early age that anything we grown-ups were eating had to be

Encourage your children to participate. Even simple jobs will make them feel useful.

something special. Our daughter Gwyneth rejected baby food altogether, preferring to sample the fare her older brothers were enjoying.

Dishwashing

Another liberating aspect of family camping is in the dishwashing department. With so few dishes and cooking utensils, there simply isn't much to wash. Nevertheless, a first encounter with washing-up, bereft of a kitchen sink, hot running water and a dishwasher, might cause a momentary setback in your camping enthusiasm. The following tips should prove helpful in setting up a system for yourself.

—Rinse all dishes first: under a pump or spigot, in a pot of cold water or at a sink. North American campgrounds usually have water spigots at various locations among the sites. Overseas campgrounds often have washing-up areas with sinks and drain boards, very convenient for rinsing dishes.

—Heat a small pot of water to boiling for washing dishes. The temperature of the water is more important than the quantity. Cooler water (comfortable to bare hands) will not sterilize and clean dishes as well. Wear rubber gloves to cope with hot water.

—For dish soap, try Dr. Bronner's, Lifetree, Campsuds, or other biodegradable, non-toxic, concentrated washing liquid that requires no rinsing of dishes after washing. Add a few drops to hot water. Don't expect it to make soap bubbles. For greasy dishes, apply full strength directly to the item. These soaps are available at outdoor equipment outfitters and natural food stores.

—Wash dishes in ascending order of cleanliness: mugs first, then cutlery, bowls, and finally cooking pots. This keeps the water clean the longest.

—Dry dishes with a dishtowel. Dry cooking pots with a sponge or dishrag. These are good jobs for children.

Refrigeration

Some means of refrigeration is only possible on a camping trip if you travel with your own vehicle. Otherwise, you'll have to make due with none, a situation that isn't nearly as bad as it sounds. Only a few foods actually need to be refrigerated for short term storage. Butter, cheese, eggs, yoghurt, mayonnaise and fresh produce all keep fine unrefrigerated. Milk, bought in the evening, will keep until morning if nights are cool. Whole milk lasts better than low-fat. Fish will last for a day if fresh and left in a cool place, but meat should be eaten shortly after purchase if left unrefrigerated. With small cooking pots, leftovers are rarely a problem. If you have some, incorporate them into the next day's menu.

Buying foods for immediate consumption is rarely a problem when camping unless you're in a wilderness area. Campgrounds are usually located near a town or come equipped with a small market right on the premises where you can buy fresh foods.

In areas where people habitually live without refrigeration, alternatives are available. Both powdered and "long-life" milk are sold all over the world, particularly in warm climates. Unlike the powdered milk sold in North America, this is a top-quality, whole milk product sold in tins and marketed throughout the developing world. When reconstituted, it tastes very much like the fresh product, close enough to please any child. Long-life milk is sterilized fresh milk sold in pint or quart size cartons. Long-life cream is also available. Campground stores usually carry fresh milk as well, packaged in everything from the familiar cartons of North America to small plastic bags (a real challenge when it comes to opening and pouring them). Yoghurt is a popular item in hot countries due to its lasting quality. Unrefrigerated, it lasts quite a long time and is usually sold that way in areas like North Africa and the Middle East. Fruit juices, when available, are also sold unrefrigerated and in small cartons.

In a pinch, you can probably find a source of refrigeration if you suddenly find yourself with a hunk of meat in 80 degree temperatures with hours to go until dinner. Ask a fellow camper with an RV, or at the campground store. We bought some meat at an open-air market in Morocco one morning before remembering we had no means of refrigerating it until evening. The campground store owner came to the rescue by popping it into his cooler for the day.

Laundry

Laundry is best dealt with on a frequent basis, a probable necessity anyway with so few clothes. If you're traveling in the United States or Canada, the chances are you'll have access to a washing machine when needed, sometimes even at the campground itself. Use the machine for washing, but skip the dryer and hang dry instead if the weather is good. This saves tremendously on time, money and wear and tear on your clothes. Outside North America the chances of finding a washing machine diminish, thus increasing the need for an efficient, non-strenuous system for dealing with laundry. One has only to see women from any number of countries bent over streams beside piles of laundry to realize how time-consuming this task can be.

Handwashing laundry. The kind of facilities you find in campgrounds abroad.

Handwashing

Washing clothes by hand is never going to be fun, but it can be made fairly painless. I've learned not to let laundry accumulate more than three days. With young children it's probably best to wash every other day if possible. Morning is the best time when energy level is high and the whole day is ahead for drying things on a line. Laundry can be done either in a sink, bucket or plastic tub, depending on what's available. In countries where washing machines are not prevalent, campgrounds usually come equipped with deep stone laundry sinks with built-in washboards. If you're traveling by car, bring along your own bucket or tub. Otherwise, you'll have to skip the pre-soak stage if monopolizing a sink is inappropriate. If pre-soaking, leave laundry in warm, soapy water overnight (when possible).

Laundry detergent can be bought almost anywhere. Tide must have a monopoly on the world detergent market for even the most remote, understocked, hole-in-the-wall shops out in the middle of nowhere have boxes and boxes of it. Besides detergent and possibly a bucket, you will want a stiff brush, the kind you can envision some 18th Century scullery maid scrubbing the floor with. Nothing gets clothes cleaner or saves more on wear and tear to your hands.

Wringing out the laundry is the most tedious part. Children can help with small items like underwear and linen napkins. If you were smart and didn't bring any blue jeans, congratulate yourself. Otherwise, you will now know why you shouldn't have.

Clothes dry much faster on a clothesline than draped over items like bicycles, tent poles or car doors. With about eight clothes pins you should be able to hang a full laundry, or approximately fifteen items. Overlap edges of clothes to double up on pins, then hang small items like underwear or socks from each pin. Underwear can also be looped over the line and through itself. If the laundry isn't dry by night, hang it from a line inside the tent. Most clothes will finish drying this way by morning. This inside clothesline also comes in handy if you're caught in rainy weather and desperately need some clean clothes.

When A Laundry Crisis Strikes

Even with the best preparation, an adventure with children is bound to give rise to some unexpected crisis that will put your laundry system to the test. While camped in Spain on a bicycle trip, our sons suffered a momentary lapse of control and wet their beds during a thunderstorm. By morning I found myself in a tent with two sopping sleeping bags while it poured rain outside. Fortunately, this particular campground had the most elegant, hi-tech bathroom facilities we've yet to see anywhere, complete with wall-to-wall mirrors, banks of sinks, rows of hot shower stalls, domed skylights, piped-in soft rock music and no one in sight. With the assistance of four sinks for washing, two shower stalls for drying and some skylight generated heat, the sleeping bags were clean and dry by evening.

At times like this, it always seems as though you just happen to be in the right place at the right time. More than likely, the truth is that on an adventure, your ingenuity develops to a point where you are never at a loss to know what to do next. This is one of the joys gained through adventuring—knowing that you have the ability to cope with whatever fate throws in your way.

Bathing

Children, as every parent knows, have a tendency to get dirty. Puddles hold a fatal attraction for them, as does dirt, sand, mud and water in general, all of which renders them into a state of filth at fairly regular intervals. Depending on the age of your children and how and where you travel, a number of bathing techniques can be put into practise.

Most campgrounds come equipped with showers. In developed countries like the United States and Canada, this means hot showers and an easy source of bathing. One exception are the National Forest and Provincial campgrounds, most of which have only the most basic of facilities. Beyond North America the availability of hot showers varies from country to country. If your children abhor cold showers, try leaving your water jug filled and

When camping in a hot climate, bathing from a water spigot can be the easiest way to keep children clean.

in the sun for the day. The water will be just the right temperature for bathing by late afternoon. If you have the room, carry a sun shower, a popular item with boating people and available at boat supply stores or through catalogs. These can heat up to five gallons of water in a relatively short amount of time.

If there's a clean, natural source of water around, use it. The ocean, a lake or a stream can all be used for bathing. If your children are swimming regularly, bathing won't be necessary other than the occasional hair wash. Most shampoos work well in salt water. It's helpful to rinse off salt water with some fresh at the end of the day to prevent salt from getting on clothes or sleeping bags. Use the water jug or sun shower, if you have one.

Children have a lot more tolerance for cold bathing if they are outdoors and having fun. Another way to avoid subjecting them to a cold shower (an experience that always elicits high pitched screams from ours), let them wash off and play under a water spigot in the campground. Give each child a plastic eating bowl and let them have a game of dousing each other with water.

Before you know it they will be thoroughly clean and hardly aware that the water was anything but warm.

When abroad, don't hesitate to strip your children naked for bathing. Attitudes towards nudity in children are usually very relaxed.

Camping Abroad

Camping abroad makes up for in congeniality what it sometimes lacks in aesthetics. Most campgrounds place their emphasis on inexpensive accommodations rather than natural surroundings. Space can be at a premium, not in terms of finding a spot, but in terms of how much of that spot is actually yours. Sites are rarely designated and space occupied on a first come, first serve basis. Just because you have parked yourself under a nice shade tree and staked your claim, so to speak, won't prevent someone else from arriving and stationing themselves inches from you under the same tree. The more popular the location and well-equipped the campground, the more crowded it will be. Sunny, coastal locations are the most crowded and have recently spawned a new breed of "camper", the seasonal resident who uses his permanently booked site as a second home. Here's some helpful hints for camping abroad:

Going Off-Season

The best way to enjoy camping abroad is to do it off-season. Small, intimate campgrounds that would probably be a nightmare when filled are much more enjoyable when shared with a reasonable number of people. We stayed in one lovely, wooded campground beside the ocean in Portugal that we shared with ten other campers. In season it boasts five thousand sites, all filled to capacity.

Meeting People

What overseas campgrounds lack in privacy and aesthetics, they make up for in social interaction, one of the main pleasures of

In some parts of the world travel with children is easier by camper. This Swiss family adventured throughout North Africa in a camper they outfitted themselves.

camping abroad. Nowhere is it easier to meet people. As no one is there to commune with nature or retreat into privacy, friendliness between campers is the norm. Your children will find it easy to meet others and find playmates in such close quarters.

Campground Facilities

Campground facilities are somewhat different from those in North America. For a start, there are usually no picnic tables. Although we haven't by any means camped everywhere, we have yet to find tables outside North America. Foreign campers bring their own folding table and chairs. If you are traveling by vehicle, do the same. Otherwise, to avoid wallowing in dirt (especially in hot climates where campgrounds with grass are almost non-existent), bring something to spread on the ground. We like to carry four lightweight, woven mats, the kind that are popular at the beach. Many countries sell them at beach resort areas. Spread on the ground in front of your tent, they offer a nice, clean area for seating, playing, eating, or cooking.

Having a tent of their own gives children a measure of privacy. The beach mat in front supplies a clean place to sit and play.

As mentioned earlier, laundry facilities usually come in the form of basins for handwashing. There are often two areas, one for washing laundry and another for washing dishes. Showers range from cold to hot, the latter for a fee. When available, hot showers can be an adventure in themselves. Some have women guarding the door and dispensing towels. Others are dependent on the sun or someone firing up a stove to get them hot. Some have machines that might or might not work or require tickets purchased at the office. "Hot" can range from boiling to tepid and water pressure is anyone's guess. This, of course, is all part of the fun.

Campgrounds almost always come equipped with small convenience stores and often a cafe as well. Nothing reflects the congenial atmosphere of this type of camping more than the presence of a cafe. This provides the campground with a social focal point and lends a nice touch of luxury to an otherwise basic life-style. For parents traveling with children, some relaxing moments at the cafe offer a beneficial respite from parenting.

In exotic locations, a campground can provide an oasis from feeling like you are always on display. In some countries this might be the one place women can comfortably wear a bikini or children play without drawing a crowd. Where cultures are wildly different between tourist and inhabitant, the interests of the visitor are firmly protected within the campgrounds. In areas where theft is a problem, guardians are the norm.

For low-cost travel to foreign destinations, camping is the best choice for families. Less confining than a rented room, more sociable, and usually amply equipped, camping offers an adventurous way to see the world with children.

Pitfalls To Avoid

Overpacking—Take less than you think you need. Camping should be different from life at home.

Too much travel—Avoid repeated long hours on the road where campgrounds are just a place to spend the night. Nothing creates boredom faster in children.

Overambitious cooking—Keep meals simple. Everything is going to taste good. Reserve fancy menus for celebrations or treats.

Defusing your children's enthusiasm—Let them participate in everything, even if it means more work for you: pitching tents, building fires, preparing meals, hanging laundry. Camping can be a wonderful education for children, both in skills and character development.

Taking the wrong equipment—avoid the wrong equipment for the wrong climate or terrain: sleeping bags that are too hot or not warm enough, tents without an annex in wet climates, sneakers for hiking in the mountains or hiking boots for easy walks.

No place to play—bring along a table, a mat, some chairs, whatever you need to provide a clean space just for children.

Chapter
4
Hiking & Backpacking

When our twins were eight years old we spent two months exploring the Portuguese island of Madeira on foot. Already well versed in family hiking, Tristan and Colin were undaunted by the four, five and six hour hikes over occasionally precipitous terrain that typifies hiking on this island. In their opinion, exploring the countryside on foot was infinitely preferable to exploring it by car, a form of travel both children will go great lengths to avoid. Our choice of Madeira for a family hiking adventure couldn't have been more fortuitous: spectacular mountain and ocean scenery, exotic flowers, hillside villages and an abundance of trails alongside the traditional levada, an irrigation system that extends over 1,500 miles throughout the island. With each trail flanked by a rushing stream of water, the children were provided with an endless source of entertainment. Aided by stick "boats", the miles flew by as each child launched his in the levada and rushed off down the path in hot pursuit. If there had ever been any doubts in our minds about the hiking capabilities of young children, this trip would have dispelled them.

The Advantages

Children make ideal hikers. Always energetic and possessed of a love of the outdoors, children quickly develop an interest in hiking if it's made fun. As a family on an adventure, hiking brings you into intimate contact with an area in a way and at a pace that children can enjoy. The physical activity, outdoor focus and unlimited opportunities to stop, linger and explore are all more attune to children's needs and interests than travel experienced from the confines of a car.

More places in the world have the potential for enjoyable, safe family hiking than for any other outdoor activity. Hiking can be done in so many ways: on a mountain trail, a donkey path, a country road, a coastal footpath. By choosing to hike when traveling to a foreign country, you will endear yourself to the locals and see and experience things far beyond the resort facade presented to most tourists. In Madeira, instead of hotels and shops and crowded streets, we saw families working in fields of sugarcane and bananas, women washing clothes in streams and children carrying home bundles of wicker. Sharing the paths with us were shepherds and wicker workers, school children and grocery shoppers. The footpaths of the world are often an integral part of the country and hiking them will be more than just an energetic, outdoor way to experience a place. Whether you are exploring the wonders of nature or experiencing a foreign culture, hiking offers you an inside view that the whole family can enjoy.

Children's Capabilities

Infants & Toddlers

No child is too young to enjoy hiking. Although hiking potential varies according to age and to some extent from child to child, don't underestimate your child's capabilities. Infants and toddlers can be carried in backpacks. Take along enough food and diapers and your child will ride happily on your back all day. A good backpack makes the difference between an enjoyable hike with your baby and an exhausting one. Packs come in a variety of styles, from ones designed solely for infants to those capable of carrying an active four year old. For the serious hiking family, consider choosing a pack capable of handling a child up to five years. Although an older toddler will enjoy walking, the availability of periodic rides in a pack will make lengthy family hikes a viable option without anyone ending up miserable.

Older Children

By age 5, children can, with encouragement, put in a decent day's hike. By age 8 a child with hiking experience is capable of the same performance as an adult. Although a child can usually match an adult in terms of physical output (after all, think of all that running around and playing they usually do), uninterrupted hiking is alien to them. When playing, children frequently stop, even if only for five or ten minutes before jumping up to play again. This is a natural need for them and one you will have to incorporate to some extent while hiking if the children are to stay enthusiastic and energetic.

The Importance Of Food

One key to success is bringing along enough food to refuel your child at critical moments. Without sufficient food, a child's energy will drop rapidly. Pack more than you would for yourself. The amount they eat on a six or seven hour hike can be astounding. Include some special treat for later in the day when your

Children of all ages can enjoy hiking, from infancy to teenagers.

children begin to tire. It may be psychological, but children always seem to lose their energy and interest just short of a destination. A few pieces of chocolate or some other surprise treat can provide just the right lift to a child's energy level and morale to get them over that last half mile.

Be Prepared For Frequent Stops

The more children you have, the more stops there will be, for children rarely synchronize their needs. One way to minimize endless interruptions is to have each child carry his own daypack. Even little ones will derive a sense of self-importance from carrying their own pack. Include something special to eat, a drink, a book or toy for breaks, and room for all those treasures they love to accumulate along the way. Early introduction to wearing a pack will also prepare them for larger frame packs as they get older and are capable of more weight carrying on overnight hikes.

Equipment

Although hiking with children can be done with nothing more than everyday apparel, a few basic items can add to your pleasure and increase your scope. Depending on the ages of your children and type of hiking you intend, recommended equipment includes infant carriers, daypacks (for children and adults), hiking boots, framepacks and camping gear. For a complete list of child carriers, see Chapter Ten.

Footgear

Footgear is the first thing that springs to mind, as your feet are what will be doing the work. Most parents' initial reaction is a reluctance to spend much money outfitting their children in yet another pair of shoes, especially ones designed for only one activity. Footgear is the bane of many a growing child's parents. It doesn't take long with a sports oriented child before you find yourself spending quantities of money on items destined for your child's feet, all of which he will outgrow within the year.

Hiking boots aren't always necessary, nor need they cost much. Toddlers are best off wearing their everyday sneakers. Any hiking trail that is too strenuous or precipitous for regular shoes will probably find them riding in a backpack. By age 5 or 6 a child can switch to some sort of lightweight boot with a hiking tread and sufficient ankle support. Children's workboots, the inexpensive brown kind sold in many shoe stores, are ideal for this age. They're not too heavy and have an adequate non-skid sole. Most shoe stores carry at least one inexpensive model of children's hiking boot, any of which are fine provided your children are comfortable in them. I have worn these after discovering that boys' boots fit me just as comfortably as more expensive models.For more authentic hiking boots, check with your local outdoor outfitter.

Children's Daypacks

Daypacks for children come in all sizes, beginning with ones small enough for toddlers. Due to the popularity of daypacks as school bags, children's models are widely available at reasonable prices. You can usually find them at department stores, toy stores, and outdoor equipment outfitters. As children's daypacks come without any back support or waist belt, keep the weight in them to a minimum. If your children fill them up with heavy items collected along the route, that's their own choice. By age ten, a child can wear full-sized daypacks. These feature built-in waist belts and padded straps, making them better load carriers.

Framepacks

For overnight and longer hikes, a child about 6 years and up can carry his own framepack. The following packs are made especially for children:

 • **Camp Trails Skipper**: Easy to open main compartment with three exterior pockets. Fits children 4 feet, 9 inches to 5 feet, 6 inches. Six height adjustments.
 • **Jansport Shenandoah 2**: A versatile child's pack. Flexible frame. Two easy-to-open main compartments and five exterior ones. Adjustable shoulder straps and hip belt. Fits children from 4 feet to 5 feet, 4 inches tall. Largest carrying capacity.

- **Kelty Junior Tioga:** One large and two small compartments. Five position telescoping frame. Similar in construction to the adult Tioga pack.
- **Kelty Ridgeway Shasta:** Adjustable shoulder straps and belt. One main compartment. Fits from 4 to 5 feet tall.
- **REI Junior Cruiser:** One easy to close main compartment. Extendable top for larger loads as child grows. Two big exterior pockets. Well padded straps and belt. Fits children with torso length of 9 to 16 inches.

Other equipment for hikes of any length:

- water flasks (minimum one per person)
- warm clothing (sweatshirt, hat, long pants)
- first aid (band-aids, ace bandage, tweezers, first aid cream, sunscreen)
- Swiss army knife
- sunhats
- bathing suits/towel
- rain gear
- snack food
- a toy and/or book for each child.

Take along bathing suits if you will be hiking where there is water. If the hike leads to an exposed mountain top or will last until late in the day, remember that it will be colder and require more clothing than when you began. Temperatures are always cooler in higher altitudes, in some places ranging as much as a whole temperature zone. To avoid any risk of hypothermia, take warm clothing even when you can't imagine using it. Rain gear is also a good idea anywhere except obvious tropical climates where even rain fails to cool you off. Bring along a toy and/or book for each child to keep him happy on the bus or car ride home or while you unwind after the hike over a cup of coffee or cold drink at a cafe.

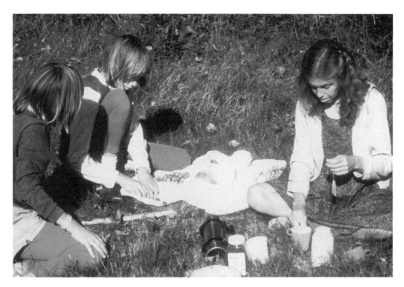

Bring plenty of food and water. A relaxing "tea time" is a nice way to end a hike.

Safety

When it comes to safety, your child will probably score higher than you. With their low center of gravity and innate fearlessness, experienced hiking children can safely navigate even difficult, vertiginous routes. I remember one ten-foot stretch of trail on the north coast of Madeira where the metal railing that was normally secured to the outer edge of the path suddenly disappeared. While my fertile adult imagination was busy conjuring up images of bodies strewn at the bottom of the ravine below, eight-year-old Tristan and Colin crossed the dubious stretch and stood looking back at me with pitying glances.

If a trail is very tricky, a young child can be roped between two adults or competent teenagers. We've seen this system used in the Alps where trails can negotiate steep, mountainous sections. While young children with hiking experience will still usually have no trouble, this eliminates any danger of slipping and falling.

Making It Fun

Making it fun, as always, ranks high on a list of parental concerns where children are involved. Like all forms of adventuring, hiking requires children and families to create their own forms of entertainment. Taking some things into consideration and employing a few tactics can quickly make hiking an activity children enjoy as much as any home-based entertainment devise.

Make-Believe

Young children rarely appreciate exercise for its own sake, seeing it merely as a vehicle for some game or sport. Allow for this difference in attitude and encourage imaginative games that work into the context of a hike. Transformed into pirates, elves, animals or orphans, children exhibit a capacity to hike forever. Many have been the hikes when Kevin and I have found ourselves accompanied by mountain goats, attacked by pirates, befriended by orphans or herding sheep. As we are also expected to converse with them, properly interpreting their multitude of bleats, baas and blood-curdling howls, hikes can take on an element of hilarity as well.

Choose Visually Stimulating Hikes

Children have short attention spans and are fascinated by changing areas of interest. The trails on Madeira, for instance, offers the optimum hiking conditions for children; domestic animals grazing in fields, men cutting wicker, women hoeing gardens, children gathering firewood, rushing streams, forests and glimpses of the sea. There are wild flowers to examine, waterfalls to pass, bridges to cross, and even here and there a tunnel to pick your way through. In comparison, a hike in the White Mountains of New Hampshire presents the same forest scene as you toil uphill towards an elusive mountain vista. Hikes like these require more ingenuity to keep your children motivated and entertained, disinterested as they usually are in the mere merit of an eventual "view".

Take Time To Converse With Your Children

Talk about anything—about nature, about the culture you're hiking through, about life in general. In the rush of everyday living many parents spend far too little time communicating with

Children are adept at finding fun things to do on a hike.

their children on a level beyond daily concerns. Hiking is a great time for discussions, for swapping ideas and expressing opinions. Pick any topic. "Let's talk about something" is a frequent request by our children on family hikes. "Something" might mean anything from the basics of nutrition to the origins of prejudice.

Story Telling Is A Favorite Activity

Try weaving a theme around wherever you are hiking. Tristan and Colin will never forget the story Kevin made up while we were hiking to the Curral das Freiras, a valley deep in the mountains of Madeira where nuns once hid from marauding pirates. As you can imagine, the scope for a good, action-packed story, the kind eight year old boys lust after, was immense. Kevin had no trouble that day keeping the pace going as both children scampered along, eager to hear every word.

Other Helpful Hints

Begin with easy hikes, gradually working up to longer, more difficult expeditions. This will allow your children to develop both their physical skills and their ability to entertain themselves. Don't rush them, but also don't underestimate them. Allow them time for breaks, games and diversions. By cultivating an aura of hiking as a joint family undertaking with everyone equally involved, making it fun and entertaining will evolve naturally. Putting a hiking stick in your child's hand and promising a notch for every completed hike (double notches for extra hard ones) will go a long way towards sustaining interest. Take a break beside a stream or pond if you come to one. No matter what age, children are drawn to water and will wade or paddle around in even the coldest mountain pool as long as you'll let them. If you're traveling during the school year and doing homeschooling, try incorporating mental arithmetic, spelling, science studies or geography questions while hiking. Children perform better mentally when they can be physically active and will surprise you with their quick response and interest in educational exercises of this type when hiking.

Backpacking

An overnight backpacking trip is always exciting for children. There's no sense of having to hike back again at the day's end or concern for what happens tomorrow. As the outdoors is a child's natural environment, the prospect of staying out all night is always alluring.

Children's Backpacking List

Children big enough for a framepack should carry no more than 20% of their bodyweight. Have them carry their own possessions, a guaranteed way of generating more enthusiasm in their role as load carriers. Include some lightweight camping items. The following is a sample of what a child might carry on an overnight backpacking trip:

- 1 sleeping bag
- 1 sleeping pad
- 1 plastic bowl/mug/spoon
- 1 water flask (qt. size)
- 1 sleepy friend
- 1-2 small toys
- 1 paperback book
- 1 pocketknife
- 1 handtowel

- 1 long pants
- 1 long shirt
- 1 sweatshirt & hood
- 1 light wt. rain jacket
- 1 pajamas
- 2 underwear
- 1 bathing suit
- 1 socks
- 1 washcloth

This assumes that the child is hiking in shorts, T-shirt, socks, hiking shoes and possibly a sunhat. For longer trips you would want to include extra socks and underwear, a second pair of shorts and T-shirt and a few more books. On any trip extra space can be used for carrying lightweight items of food; bread, crackers, cereal, spices, packaged soup, cookies. Despite trying to reduce things as much as possible, we always include pajamas because we find they convey the message to young children that it's time for bed.

Although a toddler would not be able to carry his own framepack, have him wear a small child's daypack with a few personal items in it. This will make him feel more important and help lighten everyone else's load a little.

A sturdy framepack designed for a child's "frame" is essential for backpacking.

Backpacking Abroad

In Europe it's possible to do lengthy hikes without carrying anything more than your clothes and lunch food. A number of countries have a system of maintained, fully staffed huts placed strategically along the routes for easy access as you hike. All are run by the various national alpine clubs and are open to anyone hiking the trails. Membership in any one club gets you a significant discount in all other European club huts. While Europe has the most well-developed system of huts, other countries often offer similar accommodations along some of their trails. It's also possible in some places, like England's coastal footpath, to spend each night in a bed & breakfast place or small inn, thus giving yourself the adventure of a continuous hiking experience without the added burden of carrying all your gear. For this type of hiking, the use of soft-framed daypacks should be sufficient for the whole family.

Pitfalls To Avoid

Long drives to short hikes—If your children are like ours, they will remember little of the hike and too much of the drive.

Starting too late—Children flag quickly in the afternoon or in the heat, so do your most strenuous hiking early. A picnic breakfast a few miles into the hike is a good way to ensure an early start. Have something short range to look forward to and provide a rest stop.

Too many "No"s—No, you can't have another drink; No we can't eat yet; No, you can't bring that rock, stick or pile of pinecones. Pack each child's daypack with something special to eat, a drink and room for all those things they want to keep. This way they can ration themselves and make their own decisions.

Not involving older children—In hike selection, pace setting, trail finding, picnic spot choosing, weight carrying. Children five and up want to please, contribute and feel like an integral part of any family outing. The greater their involvement, the greater their interest.

Too little to eat—Active children need an extraordinary amount of food at frequent intervals. Choose high energy, nutritious foods like nuts, dried and fresh fruit, peanutbutter, sunflower seeds, cheese and whole wheat products. Avoid empty calorie, high fat, unhealthy foods like chips, candy, too many cookies and any of the other junky foods children are continually bombarded with. Carry half again as much food for your children as they normally eat.

Too little to drink—"I'm thirsty!" is always a frequent cry, with good reason. Children don't sweat as efficiently as adults and overheat more quickly. Take one water flask per person, more if you are hiking in an area like the tropics. Avoid sweetened drinks like soda pop and sugared juices. Water is still the best thirst quencher.

Too quick a pace—A sense of pace doesn't exist with young children. Instead of getting frustrated by their erratic progress, work out a compromise: If they go up that hill without stopping, they get a break at the top.

No time to play- Pick about three good times for a play session on a five hour hike. Allow a half hour for each, plenty of time to a child. Save special snacks for times when you are walking, not during play breaks. This distributes the treats. On the other hand, try to be flexible. If children see a wonderful place for some play (a bridge over a stream, a clearing in the woods, a pile of boulders beside the trail) indulge them to a reasonable degree. After all, they love that as much as you love the actual hiking.

Chapter
5
Bicycle Touring

Most children love to ride a bicycle. The pace is fast and the scenery constantly changing. Little ones sit happily, fascinated from the vantage point of their bicycle seat or trailer. Older children enjoy the thrill and independence of riding on their own. Given the near universal appeal of bicycling as an inexpensive mode of transportation, plus its status as one of the most popular activities with children, a bicycle tour is an excellent choice for a family adventure.

The Advantages

Family bicycle touring can range anywhere from day outings to long-term trips. Some areas have designated bicycle paths, others country roads that lend themselves well to bicycle travel. Even in countries where large distances must be covered between areas of interest, most public buses and trains can accommodate bicycles for a small fee. With bicycles on an adventure, it's possible to explore a far greater area in an enjoyable, low-cost way than if you were solely dependent on walking or renting a vehicle. More than any other form of adventure travel, bicycling has the advantage of giving you an inside exposure to the places you are traveling through. In poor countries where bicycling is often the primary mode of transportation, traveling this way helps alleviate the disparity between your life-style and theirs. As a family on bicycles, shopping in local markets, eating local foods and traveling at a pace that matches that of the country you are in, you will be treated to a genuine hospitality that differs greatly from the normal relationship between tourist and local inhabitant.

In Morocco, during our two-month bicycle trip when Tristan and Colin were nine, we camped for a few days in a small mountain village where local Berber children soon befriended us. As the village was also the site of a famous waterfall, a number of tourists were bused in daily and quickly targeted by the children as a source of money. When we asked the children why they didn't treat us in the same way, they assured us that we were their friends. The presence of our children and simple traveling lifestyle made them identify with us in a way they couldn't with the other tourists.

Bicycle touring with children is a surprisingly untapped source of travel. Despite the fact that nearly all children love to bicycle, few parents realize the potential to channel this enthusiasm into a family bicycle trip. Long-term travel with children is almost always done in a car or camper. Children (not to mention adults) easily become bored, frustrated and fractious when confined for hours of inactivity in a vehicle. On a bicycle children are too busy, too active and too visually stimulated to become bored or irritable. As constant participants rather than observers in the trip, their interest is continually aroused.

Children's Capabilities

Any child big enough to ride a ten-speed can go touring and carry full children's bicycle gear. Younger children are best off pulled in a trailer. Expect a child approximately nine years or up to cover an average of 40 to 50 kilometers a day, a pace that leaves plenty of time for breaks, sight-seeing and play after reaching your destination.

Although most children are avid bicyclers, be prepared for frequent stops. Children have a way of continually needing something: a drink, a snack, to go to the bathroom, to put clothes on, to take clothes off. Leave room in their handlebar packs for easy stowage of whatever items of clothing keep coming off and

Exploring back roads gets you away from traffic and into the countryside.

on. Another way to cut down on delays is to give each child his own water bottle, preferably the type mounted with velcro, an easy release mechanism. Mastering the art of taking a drink while underway is just the kind of challenge children like.

Despite all efforts on the parents' part, a certain amount of stopping is inevitable, as children have no sense of time. Ask them if they are thirsty and they will say no. Five minutes down the road they will insist they are thirsty.

"But I just asked you five minutes ago!" you'll exclaim.

"Well," they will say, "we weren't thirsty then."

Hills are always going to present the major stumbling block when it comes to keeping your children moving. Since nearly everywhere has hills, avoiding them is almost impossible. Even places that you could have sworn were flat as a pancake will reveal hidden inclines when viewed from the vantage point of a bicycle. Figure that any hill that looks big to you looks twice as big to a child. The key here is to get them up it fast by whatever means works best. Going down the other side is never a problem. Children have an insatiable lust for speed. To a certain extent the downhill ride on the other side can serve as sufficient motivation for getting your children up a hill, although eventually they will figure out that the time ratio is unequal. As an indignant Colin remarked one day, "It takes us half an hour to go up a hill and five minutes to go down. That means most of the time we're going up."

Traffic can also cause a temporary interference with your bicycle pace as well as your enjoyment. Biking in traffic is never fun and a child's interest in it will lag as fast as yours. Only once in our experience has the presence of traffic provided the stimulant to an otherwise dull ride. Bicycling down the breakdown lane on our way to the airport in Lisbon we lived out one of our wildest fantasies, passing miles and miles of bumper-to-bumper rush-hour traffic. Despite the number of cars, the situation was hardly hazardous as we were the fastest thing moving.

Perhaps because of the fast pace, children on bicycles soon develop an adult sense of accomplishment in achieving a goal: reaching a destination, making it up a steep hill, covering a major distance. All these become as gratifying to them as to their parents and are a motivating factor on any bicycle tour. Getting your children excited about the day's bicycling should rarely be a problem and no matter how long the ride, they will rarely be too tired to play afterwards.

Equipment

Bicycling is one of those sports where equipment can be as expensive or low-cost as you want to make it. Day-outings needn't require anything more than the bicycles themselves, some type of child carrier for any children too young to bike, a roof rack or rear bike rack, and a few spare parts. Bicycles vary from basic ten- to fifteen-speed road models in the $150-$200 range to expensive touring models or high-tech mountain bikes that will take you almost anywhere. More expensive bicycles usually have a lighter frame, alloy wheels and better quality components. Longer bicycle tours will require some specialized equipment for carrying gear. Beyond that, what money you spend is your own choice. Like

running gear shops that have turned a simple sport into a potentially high-cost activity, bicycle dealers can overwhelm you with
an arsenal of gear, clothing and accessories, none of which you
actually need. In the interests of keeping things simple, a key
feature to adventure travel, we have covered gear that we feel is
integral to family bicycle touring. Other, more expensive choices
are available, but none are actually required for a family on
bicycles. All the listed equipment that follows should be available
through your local bicycle shop.

Bicycles

Any bike with a good set of gears and road tires is going to be
fine for a family, whether bicycling short-term or on longer tours.
A child's one-speed isn't appropriate for anything except the
shortest of trips because it's so much harder to ride. Every minor
hill will require the child to stand up and pedal, an exhausting
process in the long run. The major decision when choosing a
bicycle for children is between a basic touring model, a mountain-
style bike, and a cross bike which is a cross between the two.

*Enjoying a moment of solitude on the coast of Nova Scotia. Both children's bikes
are loaded with full camping gear.*

Expensive mountain bikes with excessive numbers of gears really aren't necessary unless you plan extensive off-road or mountainous bicycling. We fended off various bicycle dealers anxious to sell us prohibitively expensive mountain bikes for our young children before purchasing two basic Schwinn child-size ten-speeds at a fraction of the cost. These bikes served the children well over 3,000 miles through Spain, Portugal, Morocco, Newfoundland, Nova Scotia and Prince Edward Island without a major breakdown. We bought them cross bikes when they hit the teenage years, but they still preferred a true touring bike for trips.

One thing to consider when choosing a bicycle is the desirability of bicycling back roads to escape traffic. Children's touring bikes are built with a heavier frame and wider tire size that, when coupled with a child's overall lighter weight, help them hold up well in rough road conditions. For parents and older children who need adult-size bicycles, a cross bike is a good compromise between the features of both the touring and mountain bicycle. The frame is sturdier than a touring bike and the wheel rim made to accept anything from a narrow touring wheel to a wide mountain one, allowing you a flexibility in choice depending on where you plan to bike.

Used bicycles at relatively low prices are another option and often available at bicycle shops. Don't hesitate to buy one if the price is right. Kevin purchased a really excellent used ten-speed for about $80, and it held up fine during our first few bicycle tours. If a bicycle dealer is selling a used bike it should be in good condition. Tell him what your intentions are so he understands your need for a bicycle that will hold up under the rigors of touring as well as be a good weight carrier. Children's ten-speeds are rarely available used.

Children's Bicycles

When choosing a child's bicycle, pick one with a large enough frame to carry 2 small rear panniers, a backrack and a handlebar pack. The smallest standard touring bicycle has a 16" frame and can be ridden by an average-size nine-year-old (or approximately 4'-6" tall). Since this type of bike usually has a smaller diameter wheel (24 inches vs. 26 or 27 inches), it's a good idea to carry some spare inner tubes and a spare tire. These are difficult to find other than at bicycle shops that handle this size bike. By age twelve to fourteen most children can fit an adult bike.

Bicycle Seats

A child's bicycle seat is a good choice for a family with a young child who is just interested in day outings. It's lightweight, easy to pack in a vehicle and considerably less expensive than a trailer. Although carrying a child on the back of your bicycle will certainly make a difference to your performance, a slightly slower pace isn't going to matter in the long run, especially if you have other children riding their own bikes. Whoever isn't carrying a child should remember that the other parent is working harder and bicycle accordingly. A wide variety of bicycle seat models are available, from basic plastic seats to cushioned ones that recline. Most large toy department stores, bicycle shops and bike catalogs carry at least one type of bike seat.

Bicycle Trailers

Special bike trailers designed to carry children are the best choice for longer trips because they leave the bicycle free to carry extra gear (what doesn't fit in the trailer) and they get the weight of the child off the bike and back where it's easier to handle. Trailers also allow children to play or sleep comfortably when underway. The following is a list of bicycle trailers designed for carrying children.

• **Bike Burro Classic**: carries two children facing each other, weight 38 lbs, seat belt, optional sun canopy, attaches to seatpost.
• **Blue Sky Cycle Cart**: carries two to four children facing forwards, weight 31 lbs, baby harness, optional rain cover, seat belt, attaches to seatpost.
• **Burley**: comes in two versions for carrying children—*Burley Roo* and *Burley d'Lite* (collapsible model), carries two children facing forwards, weight 19-21 lbs, side panels and screening, splash guards, lap and chest belts, bottom bag, attaches to rear frame.

A bicycle trailer makes even long tours possible with young children. These vary from simple two seaters to deluxe folding models. Any bicycle intended to pull a trailer will need good low gearing to cope with the extra weight.

• **Cannondale Stowaway**: carries two children facing backwards (maximum height 40"), weight 23 lbs, high visibility yellow/red exterior, five-point safety belt system, optional sunshade and rain canopy, attaches to rear frame.

• **CycleTote Family**: carries two children facing forwards, weight 23 lbs, screening, seat belt, weatherproof exterior, attaches to seatpost.

• **Equinox Tourlite**: carries two children facing either direction, weight 19 lbs, collapsible, high visibility exterior, side panels, seat belt, bottom bag, optional rain or sun cover, infant sling, attaches to rear axle.

• **L.L. Bean Kiddie Kart**: carries two children facing backwards, weight 23 lbs, seat belt, optional sun canopy and seat cushion, attaches to seatpost.

• **Winchester Original**: various models, seats two children facing each other, neon exterior, side panels, five-point safety harness, reclining seats, large storage compartment, collapsible option, attaches to rear frame.

Bicycle Gear

Children riding their own bicycles can carry a scaled-down version of what you carry. Although carrying gear does effect bike performance and balance, children adapt as quickly as adults. Avoid putting any significant weight in the handlebar pack to prevent interference with steering. Our twins have carried their two stuffed friends, a reading book, a few items of clothing and a couple of small toys up there, plus any treasures they acquired along the route. Heavier items are always in the rear panniers where their weight is much less noticeable.

Child's Bicycle Gear For Touring

The following is a list of what our children carried at age nine on their first bicycle tour:

- 2 small rear panniers (type intended for front fork)
- 1 handlebar pack
- 1 sleeping bag with pad on back rack
- 1 qt. size water bottle (attached to bike)
- 1 long pants
- 2 shorts
- 1 tights (excellent cold or wet weather combination; shorts with cotton tights)

- 1 heavy sweater or sweatshirt
- 1 rain jacket
- 2 long sleeved shirts
- 2 T-shirts
- 7 underwear
- 4 socks
- 1 sneakers
- 1 sandals
- 1 bathing suit
- 1 pillowcase
- 1 small towel
- 1 hat w/ gloves
- 8 paperback reading books
- drawing and writing paper, pencils, pens, sharpener, scissors and a few toys

In addition, each child carried 1 plastic bowl, 1 plastic mug, first aid equipment, 2 inner tubes, 3 candles, some lightweight food and all necessary school material. Total weight of gear was approximately 20 pounds.

Spare Parts & Tools

Carrying spare parts is a good idea, even on short day trips. For longer tours it's imperative, especially in areas without bicycle shops. When we planned our first bicycle trip, one that would take us to Morocco, we were concerned about carrying enough spare parts in case of breakdown in such a remote area. Unfortunately, we had no idea how much to carry. In the end we took far more patch kits and spare inner tubes than were needed, despite the often rough roads.

The biggest necessity is parts for specialized equipment like child size bicycles or trailers. Two spare inner tubes per bike should be enough. To help avoid unnecessary flats, add an inner lining of "Tuffy Tire" (a plastic strip that protects the tube) to each tire, especially on the children's bikes. Children rarely have their eye out for broken glass, sharp stones and other potential tire hazards. With this protective layer, most flats can be avoided. In three months of bicycling over roads that sported more high-risk materials to tires than one would believe was possible, we had six flats, four of them on the one bicycle with no protective liner.

Include one spare tire for every two bicycles. This is most important when traveling to remote areas or with a child's size bike when you might not be able to find a replacement. Finding some place to carry them isn't really that difficult. We folded ours in a figure eight and tucked them in under the sleeping bag on the back rack. Children will have a lot of fun rolling the tires, so taking them along is no hardship.

The following is a list of the tools and spare parts we take on all our bicycle trips, no matter for how long or to what destinations. A few have not been used, but all have given us considerable peace of mind. As a matter of possible interest we have had numerous flat tires, two squeaking wheel bearings, two clacking pedal bearings, one stripped seat bolt, one ripped seat, one ripped pannier, one faulty derailleur and one exploded derailleur in the course of our family bicycling career, the last being the most challenging as it happened the first day we were in Morocco. That Kevin was able to reconstruct it on the spot does much to attest to the importance of bringing along an ample supply of wire, string and duct tape.

Other than checking tire pressure and changing the occasional flat, the most frequent maintenance job was brake adjustments, something that needed to be done about once a week. One tire also split soon after we returned home from a trip, letting us know that it was finally worn out after about 3,000 miles.

A basic repair kit of tools and spare parts for a bicycle tour includes:

- spare tire
- spare tubes
- tube patch kits
- plastic set of 3 tire "irons"
- channel lock pliers (small)
- small adjustable wrench
- screw driver/allen wrench set
- small vise grips
- "Y" socket tool (6,8,10 mm)

- spare spokes
- spoke wrench
- chain link tool
- chain lubricant
- tube of teflon grease
- duct tape
- coil of light gage wire
- small ball of string
- misc. spare nuts and bolts

Safety

Many parents are understandably nervous about children on bicycles, particularly riding on roads with no sidewalks. The thought of bicycling in foreign countries where rules of the road and speed limits are sometimes next to non-existent makes them even more nervous.

Bicycling Abroad

Bicycle touring with children needn't be any more dangerous than bicycling around your neighborhood or riding in a car. In fact, riding in a car is probably a lot more dangerous, yet no one even thinks about it because it's such an accepted part of our life. Many foreign countries, while seemingly populated by nothing but maniacal drivers, are safer for bicycling than North American roads. Cars are fewer and back roads often almost deserted. Unlike North American drivers, who usually aren't on the look-out for anything other than cars on the road, foreign drivers have an eye out for anything that moves—children, goats, chickens, donkeys and cows all frequently spill over into the roads, keeping drivers ever alert to the unexpected obstacle. In places like this where driving is something of a free-for-all, the one thing a driver can do faster than accelerate is brake.

Bicycles, the most widely used mode of transportation throughout the world, are always treated with respect, given ample berth when passing, and spared the seemingly diabolical intent of many drivers towards each other. By choosing your route intelligently, most places can be enjoyed safely on bicycles with children. Children have a well-developed instinct for self-preservation and will exhibit an admirable ability for staying out of trouble. Bicycle touring will sober even your wildest "wheelie" enthusiasts. Once off their BMX-style bicycles and onto a loaded touring one, they'll cultivate a whole new set of criteria for what's challenging and exciting when riding a bicycle.

Spare tires make wonderful toys when rolled with a stick.

Safety Precautions

What safety precautions to take are really up to the individual parents. The following are some basic guidelines for bicycling together as a family.

—Try riding with one parent in front, one in back and the children in between. Competent children can lead if they want to, but an adult is always best in the rear position for higher visibility. The leading adult should have a handlebar mirror for checking on the others.

—Bicycling should always be done in the same direction as the flow of traffic. This allows oncoming cars to slow down and follow behind you until there's a safe moment to pass.

—Children should be taught to abide by the same traffic rules as cars when it comes to obeying traffic lights and signals, riding down one-way streets and turning. This is mandatory in countries where bicycles are a major source of transportation.

—Use hand signals for turning to let cars behind you know your intentions.

Bicycle Helmets

Helmets should worn by everyone when bicycling on busy roads. Children in bicycle seats and trailers should also have a helmet for any major bicycle tour. How much you decide to use them is up to each family's discretion. On back roads we often dispense with them when traffic is next to non-existent. Other families might prefer to have children wear a helmet at all times.

Helmets are now made to fit even very small children. Make sure the helmet you choose meets ANSI Z90.4 Bicycle Helmet Standard. The following are excellent choices for children:

- **Rhode Gear Rhodester:** Available in small and large sizes.
- **Pro Tec:** Infant helmet fits babies from infancy to three years.
- **Pro Tec:** Youth helmet fits age four to ten years. This generic type of headgear can also be used for other sports that require helmets.

Children over the age of ten can fit an XS adult-size helmet. All helmets come with different sizing pads for the inside that can be changed as a child grows bigger. Helmets should fit snugly, but comfortably, to the head and not be able to move easily. For maximum protection, have children wear them flat across the top of the head rather than tilted back.

Bicycle Camping

To keep cost down and lend an added element of adventure to a bicycle tour, carry camping gear so you always have a place to stay, even if it's a deserted field or someone's backyard. With camping gear you still have the option to duck into an inn if the weather turns bad or you just want a bit of luxury. Children are always more comfortable camping, preferring the freedom of the outdoors to the confinement of a room in an inn.

While helmets are recommended for any type of cycling, they should definitely be worn when on roads with moderate to heavy traffic.

Camping Gear

Carrying camping gear needn't add much additional weight to your load. All equipment listed in Chapter 3 can be carried with relative ease. A child riding his own bike should be capable of carrying a sleeping bag, pad, mat, plus his own bowl/mug/spoon. Make sure all items are lightweight and made for backpacking. An infant or toddler's gear will have to be carried either in a trailer or on an adult bike.

Food

Carrying food requires a little forethought to avoid finding yourselves laden down with extra weight or caught miles from nowhere with a bunch of ravenous children and nothing to eat. For meals, buy dinner and breakfast food near the end of your day's biking. In the absence of refrigeration, everything should keep well overnight except fresh milk in warm climates. Lunch can be bought along the route in the morning. When bicycle touring as a family you will begin to feel as though you spend an extraordinary amount of time replenishing your food supply. It never ceases to amaze me how often we stuff quantities of food into our panniers only to have it all vanish a few hours later. The truth of the matter is that you can't carry much food when bicycling, so just keeping the family fed is going to involve repeated trips to the store. Fortunately, because bicycling is done along roads anyway, finding shops should be fairly easy, even if they are nothing more than small, village general stores. Versatility in meals will have to be foregone for the duration of most bicycle trips. By the end of long family adventures we always find ourselves fantasizing about favorite foods back home; not enough to make us want to stop, but just enough to whet our appetites.

Free-Camping

When bicycle touring, you won't always find yourself near a campground at the end of the day. Some countries or areas permit free camping provided it isn't near anyone's home and you don't leave trash behind when you leave. Some places have strict rules against free camping, although even these places seem to have more tolerance for it where bicyclers are concerned. If you need to free camp, ask if possible before just pitching your tent on someone's property. They will usually say yes. If not, they may tell you where you can camp for the night. Some will welcome you with open arms, inviting you to stay as long as you want. With children, as always, the reception is more likely to be a welcoming one.

For the most part we have avoided much free camping when touring because we find we like the convenience of bathroom and bathing facilities and a ready supply of water. When camping out on our own we have to be very careful with how much water we use, not always an easy thing to do with young children. The best option for families is finding a restaurant, Bed & Breakfast or someone's land where you can work out an arrangement to use their bathroom and water facilities for the night. In remote areas you can also find somewhere to camp beside a stream or other natural water source. Be sure to purify any water that might be contaminated, especially in foreign countries where most rural areas have grazing animals.

Making It Fun

It's the rare child that doesn't enjoy bicycling. How to prolong that natural enthusiasm to last four or five hours of continual bicycling with a fully loaded bike is not much cause for concern. With a little parental in-put, some well honed imaginative skills and a few entertainment devices, children should be able to stay happy during any bicycle trip.

Ideas for making it fun:

—Encourage imaginative play. Even when bicycling, children can devise much of their own entertainment.

—Conversing and story telling are always popular pastimes, often sparked by the surroundings you are bicycling through.

—Store a reading book, small toy and a ball in a child's handlebar pack for quick access during breaks.

—Children can have a wonderful time during breaks or at the end of the day rolling your spare tires (if you carry them). Their proficiency at this old-fashioned game will amaze you.

—Pick an interesting route; as always, children are most interested in a route through changeable scenery: farmland with

Free camping in an olive grove. People are usually generous about letting bicyclists camp for the night.

animals, country towns, fishing villages, coastal roads along the ocean. Any route with a long downhill ride or series of small roller coaster hills will be greeted with excitement.

—Play games like "finding things"or guessing what comes next or who can find a good picnic spot or somewhere to swim? Getting children to enter into the spirit of things goes a long way towards keeping them interested.

—Children riding as passengers can be kept entertained much the same way they are in a car seat: with books, toys, food, taking a nap. If your child is right at that age when throwing things is at its pinnacle, choose one of the trailers with screening.

Pitfalls To Avoid

Too fast a pace—Don't treat family touring like training for the Tour de France. Keep the pace relaxed even if one of you is a seasoned bicycler. Children will lose interest fast if continually told to speed up. Let them set the pace.

Too ambitious an itinerary—Even on a long bicycle tour, keep the focus on having fun rather than miles covered. On our 1,500 mile trip with nine-year-olds we took three months to cover the distance. We rarely bicycled on days when the weather conditions were poor or for too many days in a row. Any distance can be covered with children provided you leave sufficient time to make it relaxing instead of rushed.

Too few breaks—Keep the breaks short, but coming often. Breaks are natural to children. They take them all the time when playing, so incorporate as many as possible. Some can be short food or drink breaks, a few longer ones for play and picnics.

Overanxious parenting—Pick a safe route, teach them the rules of the road, then let them go. Children don't need to be over protected or continually told to be careful. Stop worrying about all the 'what ifs' (what if a car comes around that corner, what if they hit a rock halfway down that hill...). As our boys once said, "If you worried about all the 'what ifs' you'd never do anything!"

Starting too late—As with hiking, start early and end early. This capitalizes on a child's high energy level at the beginning of the day and need to play at the end.

Chapter
6
Sailing

Children are naturally boat people. To them a boat is not cramped, only cozy. They love small, intimate spaces to play in, the close proximity of parents, the continual visual stimulation, the predominantly outdoor environment.

The Advantages

Perhaps no type of adventure travel is easier to incorporate children into than a sailing one because your home goes with you. Only a boat allows children the freedom to move around freely when underway. Sleeping areas, play places, mealtimes and schedules all remain intact as the whole family experiences the thrill of exploring coastal areas, inland waterways, lakes and islands. Places that might once have seemed crowded when viewed from land become an oasis of natural beauty from the water. Tourist meccas are easily escaped as you poke into coves, anchor at islands and enjoy beaches accessible only by boat.

Three basic options are available for families eager to try a sailing adventure: small trailerable boats, larger cruising boats, and chartering. Each has its merits, its share of adventure and room to grow from one to the other. Starting with a small, trailerable boat a family can learn to sail easily, discover whether they enjoy cruising, explore some otherwise inaccessible areas of nature and prepare themselves for a larger craft and more ambitious destinations. Once the basics are learned and some experience accumulated they can try chartering on a larger boat in a more exotic location. From there, if bitten thoroughly by the boat bug, a family might want to either charter in a variety of places or buy a reasonably sized sailboat. Sailing gradually from place to place and exploring the waters of the world are the culmination of family adventuring on a sailboat.

What Type Of Boat

If you've never sailed before, starting small is always best, although small doesn't have to mean daysailers. Larger sailboats in the 25- to 35-foot range are often just as easy, if not easier, to learn to sail and most practical with young children. I grew up sailing a 12-foot Beetle Cat with a gaff rig, enormous boom and a sail area big enough to give any first time sailor heart failure. Our first family cruising boat, a 26-foot catamaran, was far easier to sail and most forgiving to learn on as we anchored backwards, raised the wrong sails, snapped battens, accidently jibed, broke a shroud, ran aground and committed just about every possible beginner's mistake, all while accompanied by our one-year-old twins.

Chartering

Chartering is available in all the most popular cruising grounds throughout the world. When deciding what boat to charter, don't equate boat size with house size and charter something too big. Separate sleeping areas, buffer zones between adults and children and spacious facilities all acquire a minor role on a boat where the focus is on the outdoors and each new anchorage becomes another backyard. The more compact and efficiently run the craft, the more you will enjoy your adventure.

Charter boats come equipped with all the basic essentials plus a few luxuries. Easy sail rigs, cockpit suncovers, comfortable seating, a well-designed galley, refrigeration, ample lighting, showers and pressurized water are all usually inclusive. Beyond adding some food and personal belongings, little is needed for a one or two week cruise.

A cruising catamaran's broad beam, level sailing and spacious accommodations make it ideal for family cruising.

Owning A Boat

Owning your own cruising boat is a third option, one that an increasing number of families are enjoying. After years of traveling on bicycles, with backpacks, in canoes, and on foot, sailing on our own boat is still our favorite choice for long term adventuring with children.

Boat designs vary greatly, some lending themselves more to incorporating children than others. Look for boats with small, manageable sail areas and comfortable, modern interiors, not boats that heel at the first puff of wind or look like they were built to set a new transatlantic record. While children can be accommodated on just about any type of boat, some are going to make more work for you than others. Many classic sailboats were designed in the era of macho sailing when galleys amounted to nothing more than a cubbyhole at the base of the companionway and sailing wasn't really sailing unless you had the lee rail under and everyone clinging to his seat. While beautiful to see, these boats can be hard on family life. Nowadays, practically all the conveniences of home are possible on a sailboat. Instead of roughing it, you're simply enjoying modern amenities on a modest scale.

Trailerable Boats

What kind of sailing you plan to do will help determine what type of boat you need. Small, trailerable sailboats present a whole realm of cruising possibilities on inland and coastal waters. With some basic camping gear, they can take you almost anywhere in protected waters, a unique form of sailing adventure. While sailing conditions will usually be simple to deal with, this type of craft will make things a little harder with very young children. Beyond the toddler stage their interest in their surroundings increases, as well as their willingness to help, ability to entertain themselves and aptitude at swimming.

Multihull Sailboats

Having taken up adventuring under sail when Tristan and Colin were only a year old, Kevin and I looked for the type of boat most appropriate for cruising with very young children, a criteria that led us to cruising catamarans. Unlike small day sailing catamarans in the Hobie Cat mode, ones designed solely for cruising never lift a hull out of the water, hardly heel at all and offer tremendous space in relationship to overall length. Built more like floating cottages than speed machines, they still perform well on all points of sail and can satisfy even the most ardent sailor. As a family with twin babies, this seemed the obvious choice for us. Without any significant heeling there's no need to worry about children falling out of bed, food flying off the tables or toys spilling onto the floor. Even in rough weather our children could play in the cockpit or on the foredeck with little regard for sailing conditions. While some boats require a fair amount of ingenuity and input to accommodate children, ours needed nothing more than some netting attached to the lifelines. Cruising catamarans come ready-made for children of any age.

Trailerable cruising trimarans are another good option. They offer stability and speed to cruising families, and most have outer hulls that fold or swing in for low-profile docking or trailering. If multihulls interest you, a complete review of over 150 multihull sailboats currently on the market and helpful advice from industry experts can be found in the *Sailor's Multihull Guide*, available from Menasha Ridge Press (to order call 800-247-9437 or fax 205-967-0580). A good periodical to read is *Multihulls Magazine* (to order call 800-333-6858 or fax 617-471-0118).

Safety

Harnesses

Safety is the biggest consideration when sailing with children. A harness is one way to keep a young child safely aboard yet free to roam the boat. Snapped amidships, a harness allows children with a sufficient tether line to play abovedecks without danger of falling overboard. On our catamaran the children could be snapped to the cockpit and still have enough scope to move both above and belowdecks without having to be unsnapped. Safety harnesses can be purchased through marine catalogs or made yourself with mountaineering quality webbing, buckles and snap clips. Tethers should have a snap at each end so the child can wear the harness all day with or without the line attached. We kept the lines permanently attached to the mast and snapped the children on each time they came outside to play.

As parents of young twins, we always used safety harnesses when under sail with our children. Since then we've noticed that few parents use any safety feature, preferring to always accompany their child or keep him occupied below. The use of a harness is such a simple means of guaranteeing your child's safety, freeing you from constant vigilance and allowing him freedom on board. The slight inconvenience of occasionally disentangling your child is well worth the piece of mind and element of independence both for you and your child.

Lifejackets

All children on a sailboat should have their own lifejacket, whether they wear it when under sail or not. A variety of types are available for children. Make sure the one you choose has leg

A good rowing dinghy gives children the independence of their own boat to explore and play with. By age six or seven a child is old enough to row alone.

straps, a flotation collar for keeping the head above water and some kind of strap to grab hold of in the event of having to retrieve a child from the water. A lifejacket should always fit snugly so the child can't slip out of it. We attached a plastic whistle to each child's lifejacket and instructed them how to blow it if they ever fell overboard. In the happy event that you don't ever need the whistle for that purpose, it also comes in handy when your children are off playing and you want them home.

Older children proficient at swimming shouldn't need anything unless conditions are rough. One exception might be the use of lifejackets in a dinghy when rowing on their own. Lifejackets should be standard equipment for any young children when riding in a dinghy. We dispensed with them when our children's rowing and swimming proficiency matched our own.

Sailboats Present Few Risks

Beyond the risk of falling in the water for non-swimmers, sailboats present few risks, fewer than your average home. Children on sailboats generally turn into little acrobats at an early age.

When harnessed, babies can be free to roam a boat without fear of falling in the water. These harnesses were made by us with mountaineering quality materials. Netting was also attached to the lifelines for extra protection.

Don't let your adult imagination cramp their style. If shinnying up the mast or hanging off the pulpit is their passion, let them. Their ability to prevent accidents and stay on board is just as well-developed as an adult's, especially if they've been allowed to roam at an early age. The child who is continually told not to do something will soon lose interest in being on a boat. Instead, sailing, like all forms of adventure, should promote an early independence, a willingness to try something new and a sense of achievement in children. Sailboats are a wonderful environment for developing all three.

Babies On Board

While we were sailing in the Caribbean when Tristan and Colin were ten, a young couple visiting from another boat remarked that they would have children if they could instantly be ten years old as well. "It's an infant we can't imagine having on a boat", they continued, "yet we see people cruising with them all the time." As parents who had taken up cruising with not one, but two infants, we assured them that for us babies on board had been fun and easy. Babies, in fact, are about the easiest age to cruise with. The key lies in choosing the right boat, whether chartering or buying, selecting a modest itinerary and making life as relaxed as possible for yourselves.

Sailing—An Easy Way To Adventure

The irony for us is that while many couples give up cruising when they have children, we took it up because we had ours. Plans to tour around Europe on our motorcycle, at that time our adventurous mode of travel, were quickly shelved when one baby turned out to be two, more than we could envision in a sidecar. Looking around for an acceptable means of adventure travel we settled on sailboats because our whole home could go with us while we cruised. That we knew little about big boat sailing, less about catamarans and absolutely nothing about babies on boats was irrelevant. Therein lay the initial adventurous aspect of the whole undertaking.

As mentioned earlier, catamarans for us turned out to be the ideal choice. With the high bridge deck, a baby can be playing inside and still be on the same level with you in the cockpit. Accommodations are always spacious, even on a small catamaran, making it possible to sleep an infant away from the center of activity, find room to store baby things and set up a safe play area out from underfoot. Under sail the level motion will keep the baby from falling out of bed, food securely anchored to the table and playtime a safe activity both above and belowdecks.

If you're thinking of chartering, or have been asked to sail on a friend's boat, don't hesitate to take your baby along. Although you can't exert the same control over what type of boat you cruise on or how it's set up, any sailboat can incorporate a baby well enough for you to have a fun, relaxing time under sail.

Keeping Things Relaxed

Sailing with a baby, like doing anything with a baby, means a relaxed schedule. Large amounts of territory can be covered, big bodies of water crossed and challenging situations dealt with as long as you feel able to cope with them. Parents, not babies, usually make the work for themselves. An overambitious itinerary is one way a fun cruise can become a nightmare, with the baby blamed for it all.

Daily Baby Care

Caring for a baby is easier on a boat than with any other form of adventure travel except living abroad because your home is with you. Not only does a boat have a larger carrying capacity then a bicycle, canoe, backpack or vehicle, but once you're on board the baby's bed, changing place, play area and paraphernalia can all be arranged and left intact no matter how many times you raise and lower sails or anchors.

For a baby that is already mobile, by all means use a harness to relieve the tedium of either confining him below or crawling around the deck after him. For baths, use the dishpan, galley sink or bring along a small plastic baby bath if you plan to cruise for a while. This can double as a nice, safe play bath area when going to the beach is out of the question. Room for storing infant toys can always be found, objects suspended over a play area for him to look at and household items supplemented when interest in toys begins to pall.

While sailing allows more leniency in what you can bring for a baby on an adventure, it also imposes a few restrictions of its own. The following is a list of hints concerning things unique to sailing with a baby. In addition, everything covered in Chapter Ten applies to sailing as well.

—Use a harness. Begin when a baby is mobile and continue using it until he can swim.

—At bath time, use the dishpan, sink, laundry pan, or bucket. Do any final rinse with fresh water to prevent salt water rashes.

—For toys, make use of any appropriate equipment on board: measuring cups and spoons, plastic glasses, keys on a keyring, wooden spoons, toothbrushes. Hang things from a piece of line suspended over the baby in his bed, the cockpit or play area.

—Attach netting along lifelines if the baby is at the standing up stage. This will keep both the baby and toys on board. Also use along a sleeping bunk to keep the baby from falling out. Netting is available through boat catalogs.

—Sleep a baby anywhere. A basket, carrybed or carriage top allows him to be moved while sleeping. If sailing with a group, this is a convenient way to keep the baby from monopolizing an entire cabin each time he naps.

—Use cloth diapers. Keep one bucket just for soaking purposes. Add Borax or lemon ammonia to the presoaking water. If handwashing, the easiest system is to tow a batch of diapers in a mesh bag behind the boat, then wash quickly by hand with a mild soap like Dr. Bronner's, Lifetree or Ivory Liquid. Otherwise, handwash diapers every other day in a good size laundry pan. Give the diapers a final rinse in fresh water to prevent rashes. Hang dry them in the sun to complete the sterilizing process.

—Add a second painter to the dinghy (one in the stern, another in the bow) so the boat can be snugged alongside wherever it's landing. This reduces motion and keeps everyone's hands free while handing a baby in or out of the boat. For very small infants, wear in a Snugli type carrier while riding in the dinghy. Toddlers should always wear a lifejacket.

When heeling, use cushions, blankets and pillows to create a bruise-free play area. Attach netting that can be raised or lowered if the baby is lying on a bunk to prevent falling out.

No matter whether you're planning to charter or buy your own boat, whether your trip is a week, month or year long, take your baby and discover how simple, enjoyable and relaxing adventuring under sail can be with the whole family included. Away from the play pens and swingsets, the highchairs and port-a-cribs, the bouncy chairs and walkers that are too often considered indispensable these days, you'll soon be wondering what ever made you think babies needed all that. In our travels we met a sailing family with three children, the youngest a six month old baby. As the mother was Dominican it never occurred to her that babies needed any special equipment, none of which would have fit on her boat anyway. Baby Stephanie lived, played, slept and traveled in her woven baby basket whether it was on the boat, in the dinghy, on a bus or at a cafe. We could all do well to follow her example and keep sailing with a baby as easy, carefree and uncomplicated as possible.

The Fear Factor

To a young child, many inanimate things seem alive, a status that cultivates either fear or friendship with them. To quell your baby's natural anxieties about certain items, try personalizing them with names, pats, kisses, games and the like. The boat, the dinghy, the engine, the sails can all cause alarm with a sudden burst of noise or change in motion.

Our sons' initial introduction to our outboard engine occurred while we were negotiating the intricate, current-swept passage at Woods Hole, Massachusetts, hardly the ideal moment to experience hysteria in twin babies. Heaving both children into the saloon cabin, we proceeded through the passage, realizing that something would have to be done to quell their engine fears. When we arrived at our destination, we initiated a daily ritual of getting to know "nice engine", soon a favorite shipmate as the children hugged, kissed and patted it (after it was cooled) with growing enthusiasm. By giving unfamiliar items like the boat engine a name and personality and making them the object of affection, a child's fears will be replaced by friendship.

Food

As a family, you'll probably never have larger appetites or eat more than on a boat. Why is a mystery, but sailors the world over note it and attribute it to the sea air. Whatever the reason, children develop voracious appetites that demand attention with alarming regularity. I've never had to produce more food with less staying power than on a boat when traveling with our children. Even when seas are rough and the mere idea of going below is enough to make me turn green, the children are most likely bouncing around the decks sending up a desperate plea for something to eat, please.

The saving grace to this Battle of the Endless Hunger is the boat itself. Sailboats have immense locker space waiting to be filled with food. Newer designs also have galleys built like miniature kitchens with enough modern features to make food prepared on a boat seem like dining at the Ritz.

If you're cruising in North America, food is rarely a problem. There are always sources around and ample variety except in very rural or island stores. If your itinerary is planned for fairly isolated areas, fill up the boat while still within reach of a well-stocked store. This is one of the joys of family cruising, being able to stock up with food and thus relieve yourself of the continual search for sustenance that characterizes other forms of adventure travel. With a good supply of basics on board you will only need to add fresh food along the way as you find it. When sailing in the Bahamas, for instance, an idyllic cruising ground in every sense except food which is expensive and limited in variety, we loaded the boat with all the basics in Florida, then supplemented the supply with fresh produce bought as we sailed.

No matter where you sail, some fresh food will always be available. Potatoes, onions and cabbage can be bought almost anywhere in the world for a reasonable price. Eggs, chicken and seafood are also usually to be found. Cheese is easy to store on a boat if you buy the kind with a wax coating. Everywhere sells fresh vegetables and at least some kind of fruit, even if it's nothing more than bananas and fresh coconut. As with other forms of adventure travel, no one will care on a boat whether meal variety compares with that at home, least of all children. With a few basic ingredients, some familiar seasonings and a little help from that ubiquitous sea air, no one will notice that rice and cabbage are featured five nights out of seven.

Cooking for a family on a boat will seem like Cordon Bleu school if you're used to adventuring with a campstove. If not, this is a gentle introduction to producing meals for a hungry family on something other than your home kitchen range. Standard boat stoves have two burners and a small oven, large enough for two bread pans, a small cookie sheet, or a roasting pan. Our stove, an English model, also has a grill, perfect for making the toast that keeps my children going between meals. If pressure-cooking or using a wok is what you're used to, bring them along. My mother habitually takes her large pressure-cooker on cruises and produces wonderful meals for any number of people. I like to feed the family dinners cooked in a wok and have yet to see a boat stove too small to accommodate one.

The unique culinary capabilities of a boat were epitomized for us when my parents flew to the Bahamas for a ten day cruise on our boat. Upon their arrival, five year old Tristan and Colin watched in awe and delight as my mother unpacked one goodie after another: smoked almonds, imported cheeses, roasted cashews, spicy sausage, fancy crackers, Swiss cookies and the piece de resistance, a complete frozen roast beef. As a means of adventuring in gourmet style, nothing can beat a sailboat.

Bathing

Bathing on a boat is an easy affair, particularly in the warm climates where most people choose to cruise. Fortunately, children have as much enthusiasm for playing in the water and sand as for

Keeping clean is easy on a sailboat. A sunshower suspended over the foredeck is one simple method of bathing that even little ones don't object to.

getting dirty, thus eliminating much of the need to bathe them. If the water is warm, the chances are any children above the infant stage will be in it frequently. Periodic hair washes with a good salt water shampoo plus swimming will keep them clean. A good idea at the end of each day is to give everyone a quick rinse off with fresh water to prevent saltwater sores and keep salt out of the clothes, boat and bedding. A sunshower, an inexpensive shower-ing device designed for boats, is the best way to do this. Suspend it from the boom over the cockpit, or from a halyard on the foredeck. Children like the sunshower's fine spray and nice warm temperatures. If you're chartering, your boat will probably come equipped with a shower and hot water heater. If not, bring a solar shower with you. They're lightweight, easy to carry and available through boat equipment dealers or catalogs.

In areas where the water is cold and your children look appalled at the mere mention of a swim, bathe them in the cockpit if there's no interior shower. Again, use a sunshower and rig some leecloths or hanging towels along the lifelines to cut down on drafts from the wind. If it's hairwashing day, promise a treat like a hot drink and popcorn after the shower as an added incentive to get it over with fast. Children quickly enter into the spirit of things if some sort of reward is offered at the end of it all.

Laundry

Any cruise longer than a week is going to necessitate some means of washing laundry, particularly with active children aboard. Even in tropical climates where the whole family can spend a good deal of time wearing next to nothing, laundry has a way of accumulating. As a family of five I find myself doing a wash about every four or five days when handwashing, otherwise once a week. In warm climates laundry seems to consist mostly of underwear, T-shirts and salty shorts, plus the usual sheets, pillow cases, towels, napkins, dishtowels and washcloths that get used each week. With a baby on board you can figure doing a diaper laundry every three days as well.

If you are used to throwing a large batch of laundry in the washing machine every few days at home, don't pale at the thought of transposing all that bulk into handwashing. For a start, like the pioneers and people of an earlier era, you won't wash things as often. Nor will you have as many things in the first place to get dirty. With a reduced wardrobe, your laundry pile can only get so big. This premise carries over into all work-related areas when adventuring. Fewer things means less laundry, fewer dirty dishes, less to pick up and nothing to lose. If something gets misplaced, you know it immediately.

To cut down on laundry when doing bedding, remove the bottom sheet to wash, switch the top sheet to the bottom and add a new top. If you're now thoroughly confused, think of it as only laundering one sheet per bed. Wear an apron to keep clothes clean when cooking. In hot climates, let the children go naked whenever possible except during peak sun hours. Use the same T-shirt to cover up or wear in the water, then just give it a quick freshwater rinse at the end of the day and hang on a line to dry. Choose clothes that launder easily.

Laundry—An Easy Process On A Boat

An average load of about fifteen items will use approximately 3-4 gallons of fresh water. Follow the procedures for handwashing outlined in Chapter 3. One advantage to a boat is that you can pre-soak laundry overnight, then just squeeze out and rinse most things without any strenuous handwork. The best time to do laundry is right after a rainstorm when you have plenty of fresh water. This is always a popular washing time for cruisers, with clotheslines appearing all over an anchorage after a rainy day. In addition to the usual bucket technique, laundry can be done in a dinghy filled with rainwater. Make sure the dinghy is rinsed clean first so you don't end up with salty, sandy clothes. Hanging clothes should be no problem with all the bits of line and places to suspend it on a boat. Don't skimp with the clothes pins in a stiff wind or you may find your favorite outfit flying away. I also recommend not pinning clothes to the lifelines. I lost a few things that way before realizing that the pins have a tendency to slip on the smooth lines. Large towels should always be hung cross-wise to the boat or you may see them disappearing as well. Hanging fore and aft they tend to get tangled up on the line or whipped off in a breeze.

If you own a boat and are going to be cruising frequently or for an extended time, a worthwhile purchase might be the 12-volt Mini-Wash washing machine. It weighs only 17 pounds, is 20" high by 18" deep by 17" wide, fits in your sink, cockpit, or head and washes 5 pounds of clothes with only 3 gallons of water. For a family with a baby in diapers this can be a great labor saver.

Sun Protection

Protecting your children from too much sun is critical on a boat where sunlight is reflected off the water, greatly increasing your exposure. Sunscreen should always be used on a boat, even in northern latitudes, haze or when the air temperature is cool. In the tropics, special care is required to avoid too much sun on a boat. Have the children wear cotton shirts and sunhats between 11 A.M. and 2 P.M., except when in the water or under a sun cover or beach umbrella. While sun burn causes the most skin damage, overexposure through repeated tanning is not healthy either. UV radiation is on the increase and nothing is more susceptible than children's unprotected skin on the water. If they spend a great deal of time snorkeling, have them wear a shirt while swimming. There are a prolific number of sunscreens available at various ratings. SPF #15 offers a good, overall coverage, sufficient for use on a sailboat or at a beach. Although many sun screens claim to be water resistant, re-apply after extensive swimming. Some sun screens are made specially for children and can safely be used on infants over six months. Apply a lip screen as well if needed. Piz Buin makes one that is very effective against the kind of sun exposure you get on a boat in the tropics. For more information on sun protection, see Chapter Eleven.

Seasickness

Any thoughts, plans or discussions about cruising invariably get around to the subject of seasickness. For adults who have suffered from it, the vision of a boat load of seasick children is enough to keep them firmly tied to land. Fortunately, cruising ambitions needn't be abandoned at the first glimpse of an ocean swell. Remedies are at hand and children possessed of a few defense mechanisms themselves.

Babies deal with motion in the simplest way possible—they fall asleep. During our first summer as boat owners, Tristan and Colin slept their way through every sail we took. This tendency to fall asleep in rough weather, or any noticeable motion, is typical of young children. It is, in effect, their way of dealing with seasickness. If it happens, don't worry. We actually know couples who have complained about their child sleeping while they were under sail. Why, we can't imagine. There's time enough in the future as the child grows older to develop an interest and enthusiasm for the joys of sailing. To a baby or young child, a moving boat is just like one big rocking cradle.

Older children, if prone to seasickness, will experience the same symptoms as adults. As seasickness is a mixture of physical and psychological factors, diversionary tactics work the best when it comes to a cure. Children can be lying prone on their bunks moaning with discomfort one minute and flying topsides the next at the sighting of a whale or school of dolphins. The power of diversion can work wonders on a boat and never better than with children. At the first sign of discomfort, serve up some exciting nibble food, give the children some place to lie down and have them read, talk, play word games or whatever appeals. Before you know it they'll be asking for more to eat, dreaming up games to play and bouncing around the cockpit, all seasickness forgotten.

One remedy that comes highly recommended is a seasickness prevention wristband called Sea-Band that operates on the principals of accupressure. These are available through most boat catalogs and unlike seasickness pills, contain no medication or chemicals.

No matter how susceptible your family may be, remember that most cruising time is spent sailing in sheltered water and at anchor. The number of times you will actually have to deal with seasickness will be few and quickly forgotten in the glow of sailing together as a family.

Making It Fun

Keeping children of any age entertained on a sailboat is about the easiest aspect of family cruising. Babies, given the proper stimulus, can be happy anywhere. Older children, with their ever-fertile imaginations, will encounter a host of situations conducive to play. In true child-like fashion, their games will reflect their nautical environment with your sailboat becoming in turn a ferry, windsurfer, travel-lift or trawler. Instead of just a few small cabins, your home will expand to encompass the entire surroundings. The shore, the topsides and the water will all broaden the boundaries within which you live, transforming your boat from a compact, cramped area to one of infinite spaciousness.

Beaches Become Your Backyard

Most cruising is done where there are beaches. No matter whether the beach is sand or stone, big or small, by cold water or warm, children can play happily and longer there than anywhere else. With a plastic bucket and shovel, a toy boat and small net, a child can keep occupied for hours building sand castles, digging pools and forming walls, collecting crabs, minnows, shells and stones. On a sailboat almost anywhere you stop for the night will be within easy reach of a beach, each one just waiting to be explored by your children.

Keeping Young Children Entertained

The following are a few tips for keeping young children entertained under sail, at anchor or on shore when cruising. Nearly all utilize normal boat equipment. Remember that children instinctively like to re-create activities they encounter around them.

—Fender buoys or small plastic objects such as plastic "dough-nuts" tethered to lifelines to throw overboard and retrieve.

—Sailbags & sails on deck serve as camps, tents and homes.

—A bucket of water with small plastic boats (bath toys) in the cockpit, on deck, on a dock; with a sponge for "washing" the boat; with a watering can for showers on a hot day.

—A rope suspended under the boom or a bosun's chair to swing on.

—Playing pirates or Indians with diapers for loincloths, headbands, beads, scarves (be prepared to be ambushed!)

—Playing "travel-lift" or "crane" by using spare lines, blocks, and winches.

—Clotheslines and clothespins for making a secret home among drying sheets and clothes; hanging up toys, dolls, and stuffed friends.

—Dinghy games at anchor; a child's own boat to play in with toys, a picnic, a boat on a string.

—A hammock strung across foredeck in port.

—Sticks, shells, pieces of wood, and the like -very conducive to imaginative play. Don't throw overboard. You may have to sail back to pick them up.

—Dressing up in adult clothes, hats & sunglasses.

—Flying flags; have plenty of flags, pennants, kites, windsocks or whatever you can find to fly from the boat.

—Fins help make time in the water more fun; children learn to swim earlier.

—Steering the boat in a light wind; this is a favorite, so ignore the erratic course.

—Trampoline jumping on an overturned inflatable on the foredeck.

—Child's backpack for special treasures, make-believe games, walks, picnics, trips to the beach.

—For tense moments under sail, settle children inside with popcorn, books, paper and scissors, some special treat (keep something in reserve).

For bad weather in port, kids can create a blanket home on a bunk, "cook" with galley items, decorate the boat with drawings, or have a party.

Steering is usually a popular activity, especially on calm days.

Older Children

Older children should have no trouble keeping entertained on a boat. Imaginative games, reading, exploring in a dinghy, swimming, snorkeling and meeting other boat children will all become daily activities to the older boating child. Because of their watery environment, children on boats develop an early independence and proficiency at swimming and rowing, particularly if you encourage them to feel comfortable in their unusual surroundings. By the teenage years, children are capable of full adult responsibility, a privilege they will naturally thrive on.

Bring as few toys on a boat as you would for any type of adventure travel. To children, the world of a sailboat is perfectly tailored to their size and an endless source of entertainment. Don't worry if your children show next to no interest in the actual sailing of the boat. This will come with time and really isn't relevant anyway. Just because you choose to adventure on a boat doesn't mean the children are going to want to abandon their own games for a trick at the wheel or a lesson in sail-changing. To them a boat is a home, not an activity, one that they will feel comfortable on provided no one is pushing them to perform differently than they're used to.

If you continue to sail, their interest in boat-related activities will develop as they grow older. Look at it as an asset that you can cover large distances, negotiate tricky waters and have some rip-snorting sails without the children even noticing. The day will finally come when you go to raise a sail, haul up the anchor or tie off a dockline only to discover your children got there before you.

Pitfalls To Avoid

Too much sailing—Sailing can be fun and exciting for the whole family, but don't overdo it. Everyone needs to get off the boat, especially children with their high energy level.

The Captain Bligh Syndrome—Sailing has its tense moments and not everyone reacts with the precision or intelligence of a well-drilled crew. Barking out orders, something that sailors frequently do on sailboats, is the quickest way to alienate your children.

Don't expect too much—Few children exhibit an interest in sailing during their early exposure, preferring to enjoy moments under sail from the confines of a cozy spot or as the vehicle for some marvelous games rather than by steering or handling sails. Let them cultivate an interest in their own way.

Treating a day's sail like the start of a Transatlantic race— Forget precision timing, perfectly trimmed sails, brilliant anchoring procedures and number of miles covered. There's a reason why children never show up on boats like that. A few nautical imperfections are inevitable with children on board. Most fellow sailors will be more interested in viewing your young than the set of your sails.

Overcaution—Once children are comfortable on the water, they like to do daring things: hang off the pulpit, shinny up the mast, dive off the cabin roof, swim under the boat. This is all part of growing up and sure beats driving fast down the highway. Consider yourself lucky that your children feel confidant on a boat.

Most children quickly learn to feel at home on a boat, even when under sail.

Chapter

7

Canoeing

Our two canoes slipped almost silently through the water as we paddled up the stillwater. Tristan and Colin, together in the front canoe with their grandfather, watched the shore for signs of beaver. Each in turn caught sight of felled logs, nibbled to a tell-tale point. Around a corner appeared the heaped mound of sticks that formed a beaver house at the water's edge. The creek narrowed as we paddled further, the children exclaiming in delight when we encountered our first beaver dam. Once across the dam, the stillwater twisted among tall grasses, ending finally at the base of a tumbling waterfall where a sawmill once stood. Now only sawdust remained, trapped on the bottom of the creek where it was stirred up in swirls by the children's canoe paddles. At age ten, led by their canoeing veteran grandfather, Tristan and Colin were discovering the delights of canoe travel, exploring the very wilderness waters of inland Nova Scotia that I had canoed as a child.

The Advantages

Canoeing is a unique form of family adventure travel in that it combines all the attributes of hiking, sailing, and camping in a form of travel that is simple yet exciting, easy yet challenging. Wilderness areas can become accessible from the comparatively tame approach of river or lake travel. More populated, touristed places take on an added appeal when experienced from the water.

Canoe travel provides an easy escape into areas of natural beauty untouched by man.

Canoes offer the independence of boat travel without the greater expertise and financial involvement of sailboats. Even if you've never set foot in a canoe, acquiring the necessary skill is quick and rewarding.

Canoe travel can be enjoyed a number of ways: carried on your car for day outings, rented for short-term trips or used for more lengthy explorations by water. The area you are traveling to, the ages of your children, the level of your experience in both canoeing and wilderness travel plus your natural inclination will all determine which type of canoe travel appeals to you. Like all forms of family adventure travel, there is always room for continuing up the adventuring ladder, starting with easy two or three hour outings and working gradually up to overnights and longer.

Like most forms of travel with children, the pace is slow, the focus in-depth and outdoor oriented, and the exposure intimate. As a means of travel, canoeing is less strenuous than hiking or bicycling and can more easily incorporate the carrying of food, camping gear, and children as passengers. Little is needed beyond one or two canoes for a family to enjoy this type of adventure on the water.

Children's Capabilities

Children of almost any age will enjoy a day, overnight or longer outing in a canoe. Young ones can be carried as passengers provided they are old enough to understand the importance of sitting relatively still when underway. Even babies can safely be accommodated, given a little ingenuity and forethought. Ideas for canoeing with a baby have been included in Chapter Ten.

Older children of about nine years and up can paddle well, given sufficient rest periods. One of the best ways to familiarize children with canoeing techniques is to let them go out and paddle on their own for a while in a quiet cove or pond. The following few pointers can be demonstrated beforehand, then the children let loose to learn themselves. Children this age like to feel in control sometimes and develop quick enthusiasm for an activity if parents aren't directing their every move. Later, after interest has developed, is the time for parent directed refinement of their skills.

Basic canoeing techniques:

Don't rock the boat—stress the importance of sitting down, not leaning out, and making no quick movements. Canoes are tippy and possible to upset.

Holding the paddle—depending on which side of the canoe you are paddling, the outside hand grasps the paddles halfway down while the inboard hand covers the top of the paddle. Switching sides reverses the hand position.

Paddling—paddling is done with a downward motion of the top hand, not a rowing motion. Nearly all the power comes from the top hand (the one crossing your body). The bottom hand is used primarily as a guide and to keep the paddle from scraping the side of the canoe. Put your back into the motion rather than just your arms. This greatly increases the power of your stroke.

The bowman—the bowman's job is mostly pure power. Let him set the pace and determine when he needs to change sides to give one arm a rest .

The sternman—the sternman paddles in unison and on the opposite side of the bowman. It's his job to steer, properly accomplished by using the J-stroke. This takes some practice to be done correctly, even for adults. Teach your children the basic rudder effect a paddle can have, letting them master the J-stroke as they get more proficient at canoeing.

The J-stroke—this stroke is designed to keep the canoe going in a straight line with each stroke. Begin with a normal forward stroke. As the paddle enters the water, begin turning the thumb of your upper hand down and away from your body. This will force your wrist to turn out as the stroke progresses. Continue this motion as your paddle moves through the water until your thumb is pointing straight down. If additional correction is needed to keep the canoe going in a straight line, push the paddle out from the canoe in a slight rudder-like motion at the end of the stroke. Only paddle on the same side as the bowman when the extra power is needed to turn the canoe or fight a strong wind. Then be careful you both don't lean out too far, as this can upset the canoe.

Seating—there are two seats in a canoe, one set near one end of the boat, the other slightly farther towards the middle. The sternman sits in the seat set closest to the end of the canoe, the bowman in the seat set further towards the middle. The only time to reverse this is when canoeing alone.

Because paddling a canoe is so easy, children will have a wonderful time, even on their first venture out. One child can paddle alone by sitting in the appropriate seat (see above), putting a large rock or other weight in the bow and paddling as a sternman.

Once a child has learned correctly, his canoeing expertise can match an adults; a child's power, however, can not. If your child is acting as bowman for you, remember that he is working harder than you are in the stern and will tire more easily. A ten year old can paddle for about 45 minutes to an hour before needing a rest.

As with all forms of outdoor activity, the more interesting the area you are canoeing through or the more entertaining you make it, the longer a child will last. Provide plenty of rest times or easy paddling and believe him when he says he needs to change sides, take a break or stop for a while.

Equipment

Beyond the initial need for one or two canoes, nearly all necessary equipment is similar to that used for other outdoor activities like hiking and camping. There's no special clothing or fancy footgear, no mechanical devices or spare parts. For the most part canoeing is a wonderfully undemanding form of family adventure. It's what you plan to do after you reach your destination that determines what you need to bring along with you on a family canoe trip.

Canoes

Canoes come in a variety of sizes, designs and materials. What you want is one that's stable, easy to paddle and a good load carrier. Depending on family size, one or two canoes will be needed. Four persons should be considered the maximum load for a canoe, provided two are small children. Probably the best type for family canoeing are stable "tripping" canoes. A family should choose one that's 16 to18 feet long, at least 34 inches wide, with no less than a 13-inch center depth if you're planning any extended trips. This will comfortably carry a family with lightweight camping gear.

Paddles

Although using any standard length paddle will probably be fine for a day trip here or there, for extended canoeing a proper length paddle is as important as wearing a backpack that fits or having a bicycle with the proper seat height. The following is one formula for choosing a paddle length.

When sitting in the canoe, the distance from your nose to the water is the proper length for the paddle handle. Now add the length of the blade and you have the ideal paddle size for yourself. Do the same for children. A child trying to canoe with an adult paddle will quickly tire and loose interest. Standard child paddles come in 36" and 42" lengths.

Seats & Cushions For Passengers

For passengers, some sort of comfortable seating should be included, like waterproof boat cushions or folding seats. A number of canoe companies carry a folding wooden seat. Small beach chairs also work well. For a very small child a car seat would be comfortable, but don't belt him in. Having succumbed to the paddling enthusiasm of my children and been forced to occasionally take a seat as passenger instead of paddler, I can attest to the comfort of sitting with a cushion under me and a seat back to lean against.

Gear For Canoe Carries

Carries, or portages, are trails linking one body of water to another for the purpose of carrying canoes. You can expect to find them in wilderness canoeing areas. The lighter the canoe, the easier it will be to carry. When properly carried, one person holds the canoe over his head with the center crossbar resting on his shoulders and the canoe tipped slightly backwards. Some canoes are now made with an optional built-in yoke for carrying the canoe, an excellent addition if you're planning long-term travel.

Carries range from short ones that require nothing more than a quick hoist across the land to epic tests of endurance. The longest I have ever been on was a mile, sufficient distance for anyone carrying a canoe. If you plan a trip that includes any carries, bring some padding material for protecting the shoulders of the carrier and an efficient backpacking method for ferrying all your gear. Don't attempt to carry the canoe upright with the gear in it. While this may seem easier it is in fact considerably harder, especially as most carry trails are narrow and require walking single-file. Make sure to include some backpacks for your children, plus a child carrier for any infant or toddler.

Safety

Canoes are less stable than most other types of boats and possible to upset. Although this rarely happens, for most canoeing is done in calm waters, some safety precautions should be taken in the event of an accident. The following are a few basic rules and ideas for improving the safety of canoeing with children.

—Include life jackets for everyone and have non-swimmers wear them while in the canoe. For children, choose one that is comfortable to wear, even when sleeping. Ones made especially for canoeing are designed to be both comfortable and capable of keeping a child's head out of the water.

—Young children can also be harnessed, with the tether clipped to an adult rather than the boat.

—Don't stand up or switch places in the canoe when underway. This is a important rule to learn for any small boat.

—Don't lean way out over the side at any time. Two people paddling on the same side should be especially careful of this. Canoes are very stable provided the center of gravity is maintained in the center of the boat.

Letting children paddle on their own in a quiet cove is the best way for them to learn canoeing.

Day Outings

For a day outing in a canoe, pack as you would for a day hike. Remember to include swimsuits, beachtowels and plenty to eat and drink. Because exposure to the elements is always heightened out on the water, include something warm for afternoon, especially if you will be paddling home into the prevailing wind. We've done a number of day trips down a series of lakes in Nova Scotia that require a long return to windward at the end of the day. The difference in temperature is always noticeable between our hot morning runs downwind and the return trip, when the air temperature has dropped, the wind whipped up and everyone cooled off from swimming much of the day. For a child sitting in the canoe instead of working up a sweat paddling, the trip could be a chilling one without warm clothing.

Equipment list for a day outing includes:

- life jackets
- warm change of clothes
- rain jackets
- bathing suits
- sneakers
- towels
- lunch & snack food
- water flasks
- first aid kit
- Swiss army knife
- sunscreen and sunhats
- toy & reading book per child

Include some sort of bedding for any child that requires a nap. A few small toys or a book will help keep young passengers occupied if the ride is a long one. The first aid kit should have basic items like band-aids and tweezers.

Overnight Or Longer Outings

An overnight canoe trip can be a real adventure no matter where you go. Even in fairly populated areas canoe travel can quickly make you feel cut off from modern day living. Children always find this type of experience exciting, particularly in a canoe, something they associate with the days of pioneers and Indians when adventure was a way of life.

Equipment For Overnight Trips

What equipment you bring depends on what type of accommodations you plan and the area you will be canoeing through. A trip down a populated river might warrent nothing more than basic clothing and some lunch food if you plan to stay and eat at inns or bed & breakfast places. Overnight trips in more isolated surroundings will require all the equipment of any backpacking camping trip. Sometimes it's possible to canoe through fairly isolated areas yet still stay in a cabin at night, similar to hiking a network of trails with mountain huts along the route for overnight stops. These eliminate the need to carry full camping gear and make a convenient overnight destination for a two-day canoe trip.

Basic equipment for overnight outings includes:

• sleeping bags	• shorts	• bathing suit
• sleeping pads	• long pants	• towel
• 1 or 2 tents	• T-shirts	• wash cloth
• camp stove	• long shirts	• pillowcases
• cookset	• pajamas	• sunhats
• stove fuel	• underwear	• warm hat
• ground cloth	• sneakers	• sleepy friends
• grass mats	• socks	• sunscreen
• water jug	• sweater	• dish & hand soap
• Pure water tabs	• rain jacket	• toiletries
• food	• Swiss knife	• toilet paper
• kitchen utensils	• candle lantern	• first aid kit

When preparing for long trips, don't be tempted to throw extra paraphernalia into the canoe at the last moment, spacious as it may seem. An overloaded canoe is a slow one and any superfluous things are going to be a headache every time you load or unload the canoe or cross a carry. Set the goal of only taking as much as everyone can carry all at once, similar to backpacking. Even if you know you won't be carrying the canoe, it's a useful practice for that inevitable time when your family's canoeing ambitions lead you into longer, more strenuous outings.

Making It Fun

As with all forms of adventuring, children like canoeing from the start because it's active and outdoors. Boredom should rarely be a problem unless the canoe rides are too long and the children unoccupied. Young children also like canoeing through places with a variety of things to look at. While older children can derive as much satisfaction from the act of canoeing as adults, younger ones have a more limited interest and soon need some other activity or game to keep them stimulated.

Keep canoeing exciting with some diversions, including:

—Negotiate a tricky passage between rocks.

—Land for a while at a beach or large rock so everyone can take a swim.

—Explore close to shore, watching for signs of animal life.

—Let little ones sitting as passengers tow something over the side (no leaning out, though!). Small plastic boats or Playschool plastic donuts are ideal for this, tied to the canoe with a string.

—Give small passengers their own paddles to "paddle" with. Toddlers love imitating adults and will also develop an early interest in canoeing when they feel they are participating. Tiny children's paddles are available from some canoe companies.

—Play guessing games: who will see the first beaver dam, a deer, identify a kind of bird; who can guess what's around the next corner.

—Provide any child passengers with a few toys to play with, some books to read or a cozy place to take a nap on some bedding fashioned in the bottom of the canoe.

—If traveling downwind, hold a beach towel up in the bow for a sail and see how fast you can go. With two canoes you can have a race, always very stimulating for children.

Keeping little children occupied in a canoe should never be a serious problem. Canoe travel, after all, is a lot more entertaining than car travel and children are expected to do that all the time.

Paddling

Older children will always welcome the opportunity to paddle. Perhaps it's their natural affinity for water or their imaginative zest or their feeling of being in control up there in the bow of the canoe. Whatever the reason, they'll jump at the opportunity to paddle every time unless physically worn out. If you know the day will be long, bring along a good book for each child to relax with and figure this is your opportunity to do some paddling without any pint-size competition. By rotating your children between acting as paddlers and riding as passengers, you should be able to cover a good daily distance with still plenty of time for relaxation and play once you reach your destination.

At A Beach

One fun activity when you're at a beach and the canoe is empty of gear is to let older children flip the canoe in slightly deep water and try climbing on it. With a little air trapped inside, the canoe goes through some hilarious gyrations as children scramble

Loading up for an overnight canoe adventure.

to get aboard. My childhood is filled with memories of my cousins, sisters and I convulsed with laughter as we spent hours attempting to straddle a flipped canoe .

Toys For Longer Canoe Trips

For trips that last three days or more, you might want to bring some extra toys, whatever your standby is for entertainment when adventuring for long periods. Refer to Chapter Two for suggested toys.

Pocketknives

Older children might enjoy including a small pocketknife for fashioning the pointed sticks and spears that feature in so many of their outdoor makebelieve games. Tie a brightly colored lanyard on it if possible to aid in the search when your child invariably leaves it lying around somewhere. Our boys received their first knife at age eight and began earnestly peeling bark and whittling points on an endless number of sticks. A quick bout of safety instruction should prevent any accidents through mishandling. If not, one quick nick along a finger will soon teach them to be more careful. If a child acts carelessly, take the knife away for a few days to emphasize the seriousness of proper knife handling. Children are not stupid about their own personal safety and even very young ones can be competent knife handlers, as the Eskimos can attest to.

Fishing

Fishing is another popular activity with children on a canoe trip. Take along a rod or two and try trolling underway or casting up a stillwater. Even if they don't catch anything, children will enjoy the diversion it creates and the anticipation of getting a bite.

Pitfalls To Avoid

As an outdoor, physical activity, canoeing is similar to hiking and bicycling when it comes to avoiding pitfalls with children. Refer to Chapters Four and Five.

Enjoying a protected campsite during a family canoe trip.

PART III
THE ADVENTURE

The "parking lot" at a local market in Morocco

ADVENTURING WITH CHILDREN

Chapter

8

Great Family Destinations

$\mathbf{A}$lmost anywhere in the world can be a safe, exciting place for family adventuring. Children will feel comfortable and secure and happily explore even the furthest, most remote corners of the earth provided their parents are relaxed and confident. In this book we have tried to show this basic fact, that travel and children do mix, regardless of what destination you choose.

When choosing possible destinations for family adventuring, some areas and countries immediately spring to mind. The following places are only intended as suggestions and represent a mere smattering of the possibilities out there for successful family travel. Some were chosen because they are best suited for families new to adventuring or with very young children. Others are perennial favorites or good choices for low-budget travel.

The list represents a cross-section between tried and true destinations and those appealing to even macro-adventuring families. Many are areas with the potential for extensive, outdoor activities, and most offer much of cultural interest, from shopping in local markets to exploring antiquities. A number of the places were visited by us with our children, others were recommended by other traveling parents. More detailed information on 22 of the best family destinations in the world are covered in my book *Best Places To Go—A Family Destination Guide* .

The Continental United States

Appropriate for both novice and experienced travelers, the United States combines physical grandeur with a multitude of opportunities for outdoor activities. For North Americans, this is a good proving ground, a place where families can hone their adventure skills in familiar cultural surroundings. Foreigners will find it an exciting destination in its own right.

To avoid finding yourself locked into just another car trip, pick one area to explore rather than trying to see the whole country. Too many families try to take in everything in one trip, a situation similar to touring Europe, the British Isles, Scandinavia and North Africa, all at once. Avoid highways and take to the backroads, discovering areas that move at a gentler pace. Get away from your car whenever possible. Exploring the immense park system is one way. Perhaps America's greatest assets, these parks, many of them vast tracts of wilderness, extend through many areas of the country, offering numerous opportunities for outdoor adventure. Set apart from the fast-paced, development-oriented culture that has come to typify the U.S., they retain an unsurpassed beauty, a door into an unspoiled environment. Canoeing and hiking, bicycling and sailing are all possible, as well as all forms of camping, from well-serviced campgrounds to backcountry sites. Three continuous trails bisect the country, any of which can be easily hiked in part: The Appalachian, Continental Divide, and Pacific Crest. Choose an area to canoe, like Quetico National Park or one of the many navigable rivers. Plan a bicycle tour along rural backroads. Sail the Intracoastal Waterway, discovering the quiet towns and scenic beauty that lie hidden behind the densely populated, highway assaulted East Coast. By limiting the area you cover and exploring it in an outdoor fashion, you will find your travels through the U.S. more enjoyable, rewarding, and revealing than any cross-country car tour.

As with all modern western nations, travel here is easy. Food is plentiful and inexpensive, accommodations prolific, campgrounds widely available, and medical concerns minimal. If possible, avoid crowds by traveling off-season, particularly when visiting the national parks.

The Bahamas

Made up of over 700 islands, the Bahamas offers a wealth of tropical adventure at North America's doorstep. White sand beaches, coconut palms, warm waters, coral reefs, and sleepy villages typify this offshore paradise. Outside of Nassau and a handful of tourist resorts, the islands remain untouched by the pressures of tourism, the ideal destination for families escaping winter's cold. Unquestionably one of the world's prime cruising grounds, there's also plenty of scope for hiking, bicycling, swimming and underwater explorations.

Sailing is the best way to explore these islands that were made for cruising with a seemingly endless selection of tropical anchorages, coves, beaches, harbors, and deserted spots. Sailing is completely sheltered inside each island group and passages between them are no more than short day hops. The sailing is particularly well-suited to families with young children, as there's always a beach to play on, shallow water for swimming, and easy snorkeling near-by. The most popular cruising grounds are the Abaco and Exuma Cays.

Discover he fascinating difference between the architecture and life-style of the various islands, reflecting their cultural heritage, from the New England style Abacos to the cotton plantation remnants of Cat and Long islands.

As an island nation, the Bahamas possess some of the best coral reefs in the world. Sea life is abundant, from a variety of tropical fish and colorful starfish to large manta rays, barracudas, sharks, and dolphins. Children will love exploring the shallow, warm waters filled with sea life, or collecting colorful shells along the water's edge.

Inter-island transport is by ferry in the Abacos and mailboat or airplane to the south. Pick only one area to visit to fully savor the unhurried, friendly pace of the Out Islands. Accommodations on land range from luxury resorts to cottage rentals. Boat chartering is possible out of Marsh Harbor, Hopetown, Eleuthera and Georgetown.

I give insight into traveling as a family to the Bahama Out Islands in my book *Bahamas—Out Island Odyssey*.

The Alps

Shared by seven European countries and criss-crossed by an extensive network of trails, the Alps offer endless hiking in a variety of cultural settings. Groomed trails and well-equipped "huts" make hiking here easy, with no need to carry camping gear. Although free-camping is possible in most high alpine areas, spending at least a few nights in a hut is a fun, sociable occasion. Most huts are linked by easy day hikes, allowing for treks of up to a week or longer. For a significant discount on hut facilities, join one of the many regional Alpine clubs, any of which are honored by all countries. Maps and guide books are also available through individual clubs. Children will enjoy the visual splendors of hiking in the Alps: wildflowers, impressive views, grazing cows, wildlife, rushing streams, patches of snow, mountain passes. Routes are diverse, ranging from rambles through pine forests and meadows to high alpine reaches and vertiginous peaks. Most are well within the capabilities of young children. Families hiking together are a common sight here, where even little ones acquire agility and endurance at an early age.

Due to the cultural diversity of the area, walking here can be a wonderful learning experience for children as they note the differences between each country in this compact area. One interesting and scenic route that even a four-year-old can comfortably hike is the Mont Blanc Trail. Encircling this highest of the Alps, it passes through France, Switzerland and Italy, giving you a chance to savor all three countries as you stay in huts or villages along the route. The total trip takes 7-12 days. For the low-budget traveling family, Austria is perhaps the best destination, offering all the alpine splendor and hiking diversity of its famous neighbor Switzerland without the high costs or abundance of tourists. Equally enticing to high mountain regions are the foothills, dotted with lakes, forests, fields and villages. With young children, try basing yourself in a campground, then exploring the surrounding hills in a series of day hikes. Two areas that offer lakeside camping and ample hiking are at Lake Bled in Slovania's Julian Alps and Aachensee in Tyrol, Austria.

British Columbia & Alaska

British Columbia and Alaska offer some of the most beautiful, isolated, wild areas in North America. The choices for outdoor activities are boundless, from easy yet challenging itineraries to ones for hardened adventurers. Here is nature at its most magnificent, largely untouched by man and breathtaking in its beauty. The culture is as diverse as its landscape, with Indian, Russian and Eskimo heritages providing much that will be of interest to children.

British Columbia. This Canadian province is primarily a land of mountains and fjords, of inland passages and a wealth of islands. There's hiking throughout the province, from Vancouver Island to the interior parks. Try sailing up the protected waters of the coast, visiting the many islands along the way that once supported a number of communities. Now mostly deserted, they possess the haunting quality of land that has returned to nature. Hike and camp in the Canadian Rockies or plan an easy bicycle tour of Vancouver Island where experienced hikers can walk a trail once used by lifeboat rescue teams.

Alaska. Set off on its own and reaching to the Arctic Circle, Alaska remains an entity unto itself, dominated by the forces of nature. All kinds of adventures are possible: wilderness travel with a camper or car, cruising along the southeast coast by a series of ferries, hiking any of its abundant trails. Children will be excited with a hike along the famous Chilcoot Trail, originally used during the Yukon Gold Rush. For a canoe adventure appropriate for even novice families, follow the Swan Lake Canoe Route in Kenai National Wildlife Refuge along a system of rivers, lakes and streams. Avoid the pitfall of too many hours spent driving in this expansive, rugged state. For a gentle introduction to wilderness living, try renting one of the isolated cabins maintained by the U.S. Forest Service. Combine a coastal trip of both British Columbia and Alaska by ferry, bringing bicycles along for day explorations. Inland travel in both areas is mostly limited to cars or small airplanes. Camping is also available throughout much of British Columbia and Alaska.

Canadian Maritimes & Newfoundland

Few places in North America offer the physical, cultural and outdoor diversity of the Canadian Maritime Provinces. Made up of the three provinces along Canada's Atlantic coast, the Maritimes are comprised of Nova Scotia, Prince Edward Island and New Brunswick. Together with the island province of Newfoundland, they offer a wealth of opportunities for both the novice and experienced traveler. Each province has its own distinct flavor, physical features and appropriate types of adventures.

Nova Scotia. Diverse in what it offers adventuring families, Nova Scotia can be experienced a number of ways. Sailing is possible in the sheltered waters of the Bras D'Or Lake or along the cove-dotted east coast. Hiking trails and canoeing routes are prolific, from easy day outings to longer ventures. Bicycling is safe and easy on country roads with few cars. One popular biking route is a circumnavigation of southern Nova Scotia where camp-grounds and B & Bs are conveniently located for nightly stops.

New Brunswick. Again the choice is varied, from hiking and bicycling the Fundy Isles, to exploring the rural backroads and waterways of the St. John River Valley. For a gentle introduction to backpacking, try hiking to one of the many wilderness camp-sites in scenic Fundy National Park.

Prince Edward Island. Gentle rolling hills, farmland and the ever-present ocean make this another bicycler's paradise. Because of the uncrowded roads, easy terrain and abundance of B & Bs and campgrounds, bicycling is certainly the most exciting way for a family to experience this rural island. Hiking the length of the island is possible on the scenic new Rails-to-Trails route.

Newfoundland. Typified by small coastal fishing villages and a wild, uninhabited interior, Newfoundland is best experienced at a relaxed pace. Try coastal hopping by local ferry to villages accessible only by boat. Hike the trails of Gros Morne National Park in the west or Terra Nova in the east. Rent a cabin and linger in one place for awhile, an adventure in itself in this outpost of Canada. More intrepid families can take the short ferry ride to Labrador's isolated shore.

England, Scotland & Wales

For a gentle introduction to family adventuring, any one of these three countries offers an ideal destination. The language is familiar, the life-style modern and the people easy to meet and helpful. Predominantly rural despite a high population density, all three offer a multitude of opportunities for outdoor activities in a country setting.

Walking is the easiest and best way to see the countries, for walking here is a way of life. The British love to walk and have criss-crossed their countries with a myriad of public footpaths. Some are continuous and well-defined, others crop up anywhere along the roadside. Both Wales and England have continuous coastal footpaths along their southwestern shores. National parks such as Exmoor in England can be explored by a series of easy circular hikes, well-suited for very young hikers.

Another possibility for families who know how to horseback ride is exploring the countryside along England's many public bridlepaths. The trails are well sign-posted and horses usually available for hire somewhere in the vicinity.

A bicycle tour is possible on country roads almost anywhere. Choose somewhere without too many hills. England's Broads country, for instance, is ideal with its level land, sparse population and lovely network of canals. When bicycling, farmers will often allow you to camp overnight on their property. Another possibility is sailing the west coast of Scotland among the scores of interesting islands and uncrowded anchorages, all waiting to be explored on foot.

The castles, ruins and manor houses throughout the British Isles will keep children fascinated. Many are open to the public on specific days. Children have a passion for these romantic relics of by-gone eras and never seem to tire of exploring yet another castle or manor house grounds. Public transportation is extensive on trains and buses. Campgrounds and ubiquitous B & Bs offer inexpensive accommodations.

Greece & Turkey

Greece and Turkey lie at the crossroads of two continents, offering adventuring families the opportunity to sample both.

Greece. Greece is best known for its islands, each possessed of its own unique characteristics. Linked together by a network of ferries that children will find exciting to ride on, the islands are easy to reach and explore by bus, bicycle or on foot. The life-style is for the most part simple, with fishing villages, olive groves and grazing herds of goats. Children are treated everywhere with delight. Visited off-season, the Greek isles offer inexpensive lodgings, few tourists and a relaxed atmosphere. Sailing is perhaps the best way to visit the islands, with destinations close together, and a choice between quiet anchorages and busy waterfronts. As always, sailing enables you the ability to get away from it all into the beauty of each island. Hiking can be done anywhere along the donkey paths that wind through the countryside. For more adventurous families, explore the remote regions of the Pelopennese, or mainland Greece, where you can discover isolated villages, forests, mountains and deep gorges. Children will be fascinated with the many Greek ruins throughout the country, from Minoan cities to Crusader castles, all of which will appeal to their vivid imaginations.

Turkey. The gateway to Asia, Turkey is both exotic and exciting without being intimidating to families new to foreign travel. The west coast is mountainous, wooded and westernized. Travel here is easy and safe with campgrounds, modern facilities, beaches, Greek ruins and still an aura of eastern mystique, a compromise between its Muslim roots and European influences. The further east you travel, the more Asian the country becomes. Public transportation is by bus and inexpensive accommodations are available throughout the country, including in campgrounds. The sailing along Turkey's coast is some of the best in the Mediterranean. Hiking can also be done on a number of ancient paths through the interior hills. The Turks themselves are a polite, quiet people, a unique blend between east and west that makes travel here exciting without being overwhelming.

Ireland

Ireland is a country of rolling hills and barren mountains, of isolated villages and castle ruins, a romantic, rural country infused with a sense of mystique that can't help but be alluring. Don't let the prospect of Ireland's famed mists deter you from exploring it the best way possible, by bicycle or on foot. In actual fact, the climate is surprisingly mild, warmed by the Gulf Stream. Bicycle routes abound through any of Ireland's beautiful areas. This is a popular touring country and ten-speed bicycles can be rented in a number of locations, both for day outings or long term use. Bicycling is safe along sparsely used roads and the terrain hilly without being rigorous.

Ireland's extensive canal system, no longer used for commercial purposes, is a popular way for families to adventure through the countryside at a relaxed pace. Canal boats can be hired in a number of places, including the Lakelands region north of Dublin and the more rural County Leitrim in the northwest.

Like most agriculture countries, hiking is also an excellent way to explore. Villages, Bed & Breakfast places and hostels are conveniently located to permit even long treks through the countryside without the need to carry full camping gear. In addition to the many official campgrounds, camping is permitted on private land provided you have the permission of the owner. Finding inexpensive accommodations in Ireland should not be a problem. Try exploring the coastal area of Donegal in the extreme northwest where the rugged scenery and friendly people make this a good destination for families who enjoy wild places.

Children will love Ireland's castles and medieval ruins. An entire adventure could be conducted traveling from ruin to ruin. For public transportation, Ireland has both trains and buses, the latter servicing even remote areas.

Islands

Islands make wonderful destinations for family adventuring. Self-contained and individualistic, each island has a personality all its own. On an island there's no possibility of overdoing it or hurrying along too quickly. Island people themselves are unhurried, having already learned the futility of trying to get things done fast on an island. A trip planned around just one island is an excellent introduction to the pace of family travel. These are just a handful of possible islands a family could explore.

Madeira. A hiker's paradise. Portuguese culture, jagged mountains, terraced fields and a network of trails that make exploring on foot easy and fascinating. Public buses allow you to begin and end a hike anywhere.

Crete. An unspoiled Greek island. Snow-capped mountains and sunny beaches. Hiking can be done along designated trails or the donkey paths that permeate the countryside. Accommodations are inexpensive in campgrounds, pensions and rentals. Public buses make travel easy and pleasant.

The Canary Islands. Explore these on foot, by bicycle or a combination of both. Spanish by culture and long a destination of sun-seeking English, getting out into the countryside at a slow pace will show you the lovelier side to the islands. Hiking is prolific on an extensive network of trails.

The Virgin Islands. Spectacular to look at, small enough to easily explore, and graced with eternal sunshine, the Virgin Islands offer the ultimate island escape. The Virgins islands are divided among the U.S. island group and their British counterpart. Don't miss the island of St. John's in the U.S. group, principally a national park, with hiking, snorkeling, sailing and camping. A cruise on a sailboat is the best way to visit all the islands, with protected waters, numerous anchorages and good shore facilities. In the British island group, camp on small, somnolent Jost Van Dyke or explore the largest island of Tortola, with its cloud-shrouded peaks and lush interior.

Mexico, Guatemala & Costa Rica

Traveling with children through Mexico, Guatemala and Costa Rica can be a relatively easy introduction to the developing world. This is an area of contrasts—ornate ruins and life at its poorest, mountain villages and island homes, beaches lined with resorts and hillside fields of corn. The people are friendly and family-oriented, with the ingrained love of children you find everywhere in the developing world.

Mexico. A large and varied country, from its famous beaches to its wild, mountainous regions, Mexico lies next to the United States, but is worlds apart in life-style. Because of its proximity, travel by car or camper is possible. Renting a place on the beach or in a village that appeals to you is another way to get to know the country in depth. Plan a bicycle trip through the Yucatan, where level roads, Mayan ruins and friendly people are plentiful.

Guatemala. For the most part mountainous and rural, Guatemala is a lovely, rugged, fascinating country. Populated by numerous Indian tribes, the ethnic diversity of their cultures is still very much alive today. Try renting on Lake Atitlan, a lovely inland lake ringed with mountains and villages. Roads are adventurous and sometimes impassible, but hiking is possible just about anywhere in the countryside where people live. Visit the famous Mayan ruins at Tikal or hike a live volcano. Attend a language school in the ancient town of Antiqua, where the whole family can learn Spanish in a month.

Costa Rica. A tropical paradise, Costa Rica has emerged as a popular ecotourism and adventure destination. More European than its Central American neighbors, the country is both ethnically distinct, yet comfortably modern. Renowned for its rain forests and regional beauty, Costa Rica has made valiant attempts to protect its land, resulting in an ever-growing system of national parks. Travel is easy; by car, public bus, or train. Accommodations are plentiful, conditions safe and clean, and the people friendly. With its diverse landscape, outdoor activities abound, from hiking the mountains and rafting the waterways, to exploring the coastal regions.

Nepal & Northern India

Located in the world's highest mountain range, these areas have become increasingly popular with adventurers. The cultures are exotic, the scenery spectacular and trekking the ideal way to explore, making them exciting areas for adventuring families to visit. Both are probably most appropriate for families with some previous adventure experience, as the culture, life-style and level of hiking all rate fairly high on the difficulty scale.

Nepal. Trekking has long been a popular way to experience this country. Recently, trekking facilities have been expanded along some of the more popular routes, making them more accessible to a wider range of tourists. Nepal's trails are ancient footpaths linking village to village and still forming the main artery for transportation throughout the country. Although the hiking is strenuous, it's not beyond the limitations of even small children, provided they have an acceptable level of physical fitness. With the assistance of some guides, a family could go anywhere, even with a baby. As always, walking will give you an in-depth exposure and insight into the country. Children will open doors wherever you go and be a continual source of interest. Trekking routes range from remote areas to well-traveled ones equipped with hotels and restaurants serving western style food. Carrying camping gear is not necessary in most areas.

Northern India. Lying in the foothills of the Himalayas, northern India offers a spectacular introduction to this large, diverse, culturally rich country. Once the site of an annual retreat of the British from the summer's heat, northern India spawned a number of hill stations, from Shimla in the west to Darjeeling in the east. Today they remain popular vacation spots, combining an old world English flavor with modern Indian influences. Visit Kashmir, probably best known for its houseboats on Dal Lake. Both Kashmir and Ladakh, a mini-Tibet high on the Himalayan plateau, offer trekking along ancient routes. For a more relaxed style of travel, base yourself in one of the many hill stations and walk the foothills of Himachal Pradesh and Uttarakhand.

New Zealand

New Zealand is another destination appropriate for all levels of adventuring families. Isolated by virtue of its remote island status, New Zealand is unlike any other place, a mixture of contrasting forces: English and Maori heritages, tropical regions and high peaks, cities and remote farms, cricket fields and wilderness areas. The potential for outdoor activities is widespread, for New Zealanders are an outdoor-loving people.

The bulk of New Zealand's inhabitants live on the north island. Much of the south is largely unpopulated except by isolated sheep farmers, making this an area of almost unmatched beauty. From dry plains to snowy peaks, the south island is like North America before the settlers, a place for families who like to feel alone with nature.

Sailing is possible throughout the country, but perhaps most ideal in the warm waters of the Bay of the Islands on the North Island. With nearly 150 islands, the area offers a variety of places to explore between easy day sails. Many islands and coastal areas here also have day hikes. Bicycle travel has long been popular along New Zealand's uncrowded country roads. Try a bicycle tour of either island, taking in some scenic day hikes along the route. When covering major distances, bicycles can be taken on trains and buses.

The potential for hiking in New Zealand is extensive, from public walkways near urban centers to remote trails through the country's many parks. Campgrounds are numerous, many of them located beside popular hiking routes. Designated trails are extensive, with a network of shelters situated about every 3-4 hours along many routes. Carrying sleeping bags and cooking equipment is necessary when staying at huts. One beautiful trail along the coast is the Abel Tasman Coastal Track, a 3-4 day hike that follows the north coast of South Island. Huts are well placed for easy hiking distances. Other routes include the very popular Milford Trail, the Routeburn Trail close by and the various trails around lovely Lake Waikaremoana. Public transportation in New Zealand is available by bus, train or airplane.

Norway & Finland

Both Norway and Finland are made for outdoor adventuring families, from newcomers to the well-experienced.

Norway. In a country of mountains pierced by fjords, islands and tiny hill farms, nature is a constant presence, one the Norwegians themselves thoroughly enjoy. Outdoor activities are as much a way of life here as a recreation. Families can hardly go wrong in this country where beauty seems to be in-bred and every corner is worth exploring. The country's only drawback is its high cost, something even budget-minded travelers can survive by not trying to take in the whole country in one visit.

Hiking is one of the easiest and least costly ways to get out into the country. Try the popular hiking areas in the Jotunheimen Mountains where the Norwegian Mountain Touring Association maintains trails and well-equipped huts. Membership will get you a discount at the huts when staying overnight. Other areas with extensive hiking include the Dovrefjell, Rondane, and Ovre Dividal.

Some areas of this mountainous country could be explored by a family on bikes as a way of keeping down the high cost of travel in this expensive country. Try a tour of parts of southern Norway or a bicycle trip up the west coast on the system of ferries, exploring the different islands and fjord areas by bike along the way. For an unusual adventure, rent a fisherman's cottage in the remote, dramatically beautiful Lofoton Islands.

Finland. This is a land of lakes and forest, an immense island archipelago and vast stretches of tundra. As in all of Scandinavia, the people are outdoor-oriented and there is a strong physical beauty, abundant parks and numerous opportunities for adventuring. Sailing is exciting among the Åland Islands or in the inland Lake District. An extensive network of hiking trails, some of them long distance with overnight camp sites, reflect the popularity of this sport. A bicycle tour is another excellent option in this country of few cars and a predominantly gentle terrain. Don't miss some of the fascinating historic sites, including a number of castles that lie scattered across southern Finland.

Spain, Portugal & Morocco

These countries lie close enough together to make adventuring in all three a possible destination, although taken on their own, each offers enough to satisfy even the most ambitious adventuring family. All have fascinating cultures, physical beauty, areas appropriate for family exploration and potential for outdoor activities.

Spain. Away from the notorious Costa del Sol, Spain is largely unspoiled. The north part of the country will be particularly appealing to adventuring families who want to get off the beaten tourist path. Buses and trains service most areas and freelance hiking is possible. Ordessa National Park in the Pyranees has designated hiking trails and mountain huts. Accommodations are easy to come by in Spain, from well-equipped campgrounds to pensions.

Portugal. A friendly country with an emphasis on family life, Portugal is ideal for adventuring families new to foreign travel. Bicycling the coastal areas is easy, with campgrounds conveniently located for nightly stops. The west coast in particular remains unspoiled and undeveloped, but still well equipped for traveling families. Day hikes are possible throughout the countryside along animal paths. Sandy beaches dot the coastline, many of them adjacent to campgrounds. Public transportation is primarily by bus.

Morocco. Morocco is a mixture of European, Arab and Berber influences. Once a colony of France, French still serves as the second language, so some ability is helpful. As in any completely foreign culture, everything is exciting: the ancient city streets, or medinas, the robed people, the Arab villages and dramatic landscapes. For hikers there's Toubkal National Park with a network of trails that links one remote Berber village to another. The Kasbah route in the south with its many ruins and dramatic approach to the Sahara is particularly exciting. Trains and buses service most locations and are a cultural experience in themselves.

Chapter
9
Living Abroad

The year Tristan and Colin were six we spent two months renting a villa in a small village on the island of Crete. Ostensibly devised to take up the slack period between when we left home and when the weather would be warm enough to camp, the plan introduced us to a new form of adventuring. Living abroad, we discovered, can be just as much of an adventure as backpacking or bicycling your way across a country, with all the inherent challenges of adventuring plus some added ones of its own.

The Advantages

When living in a country, everything about a culture is learned faster—its language, cultural nuances, social structure, shopping procedures, and public transportation. A home is established and with it comes familiarity, understanding and ease within a given culture. Once you've settled in a place, regardless of length of stay, the area around you can be explored in an adventurous, outdoor way with the added convenience of your own home to return to each night. When living abroad, the adventure is still there, but the pressures and unknowns are less, a situation often welcomed when traveling with children.

Learning The Culture

Learning a culture consists of a combination of things. Certain aspects are researched and learned from, specific cultural practises observed and copied, and most important of all, a mental attitude adopted. To truly learn a culture, or gain the ability to live in it comfortably, certain inner resources must be cultivated. No one does this better or more naturally than children. Their innate enthusiasm, curiosity, adaptability and open-mindedness make accepting new cultures a natural process. Children, unless taught, know no prejudice. Nor are they self-conscious and shy in an adult sense, afraid of looking or sounding silly. If people respond favorably to them, and people do the world over, then they respond well in return. Children are, in effect, the perfect ambassadors. As an adventuring family abroad, desirous of touching down in a foreign setting, your experience is destined for success provided you do nothing more complex than follow your children's lead. Babies, with no conscious skills of their own, are the best ambassadors of all, for nothing elicits a more instantaneous welcome and show of affection from strangers than the appearance of a baby.

Our new friends in a remote village in Guatemala.

Each culture has its own distinctive characteristics, things that soon become evident when living or traveling there. Some can be learned prior to your trip with a little research. This helps avoid some basic cross-cultural misunderstandings, alleviate pre-travel jitters, and prepare you mentally for the culture you will be living in. Attention to little details can make a world of difference in a small community. In Norway neighbors are invited over for coffee and some kind of baked goodies. A visit to a Greek home at any hour means shots of raki for the adults and sweets for the children. Moroccans like to shake hands at every meeting and take quick offense at the casual tourist brush-off. The French have a precise way of greeting each other that never varies and causes offense if it's not done properly. Tips about behavioral patterns like these are invaluable in easing your entry into a new culture, particularly if you intend to stay in one place for any length of time and acquire some degree of acceptance in a community. Foreigners see it as a sign that you have taken the time to learn their way of doing things and respect it. Unlike North America where the diversity of nationalities has lead to a pot-pourri of cultural practises, foreign countries often have a traditional way of doing things from which they rarely deviate. To do so would often alienate your new neighbors, despite your status as an obvious newcomer.

Many tips to cultural behavior can be learned even before visiting a country either through reading or talking to someone who has been there. Guide books offer some hints. So do travel articles in magazines and newspapers. National Geographic is very helpful with insights into the culture of a country, how its people think and act, and what standard of living to expect. Back issues can be located through local libraries. Books written by people who have lived in a specific country are best of all and worth investigating at your library. Before we traveled to our first Arab country I found a book written by a woman who had lived for years among the Arabs. This was immensely helpful in developing my understanding of their culture so I wouldn't fall into the trap of judging them by our standards. Another good source of tips for us have been the Audio-Forum language courses. Developed by the Foreign Service Institute for diplomats going to foreign countries, they contain a number of hints about the socially acceptable way of doing things in the country you will be visiting. If your supply of resources is limited, don't worry. What isn't learned before your trip can always be picked up after you get there, part of the challenge in this type of adventure.

The more you travel the more you will notice shared characteristics between cultures. Climate, for instance, creates similarities in life-styles. So does standard of living, terrain and religious beliefs. Different cultures will seem more alike, not in the sense of the world becoming de-culturalized, but in the similarities of people as a whole. There are only so many ways to handwash laundry, cultivate a steep hill, prepare food, or clothe yourself.

Learning about a culture also makes it less intimidating, for cultures very different from our own can seem frightening in their unfamiliarity. By staying in one place and immersing yourself in a country, you discover that it's not the people of the world that are frightening, but only their culture if it's not understood. When we decided to travel to Morocco, friends of ours thought we were crazy. We went, secure in our status as a family. Moroccans, like people in most developing countries, love children. As a wife and mother of sons in an Arab world, I was treated with invariable respect. The longer we stayed the more we understood the nuances of Moroccan behavior and perceived Morocco as a friendly place rather than the aggressive nation we'd been led to expect.

The adventure of learning a culture for a family is a two-part affair: the initial arrival and the act of staying there. In the beginning, just finding a place to live or a market to shop in is an adventure. After a while these challenges give way to the adventure of living somewhere abroad, of adopting certain aspects of the culture and combining them with your own cultural habits. This is what we call the Peace Corps stage, oriented towards blending in to the best of your abilities.

Where To Stay

Staying in one place usually means finding a place to rent. For a family this can be both economical and desirable in terms of living space. A rental for an entire apartment or small house on a weekly or monthly basis can be cheaper that the cost of a one-room pension at a nightly rate. We paid less per night for our villa in Greece than for an inexpensive, one-room pension without even a private bath. Friends of ours, an American couple with three small sons, spent a week in a hotel in the Dominican Republic before discovering the potential for renting. The apartment they found exposed them more to the community, gave them the independence of providing their own meals, supplied much more living space, and cost less per night than their one hotel room. Another family we know, interested in spending a winter on the island of Man O' War in the Bahamas, simply went there and within two days had a small house overlooking the water for a relatively modest price.

Finding A Place To Live

Finding a place isn't nearly as difficult as it might seem. Don't bother trying to arrange things prior to your trip. This is not only a headache, but can land you somewhere you don't like for more

The villa we rented on the Island of Crete. By traveling off-season, places like this become affordable, even to budget-minded families.

than you want to pay. Pick an area that interests you and go there first. If you like it enough to stay, have one member of the family (the cleverest negotiator) go house-hunting while the other parent stays in a comfortable, relaxed place with the children. This makes the whole process as non-disruptive and enjoyable as possible.

House Hunting—Various Techniques

Try the local tourist office if there is one, or any real estate businesses in the area. We've found places both ways. Go to a town or village that looks appealing and make inquiries. There's usually something available on a weekly basis. Ask anyone you meet if they know of a place available for a reasonable price. Our best find was discovered by asking our waiter at the restaurant where we dined the first night we arrived in a country.

Check Out The Amenities

Once you've found something you like, check out all the amenities. Very few places operate with the precision you might be accustomed to at home so expect some quirks within reason. Water and electricity that get turned off periodically are typical occurrences in poor countries. We stayed in one country where the water was turned off most of the day and the electricity all night, just as it turned dark! As this happened to everyone, we could hardly complain. What you don't want is to rent a place where you discover this only happens to you. Try the faucets, the toilet, the light switches, the water heater and stove. In fact, try anything mechanical. Use your discretion to strike a balance between what seems reasonable in a given area and what's reasonable for the price you're expected to pay. An apartment we rented on the island of Madeira featured a number of mechanical quirks, all within the reasonable-when-renting-abroad-on-an-island bounds. Water mysteriously ceased at unpredictable times. Two out of four burners were nonfunctioning on the cookstove. The hot water heater took some fancy finger work to get it going. One toilet refused to flush, the front door had a tendency to lock you out instead of let you in, and the vacuum cleaner blew out more than it picked up. Most eventful of all, our initial foray with the washing machine left us with sodden, soap-filled clothes and a machine full of water. On the other hand the refrigerator and shower worked to perfection, two burners were still better than one, Kevin always did manage to produce hot water, the front door eventually came unlocked, and the vacuum cleaner got replaced with a broom. Even the washing machine was finally brought to heel with the help of some hand signal communication from our Portuguese-speaking neighbors. While mechanical perfection is hardly a universal trait, ingenuity is and increases in direct proportion to mechanical imperfection. Before renting, don't hesitate to discover what trick must be employed to make something go.

Language

Although English is not nearly as widely spoken as some tourist bureaus would have you believe, fluency in a foreign language is not necessary when going abroad to live somewhere for a short time. Living in one place is bound to familiarize you with the basics of the local language. Children will pick up phrases quickly, particularly if they play with local children. Unlike adults, they experience little embarrassment at stumbling along in a new language and have a total disregard for grammar, all of which enables them to learn quickly. English, French, Spanish and German are all used widely as either a first or second language, so some basic knowledge in any one or more of these languages will help you when living abroad.

Once in a country, practise the language any way you can. Write things down as you hear them, practise reading signs, supplement the foreign word for the English one, even when speaking together as a family. This gets everyone's ear attuned to the new language and helps you remember new words and phrases. Shopping is one place you'll learn quickly. Nothing makes you feel more ridiculous or self-conscious than trying to shop and continually having to ask "Do you speak English?" Except in a real tourist area, they usually don't anyway.

If all else fails in a serious communication gap, find a child. Beginning quite young, foreign children are usually taught at least one other language in school, often English. Children with access to television, movies and radio are also often proficient at English just because they hear it so often. Most of what needs to be said in a communication emergency is very simple, so even just a basic command of English will serve.

Communicating with locals generally covers the same basic topics: shopping, directions, the weather, greetings, where you're from , the ages of your children, how you like the country. The jump from this to a deeper level of communication takes a fluency that only comes with prolonged visits or previous study. The one exception is if your children are enrolled in the local school, in which case they'll become fluent in a couple of months. Otherwise, your ability in a foreign language will progress fast enough when living abroad for even a few weeks to allow you to get to know your neighbors and experience a level of acceptance not enjoyed by most visitors.

Shopping

Travel guide books rarely tell you how to shop for basics while abroad. Most tourists visit places briefly, bringing what necessities they need with them from home. Nor are they dealing with housekeeping and homemaking. As a family living in a foreign country, even for just a few weeks, your shopping needs will be different from that of other tourists. Instead of artifacts and souvenirs, you'll be looking for kitchen aids and cleaning equipment. Before going it's helpful to know something about what's available, what you should bring with you and what's involved with shopping.

What To Bring With You

To begin with, take the same things you would for any adventure: basic cooking gear, toiletries, clothes, books, backpacks, a few toys, first aid equipment, favorite cooking spices, plus any little items you really don't want to live without. When renting you can be a bit more lenient about what you take as weight is less critical. Arriving with a good supply of necessities allows you time to familiarize yourself with a place before searching around for where to buy bandaids, thread, toothpaste or sugar.

Finding Local Shops

Once you're settled with a place to live, asking is the most expedient way to find various shops, even if you don't speak the language. People's hand gestures are almost as expressive as words and six or seven inquiries can still get you somewhere faster than trying to find it on your own. If someone is willing to take you the first time, so much the better. A morning spent being shown the shops and where to buy everything will practically eliminate all the headaches of shopping in a new, unfamiliar place. Some communities have an obvious town center with all the local shops. A few places have shopping centers similar to those in North America. These are harder to find due to their distance from the town center. Developing nations have more shops per community than one would believe was possible. You'll find four or five shops of a similar type in a row, often grouped together on purpose. Survival seems to be a matter of community courtesy; all receive equal business through some sort of inherent sense of fairness. Due to sheer quantity, shops are often easiest to find in developing countries once you know what to look for. At first glance it might look as though there aren't any until shutters are thrown open, metal doors raised, and an assortment of items hung outside as a lure to potential customers.

What Types Of Shops Are Available

More modern countries manage to strike a balance between American-type department stores and intimate old-world shops. Supermarkets and department stores exist, but on a smaller scale. Shops are clustered together, but not in malls. Street vendors and open-air markets thrive alongside their more modern counterparts.

Even poor countries are not the unequipped backwaters tourist guide books would sometimes have you believe. In many cases their products are equal or superior to our own and almost always less expensive. Cotton clothing, for instance, is widely used throughout the world and easier to buy abroad, particularly

An open- air market in Turkey. Supermarkets and malls seem worlds away from this type of shopping.

for children's clothing. Pharmaceuticals are available in every country. The word "pharmacy" is practically universal, as is the Red Cross identification sign, making it easy to find. Most of what you could possibly want will be anywhere you go, particularly if it's an area popular with tourists. Your biggest hurdle will be bridging the language gap in order to get what you need. Sometimes I'll frequent one shop in particular just because it's set up for the customer to serve himself. Others employ the over-the-counter technique which relies on some degree of communication. When this first happened to me in a Spanish-speaking country, I memorized the names of everything I wanted to buy so I could ask for them each time I went shopping. Tourist areas are always the easiest to shop in because shopkeepers speak English, a wider selection is available and items are usually easier of access. Instead of having half the village watch in fascination as you try to convey that you want that toilet paper on the back top shelf, you can subtly take it off the rack yourself.

Clothing

Children's clothing, of course, is available everywhere, although not always in the guise in which you see local children. I spent the longest time searching for Turkish style trousers like those worn by the little girls until I realized they are all made by the women at home. Only the material was available in the shops. Western style clothes can be bought just about anywhere these days. T-shirts, sneakers, sandals, bathing suits, socks, underwear, pajamas, all the items children typically wear out or misplace can be bought in foreign countries. Foreigners have a real flair for selling clothes, one that makes our big department stores seem stale in comparison. You'll see clothes being sold in open-air markets, off the backs of trucks, on street corners and out of Gypsy wagons. Some places even have a profitable used clothes market, perfect for children who quickly outgrow things before they're worn out. Look around everywhere, particularly at market places for inexpensive children's clothing.

Household Items

Most household items are also widely available. Cleansers, dish rags, towels, detergent, plastic and paper products are all possible to find in most places. One major exception is sponges. Definitely bring a package of sponges with you as the rest of the world seems to be lacking in a good, effective version of this basic household item. Another useful thing to bring along is a supply of baking soda, not just for baking purposes, but for cleaning. Using it in place of the usual arsenal of toxic cleaning products is a nice contribution to the environmental cause and the simplest of cleansers. You'll find its versatility amazing and start wondering why all these other products were ever invented.

If aluminum is something you prefer not to cook with, bring a stainless steel camping cookset. Aluminum pots and pans seem to have a monopoly on the world at the moment and alternatives can be next to impossible to find. Inexpensive rentals that come equipped with cookware will always supply aluminum. I also bring my small supply of camping bowls, mugs, and cutlery so I know I'll at least have the basics. Even though it's possible to buy these things abroad, you may not want the added expense for such a short time. You never know what you will find in a rental. Don't be surprised if you discover a lovely china tea set, but no plates, or a frying pan and no spatula. At one apartment we rented the landlord had to go out and buy a whole new supply of things because the previous tenants had taken everything with them.

Bring along some good daypacks and a handful of collapsible shopping bags for weekly food shopping trips. These can involve a long walk or ride on some form of public transportation so the less encumbered you are the more you'll enjoy your outings. Net bags capable of handling quantities of purchases are a particularly good choice because they're lightweight and small enough to stuff in a pocket when not in use.

How To Shop

Write down the words for everything you want to buy in the language of the country you are in. Attempts at the local language always get you quicker, friendlier service. Then observe the shopping behavior of the locals. Some places operate on a strict code of etiquette with everyone standing politely in line waiting his turn. In others this kind of behavior could get you nowhere as people push, shove and trample their way past you. If bargaining is in order, don't be shy, embarrassed or put off by seemingly belligerent behavior. In countries like this, natives thrive on a good bargaining session, with respect afforded the customer who drives the hardest bargain. As a tourist you have to strike a delicate balance between emulating the actions of the locals and accepting the limitations of your status as a tourist. By all means bargain and bargain well, but don't take it as an act of faith to drive things to rock bottom prices. Paying somewhere in the vicinity of half way between the quoted price and what a local pays is a good balance. Upon conclusion of bargaining, hand-shakes and smiles are always in order. Hand-shakes, in fact, are very important throughout most of the world. Shopkeepers are not the anonymous entities they often are in North America and expect some attention. Greetings, handshakes before and after business, and social conversation are all welcomed.

Food

Food shopping abroad is a sociable occasion. Undertaken almost daily, it is often punctuated by lengthy conversations and conducted with an unhurried air. Although it can be unbelievably time-consuming compared to shopping in North America, when viewed as a cultural event, it can also be fascinating.

Food Stores

While some modern countries do have supermarkets, food shops abroad usually take the form of small, compact stores. Don't be misled by the use of the term "supermarket", loosely applied to anything that just happens to sell food. What you actually find in each store is anyone's guess. We've discovered a wealth of foods in shops the size of walk-in closets and others with almost no variety at all. The size of the shop has little to do with the variety and quality of items. Only familiarity will teach you which shops you prefer. One of the reasons the whole process is so time-consuming is because of the unpredictable nature of what's available. Even with a modest shopping list it might take visiting three or four stores to complete your purchases for the week. Then just when you feel you have the whole routine under control, your most dependable shop will run out of something critical and you'll have to go looking again. If you're also trying to find the best price, the whole process becomes even more complicated. The more undeveloped the country, the more unpredictable the procedure.

In the Dominican Republic we experienced a flour shortage of epic proportions. After two weeks of deprivation the word spread through town that the one shop that normally never carried flour now had a supply. This is typical of what one can expect in a developing nation. Another maxim is to buy today what you'll want tomorrow. Otherwise you may never see it again. While also in the Dominican Republic we experienced a two-week powdered milk shortage, one brief influx of peanutbutter and the permanent disappearance of cookies. In countries like this, the fickle nature of food shopping just becomes part of the adventure and gives rise to many an amusing situation.

Open-Air Markets

In addition to food shops are open-air markets, the main source of fresh produce. Small towns may only have market day once a week, large ones a daily market, often located under cover somewhere in the center of town. Local farmers come here from all over the area to sell their products, always at rock bottom prices. Browse around the market the first time, then choose one or two stalls you prefer and just patronize them in the future. This eliminates market day headaches and creates a measure of rapport between you and the vendors you solicit. When shopping at a market, take your own shopping bags. They rarely have them. Bring along whatever backpacks and collapsible shopping bags you have with you. Otherwise you could find yourself stranded with a load of fresh produce and nowhere to put it. Some plastic bags, the kind you get at most grocery stores, are also useful for packing dirty items in backpacks. We once watched a young tourist look on in horror as a pile of wet, filthy potatoes was dumped into his nice, clean backpack.

Produce markets like this one in Madeira are common all over the world, offering an array of locally grown fresh foods at low prices.

In many places bargaining at the market is not standard procedure. Notice what the locals do and follow their lead. Don't be intimidated into letting the vendor choose your produce. Choose your own in a friendly but firm manner. If the vendor won't let you, move on to another stall. Take the children when you shop. Vendors love them and service is always smoother and friendlier when they are along.

In addition to fresh produce, markets usually have stalls selling all sorts of other foods: meats, cheese, fresh bread and baked goods, grains, dried fruits, spices, and nuts. Towns with very little to offer on most days can really blossom in the food department when market day arrives. In large towns where there's a daily market, Saturday is usually the main market day. This is when the bulk of the farmers arrive with their produce to sell and one can subsequently find the best, freshest and least expensive selection.

What Kinds Of Food

What you find to eat is really not that different from country to country. What's different from North America is the size of the selection. Instead of six kinds of noodles you find one. Instead of thirty breakfast cereals there are only a handful. The basics are almost universal: flour, rice, noodles, beans, meat, cheese, eggs, canned foods, oatmeal, crackers, bread, spices, tea, coffee. Fresh milk is not always available, but some other source usually is—powdered whole milk, canned or sterilized. Fruit juices generally have sugar added, so rely on the abundance of inexpensive fresh fruit in most places to provide the desired vitamins. Some countries also sell a type of unsweetened orange juice concentrate in bottles to be mixed with water. Most of the world sells fresh bread baked daily, a good filler for hungry children if the bread has some substance to it. Unfortunately it doesn't always, particularly the French kind that tastes delicious when fresh, but has little staying power. A little searching and some inquiries might reveal a heartier variety. Bakeries often bake a limited supply of whole wheat bread which they'll keep for you if they know you want it. Otherwise lavish on some peanut butter or cheese to raise the nutrition value and help fill the children. If dried fruits, nuts or yoghurt are available, these are also good snack foods.

Keeping my children's voracious appetites at bay between meals is always my biggest challenge in countries where healthy snack foods simply don't exist. Often it helps to notice what the locals do. In the absence of bread we discovered fresh tortillas with beans in Guatemala and the ubiquitous Gallo Pinto (rice with beans) of Costa Rica.

Quality Of Food

Much of the world has traditionally subsisted on a healthy diet that has little to do with any nutritional know-how. Consequently, while standard ethnic cooking is healthy, convenience foods are not. Where modern trends have infiltrated, so has sugar, white flour and additives. In Morocco, a typical example of this was the wonderful whole-wheat pita bread we found cooked by Berber women in mountain villages that couldn't be bought in stores. Instead, all you could find was modern, French-style bread made from bleached white flour. In Costa Rica, prepacked, factory-made tortillas have replaced the wonderful homemade version that we savored in Guatemala. Plain, unsweetened fruit juice is almost impossible to find. I usually give up, figuring the children get the equivalent vitamins from fresh fruit which is usually plentiful. Get used to reading food labels, buying something healthy when you find it, and snacking on things like cooked potatoes, boiled eggs, peanuts and yoghurt in the absence of more familiar foods.

Adapt To Local Eating Habits

If you do find familiar items from home, they are usually imported and highly priced. Apple juice in the Caribbean, American cereals in the Bahamas, or oranges in Norway can cost you a small fortune. If you're on a family shoe-string budget, it's best to adapt your eating habits to what's locally produced. Even fussy eaters should be able to find things they like that aren't that different from foods back home. While cold cereals are almost non-existent, hot cereal is always available and very inexpensive. Sandwiches can be made from eggs, canned fish or cheese. Grains form the staple of most of the world's diet, are often price-controlled and can be bought anywhere. Producing a dinner built around rice, pasta or bread will keep costs down and the whole family well-fed and healthy.

Despite the comparative smallness of the shops and apparent lack of variety, food abroad can be just as enjoyable as at home. Selecting produce that's fresh from the fields, experiencing an open-air market, getting a fresh bread delivery right to your doorstep, discovering a special food tucked away in some hole-in-the-wall shop are all part of the adventure of living abroad.

Shop Hours & Location

One of the first things to do when you arrive in a new place is find out the hours the food shops are open and the days and location of the market. Each place is different. Some countries leave their shops open seven days a week, others close Friday to Monday. Holidays can really catch you off guard so check those too. Greece, for instance, closes down for five straight days during Easter. We got stranded on the island of Leros with no food, no open shops, no cash and no bank from Ash Wednesday through Easter Monday. If a friendly German yachtsman hadn't rescued us we'd probably still be there. In Arab countries the month-long Ramadan turns everything upside-down with shops only open at night and everyone sleeping during the day. Knowing these things before they happen can help you avoid some interesting moments you'd probably just as soon live without.

Bathrooms And Bathing

Writing about the subject of bathrooms immediately brings to mind a memorable one from our trip to Greece. On one of our adventurous escapades into the outlying area near our villa, a Greek friend had taken us to visit a monastery up in the mountains. As usual, the raki was flowing in the direction of the adults and the Turkish Delight down the throats of the children when six-year-old Colin announced a need to go to the bathroom. Climbing up some crumbling, ancient steps and ducking under a door built to the proportions of a midget, we found ourselves squeezed into a tiny, cell-like room with nothing more than a hole in the floor. After a month in Greece I thought I had run the full gauntlet of hole-in-the-floor plumbing, but this one looked like it hadn't been cleaned since the invasion of the Turks. It was one of those moments when the presence of a child provided just the right mixture of humor, lack of concern, and basic physical need.

Looking back, adventure travel with children can sometimes seem like the saga of the bathroom. Tristan and Colin still identify certain places by their bathroom facilities. Gwyneth, thank goodness, isn't old enough to need them yet. The campground at Tarazoute, Morocco, will always remain the place with the most abysmal bathroom ever, while England is permanently imprinted on their minds as the country with impeccable public bathrooms— on arrival from Turkey we actually spent our first fifteen minutes in one just admiring the premises.

Public Bathrooms

Living abroad in one place can go a long way towards mini-mizing your battle with the bathroom. In your own home you have control over just how clean it is. Sooner or later, however, when traveling with children you're bound to need a public bathroom. Foreign countries are much more open about the call of nature than America. Public bathrooms abound and are usually well marked. Some have maids dispensing towels, men selling toilet paper, and attendants waiting to sprinkle lemon scent on your hands. Attendants will usually expect a tip after you have used the facilities. Except in thoroughly modern countries, carrying your own toilet paper is a must. Be aware that in many places, water pressure being what it is (or isn't), toilet paper does not go into the toilet, but in a basket next to it.

Eastern & Western Bathroom Facilities

There are two kinds of bathroom facilities, the Western kind that you're used to at home, and the Eastern kind, principally a hole in the floor with designated places to put your feet on either side. The Eastern kind will get your thigh muscles in shape in no time. Children will have no trouble with this. In a sort of mis-guided effort at modernization, a number of places frequented by tourists have tried to incorporate the two styles with the result that you find yourself faced with a seatless toilet that won't flush. These are the places the children really don't forget. Sometimes, in an effort to make everyone happy, you'll also find both Western and Eastern kinds in the same restroom. It's worth noting that in places where the eastern type is the norm, they also tend to be the cleanest. Traditionally, Eastern-style toilets were emptied by filling a cup from a spigot in the bathroom and pouring the water down the hole. Many have now upgraded their facilities with built-in flush mechanisms that erupt out of the ground like gey-sers. The safest technique when flushing is to put one hand on the pull-chain, another on the door handle, and make a mad dash for it when you flush.

Before renting anything, make sure you check out the bath-room thoroughly. Find out if the water gets turned off periodically and if so, keep a filled bucket or jugs for flushing purposes.

Bathing Facilities

Bathing is another area that can cover a range of procedures when living abroad. Most rentals have some sort of hot water heater, often a small fixture mounted on the wall of the kitchen or bathroom. When turned on, it either instantaneously preheats the water or heats a small holding tank. Either way, it cuts down on the amount of hot water you use. Anyplace you rent should have bathing facilities of one type or another. Showers are common, but not to be expected. What you do frequently find are the hand-held type used in conjunction with a bathtub. Children love these for hair washes (rarely a popular activity) because they use much less water pressure than a regular overhead type. If your water heater only does one bathtub full, put the children in together after the grown-ups. This way you parents get the water when it's hottest and the children arrive at the tepid stage, a favorite temperature with them. As they will also undoubtedly be dirtier than you, no one is going to want to use their recycled bathwater.

Even when renting, taking along a solar shower isn't a bad idea if you're going to a country with questionable bathing facilities. Designed to be used on boats, these lightweight plastic bags hold up to 5 gallons and can heat water in a matter of hours when laid out in the sun. The shower can also be filled with stove-heated water and guarantee warm, pleasant bathing for the whole family in any location.

Avoid Shared Bathing Facilities

With children this can be a definite drawback. The first time you march your dirty, sandy, or salty offspring down to the communal bathtub only to find it filled with someone's soaking laundry, you'll wonder why you ever quibbled about the extra money. Private bathing and bathroom facilities are one of the joys of living abroad in one place instead of traveling around. Mundane as they may seem, they do make a difference. The umpteenth time you've pointed your child in the direction of the bathroom you'll be eternally grateful it's you who cleans it, uses it, maintains it, and is the only one waiting in line.

Correspondence

When adventuring abroad with children it's nice for them to maintain some link with family, friends, and school back home. This gives them a sense of security and continuity no matter how long or short your trip is. Staying in one place while adventuring eliminates most of the difficulties that beset correspondence when traveling. A permanent address can be sent home and missed mail drops avoided. Mail takes an average of 10 days to two weeks to and from the United States to most parts of the world. Even that, however, is just an approximation. Letters sent days apart can arrive at the same time. One mail delivery might take five days, another five weeks. A friend sent some air mail postcards from Turkey, half of which actually went by air and the other half by ship, arriving six months later. Predicting how or when your mail will arrive is impossible in most instances.

If you're renting and staying in one place you'll have a chance to familiarize yourself with the postal service and know what to expect in general. Internationally, mail that is sent General Delivery is addressed to Poste Restante, followed by your name and the address of the town. If there's more than one post office in town, Poste Restante mail will go to the main one. Sometimes you can receive mail directly to the place you've rented. Stress with people back home how long everything takes to arrive. Americans are used to prompt postal service and often can't conceive of anything as erratic as what you might find. If time is really of an essence, try sending a fax. The most surprising places have fax facilities these days and sending one is reasonably inexpensive and guaranteed to connect with the recipient. Arrange a fax number in advance with a local copy place near your home if you think you will be using this form of communication. If all else fails, assure your children that it really doesn't matter if birthday cards or valentines arrive late. Receiving and sending mail while abroad is always exciting no matter when it arrives.

Quelling Your Fears

By now you might be wondering why anyone would willingly choose this type of experience—dealing with sordid bathrooms, riding crowded buses, shopping at confusing markets, struggling with foreign languages. The whole experience might sound more like a nightmare than the fulfillment of your family's dreams. In actual fact, living abroad is what you choose it to be. There are always places with comfortable accommodations, rental cars, restaurants and well-stocked shops. You can rent a place in Switzerland and never be faced with a hand-laundry or water that gets turned off. There's no language barrier in England or lack of familiar foods. Living abroad can encompass any degree of living conditions. Introduce yourself gradually, the way you would with any adventurous activity. Choose a place that is exciting to you, but not scary, challenging but not overwhelming. Anywhere you go will constitute an adventure because it will always be different from home.

PART IV
PRACTICAL CONCERNS

Chapter
10
Traveling With Babies

Gwyneth Islay was six months old when we took her to the Bahamas for two months of island hopping. Happily accompanied by her parents, brothers, and indispensable "teddy", Gwyneth was never disturbed by our mobility. With minimal clothing, a supply of diapers, somewhere to sleep and me as a food source, her needs were few and easily supplied.

A child is never too young to travel. Some family adventures may require more preparation or effort than others, but all should be capable of incorporating a baby. Of all the stages in childhood, infancy is the most amenable to travel. The child is at its most adaptable, capable of accepting any change in surroundings provided its basic needs are supplied. A traveling friend, mother of an adopted one-year-old Korean girl in addition to two sons of her own, remarked one day, "She's the perfect Third World baby—eats anything, sleeps anywhere." What the Third World baby learns through necessity, the traveling baby acquires through exposure.

Sleeping

Babies will sleep anywhere: in a car, on a boat, at the beach, in a backpack. The more motion there is, the more prone the child is to sleep. In their infancy, all our children have slept their way through hikes in a backpack, sails on various catamarans, and through hikes in a backpack, sails on various catamarans, and rides on airplanes, buses, trains and ferries. Given the chance, the traveling baby will exhibit an amazing capacity to sleep through any amount of noise or activity, an ability you can nurture prior to departure by parking him in the livingroom at sleep times.

At nap or nighttime, even young babies develop an awareness of their immediate surroundings and react more comfortably to something familiar. Where your baby will sleep is dependent on the type of adventure you choose. Some, like boat or van travel, come equipped with beds while others, like backpacking or bicycling, require a tent or rented room. Woven baby baskets or carriage tops with handles are a practical way to travel with your baby's bed. If space is at a premium or the baby has outgrown the basket stage, creating a place to sleep each night with a special blanket, pillow and "sleepy friend" will give the child the same sense of security as a familiar bed. Tristan and Colin have been bedding down in odd places for years, content as long as they had their favorite pillow, quilt and stuffed toys. Gwyneth's first foreign trip at seven months exposed her to no less than fourteen different cribs, four mattresses on the floor, one playpen and a double bed.

Clothing

Keep the baby's clothing to a minimum. Three or four of each item will usually be ample for any trip. As adventure travel to certain areas can involve handwashing your laundry, you don't want to bog yourself down with piles of baby clothes waiting to be cleaned. When one item gets dirty, change the baby into another, then wash and dry the soiled clothing.

When choosing clothes for a trip to a temperate climate, take along whatever the baby wears at home, only less of it. A few play outfits for warm and cool weather, two sleepwear, some type of rain gear and a warm outdoor suit should be sufficient. Dark colored overalls like Osh-Kosh are useful for the crawling baby as they hold up well under all that abuse and don't show up the dirt. A hat or hood is important if the baby is going to be sitting out in the elements in cool weather. Adventure activities that require strenuous physical output on the parent's part often mean an immobilized baby seated in a backpack or a bicycle trailer.

In The Tropics

In the tropics a baby's clothing is needed less for warmth than for protection from the sun or dirt. A good portion of the time, clothing can be eliminated altogether provided some precaution is taken against overexposure to sun. A shady place to play is the best solution. When the baby is out in the sun, a sunhat is a must. Skip all other clothing if you want, but don't go without a sunhat. Babies have little (if any) hair to insulate them from the sun and are easily prone to overheating. In hot sun the need for a sunhat applies to all young children. For the tiny baby, a couple of lightweight, cotton "receiving" blankets are always useful, even in hot climates, for keeping the baby warm when traveling.

Choose Cotton. If possible, choose clothing that is one hundred percent cotton. This "breathes" in the heat, lessening discomfort and the chance of skin infections. When living for four years on our sailboat in Florida and the Bahamas, our twin's wardrobe consisted almost exclusively of Carter's white cotton undershirts and what we called "terry pants". These are terrycloth panties that come in a variety of pastel colors, serve a multitude of clothing purposes, and are easy to wash and dry. At that time they were about the only all-cotton baby clothes available. Since the arrival of Gwyneth, we've found a whole new range of cotton baby clothes, perfect for travel to the tropics.

Keeping Your Baby Clean

Keeping a baby clean is another consideration when choosing how much clothing to take. Some environments are cleaner than others, warranting less need for a variety of outfits. A boat or beach in the Caribbean requires less protective clothing, for instance, than a public bus or campground in Turkey. A baby's age is also a factor, for infants who haven't reached the state of mobility are easier to keep clean than babies that have learned to crawl. Some traveling parents are more casual about dirt than others. We've seen barefoot, bare-bottomed babies in Morocco and

Guatemala and others clothed within an inch of their lives. In areas of questionable cleanliness, we compromised by dressing our children in a simple item like terry pants or diapers to keep them fairly dirt-free yet minimize clothes washing.

Diapers

Nothing comes to mind more quickly when contemplating traveling with a baby than diapers. Even the happiest, most amenable, most content baby, one seemingly born to travel, is going to use a formidable number of diapers in the course of a trip. How to deal with them looms large on any parent's mental list of obstacles to overcome.

Disposables

For a number of years disposable diapers have been the preferred choice with most parents. Recently, however, the growing environmental consciousness throughout the world has begun to change people's attitude towards all that plastic being thrown away just to keep babies' bottoms clean. Disposing of them always poses a problem. Many countries deal with their trash by either heaving it any place or burning it. We've been driven from more than one foreign campground in the morning by the smell of burning plastic as someone came around and tossed a lighted match into each trash bin. Disposable diapers contribute towards this problem. Another favorite technique is simply dropping them on the spot after changing the baby, with the result that soiled plastic diapers litter roadsides and even boat anchorages. Two other drawbacks to disposable diapers are their high cost and the difficulty of carrying them in some instances. You simply can't carry many in a backpack or on a bicycle. Even a boat starts to seem swamped when stocking up for a long trip.

Cloth Diapers

Fortunately, a resurgence of interest in cotton diapers plus some new labor-saving touches have begun to lead parents back to the old-fashioned way of diapering. Cloth diapers are inexpensive, reusable, easy to carry and non-polluting. The only hardship is the washing. As laundry is something you will probably be doing every few days anyway, tossing in a bunch of soiled diapers won't pose too much of a problem, even if you are handwashing. Many places, even remote ones, offer inexpensive laundry services. More developed areas often have laundromats or washing machines at the campgrounds.

Cloth diapers come in two different types, regular and prefolded. Although the prefolded are easier to use, the regular kind dries much faster after washing, a serious consideration when traveling. Cloth diapers are also useful for throwing over your shoulder when holding an infant, putting under its head for a clean place to lie, and as an all-purpose rag, towel, and handkerchief.

With an infant under six months, about 14 diapers will be needed a day. Carry enough for 2-3 days in case you can't wash and dry them immediately. Six rubber pants or diaper covers should be sufficient for a baby at this age. After six months, the amount of diapers a baby uses decreases. During our backpacking trip through the Bahamas with a seven- to eight-month-old, I carried 30 diapers. By age one, figure on using 8-9 diapers per day plus carrying a total of four rubber pants or covers.

Diaper Covers

As a substitute to pins and rubber pants, diaper covers have been introduced to incorporate a few of the features of disposables. With these, the cloth diaper is simply folded and laid on the inside of the cover. Some have tabs for tucking the corners of the diaper under. The whole thing is then folded up over the baby's bottom and held snugly in place with velcro tabs. For parents accustomed to the ease of diapering with disposables, this is a nice alternative. Although most brands come with a plastic inner layer, a few companies offer an all-cotton diaper cover that is ideal for travel to the tropics.

Diaper covers, however, are an expensive item when compared with their counterpart, rubber pants. You can buy quite a few rubber pants for the price of only one diaper cover. As a longtime user of cotton diapers and rubber pants (I brought up my twins in them), I can't help but question the need to spend so much money just to avoid using diaper pins. Pinning diapers really isn't the high-risk, time-consuming hardship it has recently been made out to be. It takes an experienced parent about four seconds to pin a diaper, nor need you be at risk of poking the baby's bottom or your finger. Rubber pants are easy to clean (often they need nothing more than a rinse in hot water) and quick to dry. If the weather is damp, just dry them with a towel and sprinkle on some cornstarch powder. They are also considerably less bulky to carry than diaper liners on a trip.

Diapering

Keep a compact selection of your diapering paraphernalia handy for easy access during the day - a handful of diapers, some rubber pant or diaper covers, powder, a wash cloth and a bag to hold soiled diapers. Include something soft for the baby to lie on during those times you find yourself changing him on a mountain path or in a dusty train station. Double-diaper your baby when you know you'll be on the move for a while. There's no sense in having to make frequent stops while hiking up a trail or bicycling down a road.

For a list of suppliers of both diaper products and cotton clothing, see the reference section at the back of the book.

Food

Breast-feeding

For at least the first six months, food to a baby means breastmilk or formula. Breast-feeding your baby is by far the more convenient choice if you plan to travel. With the traveling baby, breastfeeding not only guarantees a clean, healthy source of food available at any time, but provides a wonderful pacifier and a sense of security when the disruption of travel might alarm him. Nor need you stop when a baby reaches six months or a year.

Many babies will happily nurse until two or older, a perfectly healthy practise and one you will see the world over.

If you've never breast-fed, drink plenty of fluids before, with, or after each nursing. This is how you make milk. Although babies instinctively know what to do, you might need reassurance when your baby suddenly cries frantically, refuses to nurse or seems more interested in what's going on around him than in eating. A number of excellent books are available, including La Leche League's *The Womanly Art of Breastfeeding* and Karen Pryor's *Nursing Your Baby.*

In very hot conditions, a baby might not get enough fluids from just breastfeeding. In this case his diapers will be continually dry. Supplement with a bottle of water if this happens, always offering it after the regular feeding so as not to interfere with the milk supply.

Baby Food & Mealtimes

Although prepared baby food is available world-wide, a baby food grinder is worth its weight in gold when traveling with a very young child. This small, lightweight, inexpensive item is capable of grinding anything adults eat into something appropriate for babies, a real necessity if you're traveling lightweight, on a shoe-string budget, or to remote places. Other useful equipment for feeding a baby include a plastic bowl, "Tommy-Tippy" cup (impossible to spill), baby spoon, wash cloth and a couple of bibs.

Finding appropriate foods to feed your baby is no more difficult when traveling than at home. Baby cereal is widely available, although often sweetened. Check the ingredients on the box. Most of the world lacks a high level of nutritional awareness and many products are sweetened that in North America no longer contain sugar. As fresh food is usually grown and sold locally, providing your baby with a healthy diet shouldn't be difficult. Even before they have many teeth, babies can do a good job of eating small finger foods, so try supplementing their regular meals with bits and pieces of whatever you are cooking for the family. Some babies, especially those trying to emulate older siblings, insist on eating only adult foods. Gwyneth flatly refused all baby food, preferring whatever her brothers were eating.

For parents used to relying on prepared baby foods, the following is a sample of what you might feed your baby while traveling. Babies rarely care about variety, making meal planning easy.

Breakfast	Lunch	Dinner
milk	milk	milk
oatmeal w/	plain yoghurt w/	oatmeal w/
banana	fruit, cinnamon,	egg yolk or
	or oats	chicken, veg.,
		& banana

Extras: 1 glass unsweetened fruit juice, biscuits or bread

At dinner the chicken and vegetable can be ground in the baby food grinder and mixed together with fruit and oatmeal—sounds and looks awful, but most babies love it. Use any type of fruit, cooked, mashed or ground. Don't give your baby any type of sweetener. This only develops an early and unnecessary dependence on sweetened food. Nor do babies need more than one small cup of fruit juice a day.

Baby Paraphernalia

Bring along as little baby paraphernalia as you can possibly manage. If you're backpacking, bicycling, canoeing or sailing, limited space will dictate what you can include on your adventure. In a car, however, the temptation is to think the baby needs more than the whole rest of the family put together. Before you know it, the roof will be piled high and the back filled with a crib and playpen, baby carriage and toy box. A mother told me one day she was considering taking the playpen on their camping trip to Prince Edward Island and what did I think. I told her she was asking the wrong person. I'd just written a book telling parents to leave things like playpens at home because they make work and take up room and aren't needed anyway. So what would I do, she wanted to know, with an active one year old who liked to wander and explore and generally stage a disappearing act every time she turned her back. I told her to take a harness; they work every time, no matter where you are.

If we were to recommend taking just two pieces of baby equipment on any adventure, they would be a backpack for carrying the child and a harness for confining it. A harness is lightweight, inexpensive, easy to use and adaptable to any form of adventure travel. It allows a baby the freedom to roam without the risk of straying too far. On a boat, at the beach or in a campground it can be clipped to something nearby so the baby can explore without constant parental vigilance. Some mothers, when I suggest this, voice a dislike of having their crawling baby get dirty, something that wouldn't happen in a playpen. First of all, most campsites aren't on dirt- grass is much more likely. Nor is sand much of a problem, as that can be brushed off at the end of your time at the beach. If dirt does seem to be in evidence, dress your baby in the same pair of overalls or whatever when playing at the campsite. This means only one outfit will get dirty instead of his whole wardrobe in a couple of days. If parents seriously added up the time their baby spent each day confined to a playpen they would probably discover it was minimal and hardly worth the bother of including it on a trip. Babies can be kept happy much longer when harnessed, rather than confined to a playpen where, even at their young age, they soon discover that life beyond those four sides is much more interesting.

A crib is another item you can leave behind, even on a trip with a car. Put the baby to bed in the corner of a tent. If it crawls around and falls asleep on someone else's sleeping bag, just move it later before you go to sleep. In the morning, there's not much difference between being woken by a baby crawling on top of you or howling from the edge of its crib.

Toys are most important for infants too young to walk or even crawl. Bring a few to string across the inside of a tent, attach to a backpack or give the baby to play with when lying on a blanket. Make use of whatever other items you have on hand that can double as toys, basically anything non-toxic that's too big to swallow: measuring spoons and cups, wooden spoons, jars, keys on a keychain, plastic containers, a wristwatch. One favorite item of teething babies is a toothbrush. Include a special one for the baby to chew on when fussiness sets in and nothing else works.

Health

Aside from the common cold, babies of any age rarely get sick. What ailments they do suffer from are infrequent and generally easily remedied. The most difficult thing about doctoring a baby is that it can't talk and tell you what the problem is. Even after learning to speak, young children will often indicate the wrong part of their body when something hurts. A good baby book plus experience will help you diagnose and treat simple problems in the absence of a doctor. Dr. Spock's *Baby and Child Care* offers a compact, comprehensive assortment of relevant baby problems and how to deal with them, from how to get your baby to sleep to diaper rash to serious illness.

A few ailments are most prevalent among babies and parents should familiarize themselves with them prior to taking the baby on an adventure. Although treatment for some serious illnesses is included, using them should by no means preclude finding a doctor at the nearest opportunity.

Diaper Rash

All babies periodically suffer from diaper rash. Failing to change a baby's diaper regularly during busy travel days, improperly washed diapers or extreme heat can all cause an outbreak on a trip. Try to keep the baby's diapers changed, even if it means changing him in some unorthodox, highly visible places. People are usually so intrigued to see a family traveling with an infant that they are most tolerant when it comes to anything relevant to baby care. Improperly washed diapers will cause a rash, so use a sterilizing liquid like lemon ammonia to eliminate this problem. In hot climates, give the baby plenty of time to air his bottom free of diapers. Beach time is a wonderful opportunity for letting the baby go naked without worrying about accidents. Leaving off rubber pants that hold in the moisture will also help.

To treat diaper rash, wash and dry the baby's bottom carefully each diaper change. Do not wash with soap as residue left on the skin increases the problem. Babies really don't need to be washed with soap, just warm water. The same applies to shampoo. Apply an soothing ointment like calendula cream (available from natural food stores and suppliers of homeopathic treatments) before putting on a new diaper. With a serious rash, lay the baby on some diapers for an airing period between changes. Sunshine and fresh air are the best cures.

Prickly Heat

Prickly heat commonly occurs in hot, humid weather. Beginning at the neck and shoulders, it can spread across the chest or up around the head. Babies, however, rarely seem to notice. The best avoidance is to keep the baby naked or dress him in loose, cotton clothing. Applying cornstarch powder will help bring relief.

Bathtime in the dishpan is one simple way to keep a baby clean when camping.

Stomach Problems

Breast-fed babies rarely suffer from diarrhea or stomach upsets, another good reason to continue nursing while traveling with a baby. In the event they do occur, the cause is usually infection or exposure to bacteria in water or food. In countries where bacteria might be a problem, first wash, then peel or cook any fresh produce the baby will be eating. Water is the greatest source of bacteria and should be avoided or sterilized. Bottled water is usually sold throughout these countries. Otherwise, boil the water before drinking or use an appropriate water filter.

In the case of an infection, stomach disorders usually pass quickly. If diarrhea persists, babies over a year old can be given Pepto Bismol. Feed the baby plain starchy food like banana, bread, rice, noodles or baby cereal until he recovers.

Colds & Fevers

Infants under a year almost never get colds. If they do, it's usually mild and hardly noticeable. Older babies become increasingly susceptible to colds, often accompanied by fevers. Warm climates where children spend most of their time in the fresh air are less likely to breed colds. As most types of family adventures involve outdoor activities, colds are a rarity.

Sick babies are often happiest when nursing. Don't under any circumstances give a feverish baby aspirin. This has been found to be very high risk. Fevers in babies are usually not a cause for alarm, but only a common side-effect to mild infection. For more serious childhood ailments like ear infections or bronchitis, see Chapter Twelve.

Skin Infections

Although not generally a common problem with babies, these can occur frequently in tropical climates where any untreated cut or insect bite can easily become infected. To prevent serious infection, treat cuts or bites immediately with hydrogen peroxide and aloe vera. In hot climates, uncircumcised babies are also prone to slight skin infections on the end of their penis unless preventative measures are taken. Once a week carefully pull back the foreskin and wash gently. In the event of an infection (you'll know because the baby will act most uncomfortable when you try to expose the tip of the penis), apply Bacitracin ointment for three days.

The following is a suggested list of medical essentials to include on any adventure with a baby:

- Cornstarch
- Bacitracin
- Pepto-Bismol
- Hydrogen peroxide
- Thermometer
- calendula cream
- Ipecac syrup
- Aloe Vera Gel
- Sunscreen
- Vinegar

The fear of a sick baby keeps many parents from contemplating travel with their young child. Ironically, babies are rarely ill when traveling. As most adventuring involves travel to warm climates and living outdoors, even the common cold is a rare thing. We've traveled with our children since they were born and almost never had to deal with an illness, a situation shared by other families we've met along the way. By employing a little common sense and giving your baby a healthy diet and plenty of fresh air, most babies will stay free of infection.

Inoculations

All babies that travel should probably be inoculated against various diseases. Inoculations against diphtheria, tetanus, and optionally pertussis are given together in a series of four shots, usually over the baby's first two years, although later is often regarded as healthier for the baby. Protection against poliomyelitis is administered orally, also in four doses over two years. Inoculating against Pertussis (whooping cough), measles, German measles and mumps is up to the parents. Some areas of the world require other inoculations, so check with your baby's doctor before departing. Keep a record of all shots in case of an emergency while traveling. Tetanus treatment, for instance, varies according to when and what the child was already given. If you are traveling when an inoculation is due, locate a doctor or health clinic; the local tourist bureau can recommend where you should go.

If you are traveling by car or staying in one place, a lightweight, woven basket provides a bed, a place to play and a means of transport for young babies. Toys strung across the top keep the baby entertained during wakeful times.

Transportation

Tristan and Colin's first means of transport on the road to adventure was the back of a VW Bug. By the time our modest camping gear, baby-related equipment and two Mexican baby baskets had been loaded, there was barely enough room for the occupants. Their next vehicle was more spacious, a 26' catamaran that would carry them over 4,000 miles while supplying all the conveniences of home. As babies, all three of our children traveled on trains, in cars, on the backs of bicycles and in airplanes. They rode ferries, were pulled in wagons, and spent hours seeing the world from a backpack.

Public Transportation

No matter how you plan to travel, there are ways to make life simpler for yourself when traveling with a baby. On public transportation, people are very solicitous to traveling babies, giving up seats, offering food, entertainment or a lap to sit on.

Airports often have changing rooms and airplanes can usually provide baby food, diapers or a heated bottle if notified ahead of time. Whenever we arrived at check-in with a baby, airport officials tripped over themselves in their haste to assist us. We were always given the seats at the front of the tourist section that allowed much more room for us, our children and our paraphernalia. Ask for these seats if you plan to fly with a baby.

Babies always ride for free on public transportation. Sometimes this means you'll have the baby in your lap for the duration of the trip, but usually an extra seat will be available. Remember to take along a bag of vital necessities for keeping the baby dry, comfortable and entertained whenever you ride on public transportation. There's nothing worse than discovering all your spare diapers or the baby's favorite sleeping friend is roped to the roof of a bus or in the bowels of an airplane. On a long trip a baby can be entertained by almost any safe object. To a baby, toys don't have to be something from Fisher Price. He can get just as excited over a bunch of measuring spoons, a set of car keys or a wristwatch.

Sailboats

With travel that relies on your own means of transport, a baby can again be incorporated successfully. Certain modes of travel, of course, are easier than others when it comes to including a baby. Sailboats, particularly multihulls, are made for babies. On a boat you travel with your home, thus avoiding many of the rigors associated with adventure travel. There's no need to continually set up a new home or reduce your needs to the bare essentials. Your baby can always sleep in his own bed and play in familiar surroundings. Tense or rough sailing moments can be handled without disruption to the baby. After years of indulging in many different forms of adventure travel, boats are still our first choice for babies.

Canoes

Other forms of boat travel, like a canoe, can also include a baby. Canoe, bicycle, and backpack transport all involve confining the baby's mobility while underway. This is not difficult. People do it every time they take their baby for a walk in a carriage or ride in a car. There's nothing more confining than a child's car seat or stroller. A baby can be just as successfully confined to the center of a canoe or the back of a bicycle.

Ideally, the baby should have reached the sitting stage. This makes life simpler for you and more interesting for the baby. In a canoe the main problem is the possibility of capsizing. Our choice would be to have the child wear a baby lifejacket and a tether attached to one parent. This way if an accident did happen, he wouldn't be able to drown or drift away. Make it clear to him that he must sit or lie down while riding in the canoe, not crawl or lean out. This really isn't as difficult as it may sound once a child is over a year old and able to understand. If the baby is at the peak of his stand-up-wherever-he-is period, have him sit in an older person's lap. Even at this stage babies usually behave when underway, because they love the motion and are very stimulated by a visually changing environment. This is why they enjoy rides in a baby carriage or bicycle seat so much. Their changing environment can just keep pace with their short attention span. Make a comfortable place in the canoe for sleeping and playing while underway. Tie any toys to the canoe unless you want to spend your whole trip chasing after things. Although ambitious canoe trips are probably not most families' choice of the ideal adventure with a baby, day outings or overnights are certainly possible and short enough to keep even an active baby from getting impatient.

Bicycles

On a bicycle there's two ways for a baby to travel, in a child's bike seat or towed behind in a trailer. Although a bike seat is fine for day outings, a trip executed by bicycle alone would warrant the use of a trailer due to the need to carry extra gear on the bicycle itself. All trailers on the market can accommodate two children, thus providing plenty of room for toys, pillows, blankets, books and sleepy friends. When very young, most babies will nap their way through a bicycle trip, lulled to sleep by the regular motion. Toddlers will need more to keep them entertained. With Gwyneth (a very active child), we found her enjoyment of the trailer greatly increased by the time she was a year and a half. Prior to that she was on happy on short rides of an hour or so, unless she was sleeping. With a baby like this, longer bicycle tours are feasible after the child reaches the age of two. If touring, choose a trailer with screening and rain cover. Our Cannondale Stowaway also has seats facing forward, interior pockets, padded seating, rear storage, and collapsibility, all desirable features on an extended tour.

Motorcycles

Although car travel is familiar to all families, motorcycle travel can be an adventurous way to see the world with a baby in tow. As long-time motorcycle travelers, Kevin and I originally planned to travel through Europe with a baby in a sidecar, an idea that evolved when we met a family touring through Colorado with their five-year-old daughter. After her initial start on the back of the motorcycle worn in a Snugli, she had graduated to a lovely German-made sidecar when, as her parents told us, she no longer fit between them. With her sidecar filled with toys, books and a comfortable bed, she rode happily for hours.

Backpacks

For the family adventuring on foot, a pack is the best way to carry a baby. In fact, some way of carrying your baby on your person is a must on any type of adventure. No matter what vehicle you chose to travel by, walking will make up a large part of your time. You'll walk for recreation or exercise or to sight-see. You'll walk to catch a bus or grocery shop or find a campground. You'll walk to the beach or through a village or up a mountain trail. We are continually amazed how few traveling families we see using a baby pack, relying instead on carrying the baby in their arms or pushing it in a stroller. Carrying the baby is tiresome, can be backbreaking and leaves you with no room to carry anything else. Pushing him in a carriage, provided you even have one, is fine on paved streets, but of little use elsewhere. An easy way to carry your baby that is comfortable for both you and the child and leaves your hands free is going to be critical.

Schedule Travel Around The Baby

To make transporting your baby as trouble-free as possible, try to plan your times of travel around the baby's schedule. Covering big distances is going to be tiring for everyone, so try to limit these as much as possible. If you are traveling by public transportation, do a large distance one day, then stay for a while and explore the new area on foot or rented bicycles. This involves the least disruption to the baby and stress to the parents while leaving plenty of room for adventurous pursuits.

For daily transport, plan your travel for times when the baby's energy is at its lowest ebb. Nap times are ideal for moving. The motion of travel will help him sleep at a time when you welcome it. When he's at his most active, first thing in the morning, for instance, stay in one place and let him play. Provide something for him to look at or play with when traveling during wakeful periods. Try stringing objects above a play area on a boat or bicycle trailer, or tying a toy to a backpack. These will keep a baby occupied for hours, especially with the motion making them move. We hung objects from the top of our children's baskets that kept them entertained over many miles of travel. Try to incorporate whatever diversions and activities you would have at home into your travel time. A canoe or bicycle or boat that looks like a traveling playpen may make you conspicuous, but it's also going to make the difference between a happy baby and a bored one.

Backpacks

Every traveling baby should have a backpack. No single piece of equipment will contribute more towards the success of your family adventure. A backpack gives a baby a sense of security, a place to rest or sleep, a vantage point from which to see things, a measure of safety in certain situations. For the parents it makes the difference between freedom and frustration.

Gwyneth spent much of the first months of her life viewing hiking trails, foreign destinations and strangers from the secure vantage point of her backpack. When exhaustion set in she simply went to sleep, so we were free to continue our outdoor activities.

Two-year-old Gwyneth showing off her LaFuma 660 child carrier, a comfortable internal-frame backpack.

A trip to an underdeveloped nation will show you that carrying a baby on your back is a time-honored tradition. Mothers are frequently seen working in the fields or shopping at markets with a baby strapped to their back. Babies of all ages will ride there for hours, held in place by a simple shawl wrapped over one shoulder and tied around the waist to form a sling. With the growing number of active parents who want to or need to include their small children in their daily activities, the need for some type of carrying device is now in demand in countries where the baby carriage has traditionally ruled. Although a simple shawl will certainly suffice, a well-made backpack is a worthwhile investment and kinder to your back.

Sling Packs

Newborn babies not yet capable of sitting up need a soft sling-type of carrier. Although a number of simple models are available, the Snugli is probably the best made and most comfortable. Criss-crossed straps and a waist band help distribute the weight while the baby rides in a pouch protected by an outer lining. Adjustable snaps help support the head of a newborn. Babies are first worn on your front, then switched to the back when the baby is older. Many parents fail to realize the Snugli is designed to be worn on the back as the child grows bigger.

I once demonstrated to an exhausted-looking mother in the middle of our local bank how to swing her baby in its Snugli on to her back. The time to switch from front to back is when the baby starts to feel heavy and pull uncomfortably against your shoulders. Don't be alarmed if your sleeping baby looks like its neck is about to break. Babies seem to be quite comfortable sleeping in a position that would give an adult a stiff neck for weeks.

Frame Packs

Frame packs are designed for babies that can either hold their head up or sit up by themselves. If you already own a sling-type, like a Snugli, the most practical would be a pack that could last your child through the toddler stage. This way you will always be free to cover good distances on foot right up until the time your child can walk the distance with you. When Tristan and Colin were babies, the Snugli and Gerry pack were the only suitable carriers for long distances and neither could handle a child over about 2-3 years of age. With the arrival of Gwyneth, we've discovered a number of excellent frame packs now available for carrying babies of all sizes.

The packs below have good external or internal support frames, adjustable back supports and seats, gear storage under the seat, and padded shoulder straps and hip belts:

Gerry Ultra Deluxe: External frame. For babies five months and up to 40 pounds.

Gerry Trail Blazer: For more rugged use. External frame. For babies five months and up to 45 pounds.

Lafuma 660: Soft nylon internal frame. Extremely comfortable and lightweight. For babies 9-36 months.

L.L.Bean Child Carrier: External frame. Good load carrier. Capable of carrying a child up to 40 pounds.

Kelty Child Carrier: External frame. Good load carrier. For babies 15-35 pounds.

Tough Traveler Stallion: External frame. For babies up to 4-5 years and 60 pounds. Well-made seat with footrests for child.

Tough Traveler Kid Carrier: External frame. For babies up to four years and 50 pounds.

A rather innovative backpack for carrying children is the relatively new Stroller Pack, available through many outdoor equipment outfitters. This device is a rugged frame pack with wheels that doubles as a child carrier and a child stroller. The design allows the stroller to be effective both in town or along country paths and tracks.

External-frame packs come with stands, useful for setting the baby on the ground temporarily (and <u>always</u> under adult supervision so the child can't tip over) for loading, unloading, doubling as a highchair at meal times or letting the baby complete its nap when you've stopped walking. The storage area under the seat is great for carrying extras like diapers, snack foods and spare clothes.

For the serious adventuring family, some way of carrying your child from infancy to three to four years is the best choice. At five a child is no longer a liability on a hike and quite capable of covering major distances on his own provided he is already used to walking. Unlike when our sons were backpacking age, it's now possible to carry your child right through the toddler stage. Our personal choice for baby backpacks is a Snugli for up to nine months, then a Lafuma 660, one of the most comfortable child carriers available. Although an older toddler enjoys walking, the availability of periodic rides in a pack makes lengthy family walks a viable option.

Backpack Tips

A couple of tricks are useful for keeping both you and the baby happier while using a pack. Mothers with long hair should wear it up or braided and out of reach of the baby's grasping fingers. Don't allow your baby to brace its feet on the bar at the bottom of a frame pack and stand up (the Lafuma has no bar and thus avoids this problem). This is horribly uncomfortable for the wearer as the baby is constantly teetering over you and shifting its weight around. Pull his feet through the shoulder straps to prevent this from happening. Put the pocket under the baby's seat to good use carrying along extras for emergencies. Spare diapers, rubber pants and other diapering essentials are always a good idea. Also an assortment of edibles for moments when hunger or fussiness sets in. I also routinely carry a baby harness for those times when Gwyneth would rather be walking than riding.

If your baby reacts negatively when first introduced to a pack, don't despair. One harassed mother told me her infant hated the Snugli.

"How many times did you try it?", I asked.

"Once", she said.

Don't give up after one try. Babies usually dislike food the first time they encounter that as well. Yet no one thinks of not feeding their baby. All babies, even fussy or hyper-active ones, can be happy in a pack. Just adapt the attitude that your baby is going to love it. Eventually he will.

Pregnancy

Adventuring while pregnant imposes the same limitations as any activity undertaken during pregnancy. Much depends on how you yourself feel. Some women find it easy to continue to be active while others tire quickly. As pregnancy advances, the tendency to tire increases, so don't plan some physically strenuous adventure after about five months. Otherwise, with a little fore-thought, adventuring can be enjoyed throughout pregnancy.

After about four months, pregnancy will affect your performance in outdoor activities and warrants some precautions.

Hiking is going to be the easiest and safest, although shortness of breath is common among pregnant women. To ease the problem, avoid hikes with high elevation gains. Be sure to drink plenty of fluids when hiking or performing any strenuous activity. Bicycling is fine, provided you can still lean over comfortably towards the handlebars. Canoeing is best avoided unless it's of the tamest variety. All that vigorous stress on the stomach isn't going to make you or the baby very happy. If you go, go as a passenger and enjoy the luxury of watching the scenery. Sailing might or might not affect you, depending on how queasy a pregnancy you are having. Although taking any kind of seasickness pill is unsafe when pregnant, try wearing Sea-Bands, a type of wristband that functions on the principals of accupressure. Sea-Bands are available through most boating catalogs (see the reference section for sources). Because any sea motion is going to amplify your queasiness, pick a protected area to cruise and limit sails to short hops between islands or harbors, with plenty of time left over for shore explorations.

Choose an adventure, a destination, a pace of travel that appeals to you in your present state. Italy has always seemed to me like the perfect place to be during pregnancy: lots of warm sunshine, an affectionate, child-oriented people and appealing food. The last is, of course, of major importance. Pregnancy usually creates a finicky stomach, so if the mere thought of hot chilies or soy sauce makes you turn green, don't plan a trip to Mexico or Japan.

A trip to an exotic, foreign place with little travel once you get there can be the ideal adventure during pregnancy. By avoiding the sterility of popular tourist spots and renting a small place in a more authentic, country setting, your adventure becomes an act of immersing yourself in a given culture rather than achieving any great athletic prowess. This type of adventure still provides plenty of opportunity for outdoor activities, like walks in the countryside, shopping at open-air markets and just living a simple, labor-intensive life-style. Your pregnancy will most likely also elicit much interest and hospitality from local inhabitants.

Travel on public transportation should be no problem, except for flying on small, unpressurized airplanes after seven months.

As lack of cabin pressure has been known to trigger premature labor, airlines are understandably reluctant to let women in advanced pregnancy on their airplanes. One acquaintance of ours found herself stranded in the Caribbean when airline officials refused to let her fly home after two weeks of cruising in the islands.

If pregnancy springs a surprise during your travels, make sure to avoid the use of any potentially harmful drugs like prophylactic tablets for malaria, water purifying tablets or seasickness pills. In areas of questionable cleanliness, wash and cook foods carefully and drink bottled or filtered water to avoid contamination from parasites that would normally require medication.

Pitfalls To Avoid

Lack of mobility—Take along a good child pack for maximum mobility.

An overambitious itinerary—A week in one place can be as meaningful and enjoyable as seeing an entire country.

Overanxious parenting—Relax with your baby. Accidents are rare, illness rarer and good doctors and medical treatment available the world over.

Too much baby paraphernalia—Babies survive just fine without highchairs, cribs, playpens, walkers, baby carriages and all the other paraphernalia considered integral to bringing up a baby these days. Keep it simple on a trip.

Inappropriate destinations—Avoid places where babies are out of place, baby-sitters a necessity, and you're destined to feel embarrassed every time your child cries. Warm climates are easier than cold, staying in one place more relaxing than moving around a lot, and places inhabited or frequented by other families the most fun of all.

Travel with a baby is always an adventure. What might seem tame to the hardened adventurer takes on a new dimension of achievement when a baby is added to the trip. Don't hesitate to start modest when it comes to adventuring with your baby. Our first trip with six-month-old twins was camping in Florida, hardly an itinerary destined to ignite the interest of a hardened adventuring family, but packed with enough excitement to satisfy us at that moment. The key to traveling with a baby is, like all adventure travel, recognizing your limitations while following your instincts. Any family adventure is appropriate for a baby provided you as a family are ready for it.

Chapter
11
Education & Learning

It has frequently occurred to us as we adventure during the school year that most families are missing out on one of the best times for family travel. The benefits are numerous—fewer crowds, a wider selection of destinations, off-season rates, the ability to travel for a longer period of time, and the availability of any time of year for a trip. Contrary to widespread belief, coping with your children's schooling while traveling is less demanding and more rewarding than most parents think. Nor is the children's education at risk. Travel is the ultimate means of education because it exposes children to things they normally only learn about through books.

The following are a variety of schooling options available to the adventuring family. While taking along a host of school books and teacher instructions is fairly common for short absences from a formal school environment, the idea of homeschooling over a longer period can be somewhat intimidating to parents, especially those with older children. Yet exposure to learning outside the classroom can be valuable, both in discovering the many ways that children can learn as well as the ease with which parents and experience alone can teach.

In an effort to encourage families to take the plunge and travel during the school year, we've included recommendations for everything from using materials supplied by a traditional school to devising your own school-style curriculum to following no set curriculum or program, a learning technique commonly referred to as "unschooling". Use the type of learning program that works best for your family and each individual child. Some children like a scheduled day, others thrive on the flexibility of unschooling. Our family has undergone the full transition of a homeschool family, from using a school program to a school-type correspondence course to unschooling, a natural course of events as we discovered the ease of learning at home. Gwyneth, our youngest, will probably enjoy a far more flexible education than her brothers, for experience has taught us just how capable children are of learning on their own once the basic skills of reading, writing and arithmetic have been mastered.

The Case for Homeschooling

While families familiar with homeschooling seem relaxed, confident and competent, those new to home education often feel overwhelmed and confused. After all, isn't that why we have teachers and schools? Isn't school the only place our children can be properly educated? Historically, the ability to learn successfully at home is proven fact. Only in the last one hundred years have recognized institutions replaced the family unit as the prime educators in a child's life. All it takes for successful homeschooling is confidence in your ability as a parent and a recognizable level of parental intelligence, something most of us accept without question. If you can read, write and do basic arithmetic, you can teach your children. Unlike the old days when compulsory education was introduced, families today have access to a wealth of learning tools, from books and writing materials to libraries, magazines, newspapers, specialty classes, and a host of other information sources.

Homeschooling comes in a variety of guises, from the full or partial use of a structured correspondence course to what's popularly called "unschooling", an approach that allows the child to initiate his own education. Having undergone the evolution of a homeschooling family ourselves, from school to correspondence school to unschooling, we recognize the value of all three, particularly when experienced in that order.

Newcomers should feel free to incorporate as many aspects of structured schooling into their day as they feel comfortable with, thus easing both themselves and their children into the life of home education. With experience and time, most will find themselves naturally deviating into whatever system works best for them as a family. As homeschooled children are highly motivated (no boring, inactive, crowded classroom to defuse their enthusiasm) and travel the ultimate vehicle for education, it won't take long on a trip to develop a strong commitment to home education. Education techniques described in Learning Outside The Classroom will form much of the basis for your schooling, techniques that can be continued at home utilizing whatever subjects particularly interest your children .

Parents comfortable with the idea of teaching younger children often express concern about coping with the education level of a teenager, yet teenagers are perhaps the best suited of all for home education. Having already mastered the core subjects of reading, writing and arithmetic, they're ready to pursue their own interests, something formal school makes little allowance for. Education at this age should include plenty of hands-on experience rather than just book-learning, an approach to schooling that does much to defuse their sense of aimlessness. Eager and in many ways ready to take their part in the adult world, many teenagers are frustrated by the inactivity of pure classroom academics. Travel, particularly adventure travel, satisfies their need to learn through experience. Let them devise their own studies, cultivate learning opportunities, and fully participate in your travels. In return, your teenager will become a competent person in his own right, comfortable with himself and thus armed against the social ills that plague today's youth.

Homeschooling Options

Extended travels with children during the school year are feasible, legal and relatively easy. Depending on circumstances and inclination, three education options are available: work supplied by the child's school, a structured correspondence program, and devising your own program, be it a set curriculum or unschooling.

Work Supplied By The Child's School

This option requires the cooperation of the child's teacher and is most practical for elementary school children where one person teaches all the subjects. Unlike a correspondence course, all organization, instruction and corrections are the parents' responsibility. Although teachers are not obligated to supply work for absentee students, many are willing to do so if approached well in advance of your trip, particularly if the rest of the class can benefit from your children's travel experience through an exchange of post cards and letters or a presentation when they return.

Correspondence Courses

These were primarily designed to educate children living in remote areas or traveling abroad. Nowadays, with the resurgent interest in homeschooling, many are used by parents teaching their children at home in lieu of sending them to school. The material is often lightweight (a serious consideration when traveling), teaching instructions clear and the curriculum organized, explicit and designed for parents with no previous teaching experience.

The most well known correspondence school in the United States is the Calvert School in Baltimore, Maryland, offering accredited homeschooling courses from kindergarten through eighth grade. Lessons are outlined daily and all curriculum materials, planning and instruction are provided by the course. Although some parental guidance is always necessary, particularly with elementary school children, all instruction beginning with grade six is oriented towards the child working alone. In addition to the Calvert School, a wide variety of other programs are now available in the United States. Holt Associates in Boston, Massachusetts publishes the bimonthly newsletter *Growing Without Schooling* containing a wealth of information on homeschooling resources, including their Home Schooling Resource List. This inexpensive publication includes addresses for correspondence schools, programs and materials, plus homeschooling organizations throughout the country.

Canada, New Zealand, and Australia all have the advantage of free, state-run correspondence programs designed for children living in isolated regions of the country. Each requires proof of residency and a permanent home address where the material can be sent. Using the program while traveling is always possible, provided the material is gathered ahead of time. England offers an excellent, accredited homeschooling guidance service through the Worldwide Education Service (WES) in London.

Devising Your Own Program

This allows for the most flexibility and can range anywhere from choosing your own subjects and devising a curriculum to allowing your children to discover and pursue their own interests. Some parental input is always necessary, particularly in the form of enthusiasm and encouragement as you guide them in directions that will broaden their minds and develop their own strengths. First time homeschoolers might benefit from the curriculum planning at the end of the chapter, but don't be afraid to deviate from any set schedule and allow the exposure of travel to serve as teacher.

Although home education has now almost reached the state of total acceptability throughout North America, be sure to check into the laws governing homeschooling where you live. *Home Education Magazine* and Holt Associates are both good sources of local homeschool support groups that can help guide you through the initial legal steps.

Homeschooling Resources

American School, 875 East 58th St., Chicago, IL 60611 High school courses.
Calvert School, 105 Tuscany Rd., Baltimore, MD 21210 Courses for Kindergarten through Grade 8.
Cambridge Academy, Petti Building, Suite B, P.O. Box 1289, Banner Elk, NC 28604. High school courses.
Growing Without Schooling, Holt Associates, 2269 Mass Ave., Cambridge, MA 02140. All types of resources for homeschooling; how-to books, supplementary materials, support groups, newsletter

Setting up a temporary classroom at a table is conducive to the more formal aspects of schooling.

Home Education Magazine, P.O. Box 1083, Tonasket, WA 98855. Good general resource for homeschoolers.

Home Study International, 6940 Carroll Ave., Takoma Park, MD 20912. Courses for kindergarten through college.

ICS-Newport/Pacific High School, Scranton, PA 18515 High school courses.

Ministry of Education, Communication Services Branch, Mowat Block, Queen's Park, Toronto, M7A 1L2. Canadian correspondence courses for all grades.

Worldwide Education Service, Strode House, 44-50 Osnaburgh St., London, NW1 3NN. Courses for elementary grades through age 14.

Learning Outside The Classroom

Impromptu Talks

Much of your adventure travel experiences can be converted into a learning opportunity. The culture, language and physical environment of the places you visit will provide continual resources for impromptu lessons. One way to help put what the children experience into a learning perspective is through discussions. Discussions can take place anywhere and most children love them. The same child that yawned his way through morning lessons will ignite with interest during a spontaneous discussion on a hike, for instance. Talk about anything you see: local lifestyles, animal and plant life, topography, agriculture, cultural habits, climate, foods. From there branch into broader subjects like political structures, history, environmental concerns, sociology. Children are wonderfully accepting of what they see. Unlike adults, they neither criticize nor compare things to back home. Instead they merely absorb them without conscious thought. It's up to you to help them put things into the larger perspective of understanding—why people farm the way they do, build houses a certain way, have a particular political structure, eat certain foods. At the risk of brainwashing your children, this is a golden opportunity to make learning come alive in more areas than a regular classroom could hope to reproduce.

Build Education Around Your Travels

Things seen and experienced through adventure travel can also reinforce the normal curriculum. Children are always going to be more receptive to learning a specific skill if it relates to something in their life. Have them research and write a report about the country they are in or some ruins they visited. Use aspects of your travels to devise math problems. Adjust their social studies, history, and geography lessons to the area you are traveling through. Any relationship you can create between what they are learning and what they are experiencing is going to make school more meaningful for children of any age.

Travel As The Teacher

Academics outside the classroom can take the place of, as well as augment, the normal curriculum. Abandoning regular school time for some travel-related experience can often be more valuable. This is what we refer to as "International School". Even the simplest acts can become a valuable learning experience when adventuring—walks through the countryside, a pick-up soccer game with local children, tea at a cafe, building a campfire. Social studies can become a way of life as children shop at open markets, ride public buses, eat local foods and play with village children. As you adventure you discover that everything your children learn during their trip—any formal school subjects, travel experiences and day-to-day living in a foreign country—become linked together into an overall accumulation of knowledge.

Scrapbooks & Journals

Some children love to keep journals, an excellent way to develop writing skills in a way children can enjoy. For some reason this seems to be particularly popular with girls. Have your child write something each day, even if it's just a small entry. Some proof reading will be necessary to determine what areas the child needs work in (paragraphs, punctuation, spelling, etc.), but the major focus is cultivating an enjoyment for writing.

For the child that doesn't like writing in a journal, a scrapbook can be equally educational and fun. This is what we did with our children after our attempts at journals became mired in boredom. Children can do this at any age, beginning as young as six or seven. Just adjust the content to the child's capabilities. Our first ones, called Madeira Books because we were adventuring in Madeira at the time, were a combination scrapbook, journal, social studies, and nature notebook. These were worked on a few times a week and contained the following entries:

—The History	—Carnival
—Funchal (the main city)	—Buses
—Wicker & Thatch	—My Favorite Hike
—Botanical Gardens	—Trees & Greens
—Fishing	—Embroidery
—Agriculture	—Easter Celebration
—Domestic Animals	—Wine
—Levadas	—Exports

Contrary to what many people believe, children can learn from their parents, particularly if both child and parent maintain a positive relationship during schooltime.

Some of the entries were based on personal experience, others on research. Included were postcards, illustrations drawn by the children, pictures cut from tourist brochures, bus and airplane tickets, pieces of wicker. There's no end to what children can put in a book like this. In a later one kept by the children in the Caribbean, they added pressed leaves collected on our many hikes. All children seem to enjoy keeping this type of record of a trip and learn a great deal while doing it.

Stamp Collecting

With their natural penchant for collecting things, children usually enjoy this activity. Have them start their stamp collection at home to help develop their interest. This is an easy way for children to glean some geographical know-how from the countries they are visiting. Have them research what each stamp represents.

Environmental Studies & Geography

This is a natural area of study for children who are adventuring. A number of resources can be used to supplement what the children learn through their outdoor activities and observations. Among the most informative and useful for children are the National Geographic publications, of which the following are just an example:

—*Action Book Series*
—*Young Explorers Series*
—*Exploring Your World—The Adventure of Geography*
—*World Magazine* (a magazine for children)

Exploring Your World is probably the best children's environmental encyclopedia available today. Another excellent selection of books is offered by Usborne Publishing Ltd., including the following:

—*First Nature Series*
—*Young Scientist Investigates Series*
—*Nature Facts and List Series*
—*Animals and Their Ecosystems Series*
—*Natural Wonders Series*
—*First Travellers Series*

Other topics covered by Usborne include conservation, ecology, geography and world history.

Some other resources for children of all ages are:

—*Wilderness Album Series* (Hyperion Press Ltd.)
—*Troll Nature Series* (Troll Assoc.)
—*Ocean World Series* (Cousteau Society)
—*Dolphin Log* (a Cousteau Society children's magazine)
—*Ranger Rick Magazine* (National Wildlife Fed.)
—*Ranger Rick Book Series* (National Wildlife Fed.)
—*National Wildlife Magazine* (National Wildlife Fed.)
—*Eyewitness Junior Series* (Alfred A. Knopf)
—*Eyewitness Books Series* (Alfred A. Knopf)
—*Library of Knowledge Series* (Random House)

—*Natural Science Book Series* (Lerner Pub. Co.)
—*The Viking Children's World Atlas* (Puffin Books)

Choose areas of study that pertain to the environment you are traveling through—marine life for trips by the sea, tropical birds if hiking in the rain forest, the trees and plants if hiking in a northern forest. Children can learn a great deal about environmental concerns by first studying the natural surroundings of an area and then observing the impact of mankind on them. When hiking in Toubkal National Park in the Atlas Mountains of Morocco, for instance, our children learned about the effects of soil erosion and overgrazing from a Peace Corps worker who was stationed there to help the Moroccans develop an effective park management plan. A similar encounter in the mountains of Guatemala was equally informative. Opportunities for environmental studies abound. National parks and nature preserves all over the world are excellent sources of information. Visit their visitor centers, collect and read brochures, and have the children ask as many questions as they want. Study and discuss the different environmental concerns of the areas you travel to. The adventuring child has a unique opportunity to experience many different natural environments, learn about their needs, and observe what is being done to preserve them. In return, this will help him develop into a person who not only enjoys the outdoors, but understands and lives in harmony with it as well.

Children's Reading Books

All the following listed books are available in paperback and well-suited to adventuring children. Some have an outdoor focus, some are good for sparking imaginative play, and some encourage a positive relationship between siblings and children of different ages, all areas relevant to children when adventuring. A number of the books are old-fashioned. Don't let this deter you from introducing them to your children. Written in an era before television, play groups and modern affluence, they foster the type of simple activities adventuring children must rely on.

Adventuring enriches a child's awareness of the environment. Simple activities such as collecting shells can be turned into impromptu science lessons.

Aiken, Joan—*Black Hearts in Battersea, Wolves of Willoughby Chase*

Alcott, Louisa May—*Little Women, Little Men, Eight Cousins, Old Fashioned Girl*

Banks, Lynne Reid—*The Indian in the Cupboard* books

Blyton, Enid—The *Five Series*, Adventure book series, etc. Although these books are not published in the United States, we have included them on the chance you have access to them in either Canada or England (where they are published). All her books are appropriate for adventuring children.

Brink, Carol—*Caddie Woodlawn*

Burnett, Frances—*The Secret Garden, The Little Princess, Little Lord Fauntleroy*

Burnford, Sheila—*The Incredible Journey*
Caudill, Rebecca—*Schoolhouse in the Woods, Schoolroom in the Parlor, A Pocketful of Cricket*
Cooper, Susan—*The Dark Is Rising Series*
Dahl, Roald—*Charlie and the Chocolate Factory, Charlie and the Great Glass Elevator, James and the Giant Peach, Fantastic Mr. Fox, Danny The Champion of the World*
George, Jean Craighead—*My Side of The Mountain*
Henry, Margerite—*Misty of Chincoteague, Sea Star, Stormy, King of the Wind, Justin Morgan Had A Horse, Brighty, Born To Trot*
Ingalls, Laura—The *Little House* books
Jacques, Brian—*Redwall Series*
Lawson, Robert—*Rabbit Hill, Mr. Revere and I, Captain Kidd's Cat*
L'Engle, Madeleine—*A Wrinkle In Time* trilogy and all other books
Lenski, Lois—*Strawberry Girl*
Lewis, C.S.—*The Chronicles of Narnia* books
Lindgren, Astrid—*Pippi Longstocking* books, *Mio My Son, Children of Noisy Village*
London, Jack—*White Fang, The Call of The Wild, Stories of the North*
Montgomery, L.M.—*Anne of Green Gables Series* and all other books
Mowat, Farley—*Lost in the Barrens, Owls in the Family*
Nesbitt, E.—*Five Children and It, Enchanted Castle, Phoenix and Carpet, Story of the Amulet, Treasure Seekers, Railway Children, The Wouldbegoods*
Norton, Mary—*The Borrowers Series*
Porter, Eleanor—*Pollyanna*
Ransome, Arthur—*Swallows and Amazons Series*
Selden, George—*Chester Cricket Series, Harry Kitten and Tucker Mouse*
Sidney, Margaret—*Five Little Peppers, Five Little Peppers Midway*
Taylor, Sydney—*All of A Kind Family Series*
Warner, Gertrude Chandler—*The Boxcar Children Series*

White, E.B.—*Charlotte's Web, The Trumpet of the Swan, Stuart Little*

Winthrop, Elizabeth—*The Castle in the Attic*

Music

If a child plays a musical instrument, adventuring during the school year needn't interfere with his continued studies. The biggest consideration is, of course, the size of the instrument. While taking along a piano just won't be possible, something like a flute or clarinet will. Many instruments are small and easy to pack except on extreme lightweight travels like a bicycle tour. Even then, a recorder or harmonica could still be included. When one of our children came home one day from school all inspired to take the cello (the music teacher had just done a demonstration of all the string instruments), we refocused him to the violin, realizing that a cello wouldn't be practical for our type of travel. Since then, the violin has gone with us on all adventures except those on a bicycle and both children have been able to keep up in their studies, even on three and four month trips.

If your child plays an instrument, tell his teacher well ahead of time about your impending travels. That way if there's anything important to be introduced soon, the teacher has time to do it. If you have access to a tape-deck on your trip, tapes are an excellent way for the teacher to provide some firsthand guidance while you're away. The boy's tapes from their violin teacher made it seem like she was right in the room with them and provided plenty of new motivation when it was needed. A musical instrument can be practiced anywhere, even in a campground where the neighbors will usually be intrigued and pleased with the sound of a little music each day. Have the child or children do an occasional performance, always a way to get them inspired about their progress. Ours like to make programs, invite everyone they know, serve refreshments, and let the audience make requests. Other fun musical activities are composing their own pieces and "Fun Night", when they get to play anything they want.

Extracurricular activities like music can be continued during your travels. Here, Colin practices the violin while sailing in the Caribbean.

Art

Art can be a key form of entertainment on an adventure and just as diverse as what children would be exposed to in school. Paper and colored pencils are lightweight and easy to carry on any trip. Get a good set of pencils with a wide variety of colors. These are much less messy than crayons or magic markers and come in lovely varying shades. Water colors are also possible to take along for some work in painting. If you're traveling by the ocean, have the children look for clay at low tide. This can be molded into all kinds of shapes and allowed to dry. Our children have made tiny pots, boxes, baskets, doll furniture, and animal sculptures from clay collected by the sea. If you have the carrying capacity, keep some in a plastic bag for future sculpting sessions.

Sports

Because of the nature of adventure travel, keeping in shape through outdoor exercise is never a problem and is a good substitute for sports provided by schools. What will be missing is team sports activities. Taking along something like a soccer ball or baseball and mitts will provide opportunities for getting up some games with other children during your trip. Take into account what sport is popular in the place where you will be traveling, as this is the one the local children will most likely be able to play. Few children around the world have the exposure to multiple sports that North Americans do. In Europe, for instance, everyone plays soccer, which they call "football". In the Caribbean and Central and South America baseball is also popular. Few foreign children play American football or basketball, although interest in the latter seems to be on the rise. Older children should be able to get involved with weekly pick-up games if staying in one place for any length of time.

Structured School Program

The following are suggestions and guidelines for parents who are more comfortable using a structured school program. Keep in mind that even this traditional approach can incorporate many of the positive attributes of unschooling mentioned earlier.

Parental Responsibilities

Parental responsibility regarding a child's education, while certainly very real, is not the major hurdle many parents believe it to be. No teacher certificate or teaching experience is required to teach your own children while traveling. Nor need it take up hours of your day or turn into a daily battlefield. The younger the child, the more teacher input you will be called upon to supply, with first grade requiring the most and high school the least. With first and second graders, your teacher input stays high because of their limited reading skills.

By fifth grade a child can follow his own instructions and assignments almost entirely without the need for parental guidance. At that point, how much travel-related improvisation you as parents want to supply is up to you. No matter what type of program you choose, familiarizing yourself with the material will be necessary, even if it's just to correct materials supplied by a school. Exposure to your children's academics should do wonders for your own education, as you find yourself brushing up on things like long division and prepositions on the sly with a structured school program, or learning about such diverse subjects as volcanoes, Egyptian tombs and whales through a more flexible educational approach.

The more hometeaching you do, the easier it will get. The first time you're faced with an armful of books and your own children as students you might wonder why you ever even contemplated travel during the school year, particularly if the material is supplied by the child's school and not completely outlined in terms of how you should present it. At the beginning of your trip, work out a weekly schedule and set a particular time of day to do school (first thing in the morning is best). Because of the intensive learning conditions, a day's material can usually be covered in half the time it takes at school. Expect it to take a little longer the first few days as you get organized and the children adjust to working at home. The children can usually complete the work in 2 to 3 hours, including recess. When teaching academic subjects in a structured school program, it's best to adhere to some type of a classroom structure: a set schedule, one place for doing schoolwork, no idle chit-chat, prepared lessons and paperwork, a recess break. This not only ensures that all required material is covered, but also helps the children readjust to a regular classroom when they return home.

If your child has difficulty in a certain area of learning, the chances are their classmates at home are also struggling. New concepts often take weeks to learn. Some concepts are introduced periodically just to familiarize children with them rather then actually teach them yet. Don't expect your child to grasp something quickly just because it's on the curriculum. Children will learn faster at home than in a crowded classroom, provided you maintain a positive relationship with them. Resist the temptation to bring them home ahead of their classmates. The lessons learned through travel will enrich their lives far more than an accelerated school program.

Academic Concerns

If your trip has been a long one, your children might experience some initial difficulty at concentrating in a roomful of children or adhering to a rigid classroom structure. All teachers have a way they like to do things that take the children some time to sort out. None of this should take long and an understanding teacher will help the child through this period. If your children are returning to the same classroom, incorporating similar techniques into your homeschooling will make the transition period easier. Have them set up their papers the same way, do math problems by odds or evens, complete a set number of exercises on each subject—whatever the teacher normally requires. This may seem incredibly silly at the time, but in the long run it will ease your child's re-entry into the classroom.

Social Concerns

Socially, children should have few problems. Some teasing or meanness is to be expected at that age when these are prevalent peer group techniques. To minimize this, encourage your children to look and act happy when they return to school, even if they aren't. Mine always had a teary moment before their return to school, then put on what Colin called a smile so big it feels like his face was about to split. By looking happy, they defused any resentment and jealousy the other children might have been harboring towards their absence. Instead, their classmates eagerly told them everything that went on at school, secure in the feeling that Tristan and Colin were the ones who had been missing out on things. As Tristan said after his first day back at school after missing four months of fifth grade, "Even the kids who don't like me were friendly!"

Curriculum Planning

The following are some suggestions, samples, and resources for setting up and supplementing a structured school curriculum while your child is traveling. No matter what type of program you choose or how long you travel, there's always room for incorporating trip-related experiences into academic studies. Included are two sample daily curriculums, one for third grade and one for fifth, plus examples of special activities that have worked well for us.

Grade Three Daily Curriculum

8:30 - 9:00	Opening Work: story work sheet multiplication quiz
9:00 - 9.30	Spelling
9.30 - 10:15	Creative Writing
10:15 -10:30	Recess
10:30 - 11:15	Math
11:15 - 11:30	Reading
Later in day:	Scrapbook/journal writing, reading, and music

Total time: 3 hours

All structured material should be able to be supplied by the children's school. If you follow a formal program like this, I suggest you get started right after breakfast—the kids will be at peak form and you'll have the rest of the day for other activities.

Opening Work. In the Opening Work, the story work sheet refers to an exercise in reading a short piece, followed by a series of five or six questions that must be answered from memory. Sometimes read the story out loud and sometimes let them read it to themselves. This is an important skill taught at this grade level, retention of what one has heard or read. Any short piece of reading could easily be supplemented for the work sheets, provided you thought up some questions ahead of time.

Multiplication Quiz. The multiplication quiz is a quick daily test on whatever multiplication table the children are working on that week. This short, repetitive exercise helps them learn their tables, the biggest arithmetic hurdle of the third grade. First the problems are given in order, then mixed up, then timed.

Spelling. The spelling exercise varies daily:

Monday:	write in alphabetical order
Tuesday:	write all words and show vowel sounds next to each word

Wednesday:	choose and write four words and illustrate meanings with a drawing
Thursday:	look up words in a children's dictionary and write page number of each definition
Friday:	final test

Creative Writing. Creative writing stresses different activities, with one story written a week.

Examples: a description of someone you know
—a description of a room in your home
—a story about animals living in the woods
—your favorite hike
—a sea adventure story

All stories should be at least five paragraphs. Spelling is not stressed in creative writing. The primary emphasis is on creativity to help develop a love for writing in the child.

Math. Math is worked on out of their school book at any rate they felt comfortable at. This is one area where homeschooling children progress faster than children in school, probably due to the more favorable conditions for concentration. From my experience children of this age really thrive on math learned through games.

Scrapbooks & Journals. The scrapbook/journals are something the children work on two or three times a week. For more information on them see the section on scrapbook and journal keeping. These are an accumulation of social studies, history, geography, science and environmental studies.

Reading. Reading takes place frequently and just about anywhere. You can never bring too many reading books for children when adventuring. If you have the space, squeeze them in. They can always be traded or given away, although you will find your children reading them again and again. Adventuring children quickly become voracious readers.

Music. Music can be a continuation of their studies begun at school, or something totally new to be experimented with on the trip. All formal music programs can be supplied by their teacher and dated according to a recommended practice schedule.

Grade Five Daily Curriculum

8:30 - 9:00	Language
9:00 - 9:45	Math
9:45 - 10:15	Spelling
10:15 - 10:30	Recess
10:30 - 11:00	Reading
11:00 - 11:45	Creative Writing
Later in day:	Social Studies, pleasure reading, violin

Total time: 3 hours (not including recess)

Again, all structured school work can be supplied by the children's teachers. Let older children choose the order in which they want to do the subjects.

Language. Language covers various aspects of grammar (nouns, verbs, pronouns, adjectives, adverbs, etc.) plus developed writing skills through the use of such things as descriptive passages, conversation, organization and topic sentences. Both a language text book and work book are used.

Math. Math is worked on out of a book and covers a variety of fifth grade math skills: long division, multiple digit problems, word problems, fractions, decimals, geometry concepts.

Spelling. Spelling uses a work book for the first two days, then a pretest to determine what words needed work, then writing and studying words misspelled on the pretest, and a final test on Friday.

Reading. Reading is an interpretive study of various assigned books. The books are read over a two-week period and a number of exercises can be built around the children's ability to interpret what took place in the story. In this type of study no one answer is necessarily the only right one. The purpose is for children to develop their interpretive skills.

Creative Writing. Creative writing involves writing one story a week, built around various ideas and writing skills. Some ideas are as follows:

—A story built around an illustration in a book
—A mystery
—A secret hide-out
—My favorite friend or cousin

—A play in three parts
—Poems
—A sea chanty
—Creating a setting for a story
—Supporting an opinion
—Developing a character

Week's curriculum:

Monday:	organize story
Tuesday:	write first draft
Wednesday:	finish first draft
Thursday:	proof read with parent and begin final draft
Friday:	finish final draft and read out loud

Special Reports

This is one exercise children enjoy doing on a trip. Researching something first-hand is always more interesting to them than using school textbooks. By Fifth Grade children begin developing organizational skills through researching and writing special reports on an assigned subject. Pick something relevant to your travels and have the children produce a written report over the period of about two weeks. The following example is a report Tristan and Colin did at age ten while homeschooling in the Virgin Islands.

Annaberg Ruins (a preserved sugar mill ruins on the island of St. John in the Virgin Islands):

Step One:	made notes from guide book on the history of St. John
Step Two:	visited ruins and took notes
Step Three:	made complete outline from notes for report
Step Four:	wrote report in pencil
Step Five:	revisited ruins and drew sketch of layout
Step Six:	revised first draft and wrote final draft in pen
Step Seven:	drew interpretive illustration of the sugar mill in its working days, based on layout sketch and information

Doing Drills

Adventure-related activities can also be converted into informal school time. Hikes, sails, bike rides on back roads and canoe outings are all excellent times for oral exercises: vocabulary drills, mental arithmetic, spelling, question and answer sessions, story telling, discussions. Bus, train and car rides, lunch breaks and waits for public transportation can be times for reading.

Putting Your Child In A Foreign School

If you're renting and staying in one place for a long time (three months or more), a fourth option is to put your children into the local school. This has the advantage of providing your children's schooling, giving them a crash-course in the local language, and introducing them to other children in the neighborhood. Even with no background training, a child will become fluent in a foreign language in a couple of months if attending school. Some cultures absorb foreigners more readily than others. How different your child looks can make a difference. A blond among dark-haired children, for instance, is more likely to have a tough time than a blonde among blondes. Children in large groups can be less welcoming to an outsider than individual children met outside school. If you want your child to attend the local school, the best thing is to have him get to know someone his own age outside school first. This will provide him with friendly support when he first comes under the scrutiny of his classmates. Then play it by ear. Some children will be miserable, in which case take them out. Others will quickly learn the language, make friends, and benefit from the whole experience.

Conclusion

When debating whether or not to take your children out of school to go adventuring, remember that the greatest educational lesson children learn through adventure travel is the one they learn effortlessly—an understanding of the world they live in. This, after all, is what education is all about—developing and expanding a child's perception of he world and everything in it. By expanding their horizons through adventuring, you will be expanding their potential for learning. Adventure travel becomes the ultimate classroom with world its text book and experience its teacher.

Chapter
12
Medical Concerns

A sick child on a trip is no parent's idea of a good time. The mere thought of struggling to locate the nearest doctor, deal with the language, and cope with the illness in a tent, pension, canoe or boat is enough to keep some families home or cause parents to leave their children behind when they travel. Despite what one might think, adventure travel gives rise to few medical needs. Instead of falling prey to a variety of illnesses or accidents, traveling children are often healthier than at home, particularly if you're traveling somewhere warm during the winter months. If a child does get sick, it's often short-lived and easy to deal with, especially in a warm climate where even a sick child can be outdoors. When Tristan and Colin contracted the chicken pox while we were living on a boat in Florida, I was able to give them showers on the foredeck, take them for rides in their wagon, and let them play outside—things I couldn't have done at home in the cold weather. Injuries are rare, despite what might sometimes seem like high risk situations. The risk is usually in the imagination of the parent and far from a real threat to the child.

Learning The Basics

Acquiring some medical background, carrying first aid equipment and taking a few precautions are always good preventative insurance when adventuring with children. Although applying the occasional band-aid or extracting a splinter are generally the most rigorous first aid you'll be called upon to deliver, knowing how to deal with more serious situations or what to expect from foreign medical services will do much to relieve anxieties when adventuring. The following is a list of ailments, injuries and preventative measures common to children. While basic remedies have been included, a doctor should still be sought at the earliest opportunity for anything of a serious nature.

Cuts

For any cut beyond the simple band-aid stage, allow it to bleed briefly to ensure cleanliness. Wash hands, then gently clean the cut with soap and a piece of sterile gauze dipped in boiling water. Allow the cut to dry, apply hydrogen peroxide and Aloe Vera, then bandage with gauze and adhesive tape. We use Aloe first, waiting a few days to see if the cut shows signs of infection that require stronger medication. Aloe Vera gel, derived from the Aloe plant, has many healing capabilities that are largely ignored by conventional medical practises. To avoid unnecessary exposure to chemicals, we always try it first whenever appropriate. If the cut doesn't show immediate signs of healing, apply first aid cream.

Burns

Immerse the burn immediately in cold water for 15 - 20 minutes. Apply Aloe Vera and leave unbandaged. For more serious burns where skin has blistered, bandage with Vaseline gauze. Change the bandage in about 6 or 7 days. Do not bandage burned areas to each other (fingers, toes, etc.). The burn will take about two weeks to heal. If the burn is very severe it might be necessary to give antibiotics as well; seek medical attention.

Skin Infections

These are most prevalent in tropical areas where even the smallest cut or bite can lead to infection. To avoid, treat any minor cut or bite that doesn't heal right away with hydrogen peroxide and Aloe Vera. Again, if there's no sign of healing in a few days, apply antibiotic cream. Wear sandals and cotton clothes to allow the body to "breathe" and lessen the chance for skin irritations to develop. To neutralize the sting of jellyfish, nettles, bees or biting insects, apply a paste made with Adolph's Meat Tenderizer and rubbing alcohol. Adolph's contains a papaya enzyme that breaks down the insect venom present in the sting or bite. Fresh papaya works as well.

Spiny Urchins

About the only risk children run when playing at a beach in the tropics is stepping on a spiny urchin, something that can usually be avoided by keeping away from grassy areas in the water. Occasionally a few will find their way to nearby sandy spots, particularly after a day of high winds and waves. If your child steps on one, pull out any large spines with tweezers or a sterilized needle as you would for splinters. The spines are very brittle; a number of them will be impossible to remove. Apply vinegar to the injured place to help make the remaining spines dissolve.

Stomach Problems

Like the subject of seasickness when talking about boats, some mention of stomach difficulties usually arises when a discussion on foreign travel is underway. Many people have their own horror story, or know someone with a horror story, or know someone whose friend has a horror story. Whatever the case, the stories are far more frequent than the actual fact and shouldn't be a deterrent from traveling to exotic places and trying unfamiliar foods, even with children. Both diarrhea and constipation can occur, particularly in the early stages of your trip. Avoiding them, however, is not that difficult.

Constipation

To prevent constipation drink plenty of fluids (six glasses a day) and eat high-fiber foods: dried fruit, whole grains, dried beans, raw fruits and vegetables, nuts. The first twenty-four hours of travel is the most critical because you're usually sitting on an airplane or in some type of vehicle. Food that's offered on airplanes or that you buy in restaurants is rarely high-fiber and just compounds the problem. For this reason I always carry a supply of high-fiber snack foods with us on the beginning of any trip to tide us over until I can start cooking our own meals. Favorite choices are peanut butter, rice cakes, trail mix, nuts, dried fruit, sunflower seeds and whole wheat crackers. If you have the room, taking along a small supply of a high-fiber cereal like grape-nuts or some kind of bran cereal will also help the cause. Once you start adventuring, the problem should disappear unless you're spending long hours in a car. In that case, keep up the high-fiber nibble foods and meals.

Diarrhea

Diarrhea is usually the result of exposure to new bacteria present in the food and water where you are adventuring. While not a threat to your health, they can upset your digestive system for a while. The more you travel, the less susceptible you become. Children also seem to be highly resistant to stomach upsets. Tristan and Colin, who have been traveling all their lives, have cast-iron stomachs capable of ingesting any foreign foods without mishap. Nor are they the exception. Friends of ours spent six months adventuring in India with their four and six-year-old children, neither of whom ever showed the slightest sign of a problem. As the mother told us with amusement, the only one to get sick was her! Some places, such as India, do require extra care when handling food and water to avoid picking up more serious types of bacteria, but for the most part diarrhea can be avoided by easing yourself into new foods gradually. Adventure travel has an advantage over other forms of travel because you are the one doing your own cooking. Another preventative measure when traveling to developing countries is a daily dose of acidophilus, the bacteria normally present in yoghurt. Acidophilus tablets are available at health food stores.

If someone in the family does get diarrhea, eat foods easy to digest (the opposite of what you eat with constipation): toast, crackers, bananas, yoghurt, boiled eggs and potatoes, noodles. Avoid any fried or raw foods other than bananas. Take Pepto-Bismol. This is a safe medication for children of all ages. Avoid giving children Lomotil, often prescribed for traveler's diarrhea, as this is a powerful drug and not really necessary in most cases. If the water is suspect, and it usually is, use a water purifier, drink bottled water or drink water that has been boiled until the problem remedies itself.

Sun Protection

Adventuring involves spending a great deal of time outdoors, often in the sun. No matter what latitude you're at, some protection should be applied to protect children from overexposure. Regularly apply a sunscreen rated at SPF#15 or higher. Some, like Johnson's baby sunblock, are made specifically for babies and children without harsh chemicals. In high exposure situations like the tropics, on the water, on a beach or at high altitudes, sunhats and T-shirts should be used between 11 a.m. and 3 p.m. when the sun is the most directly overhead.

Make sure children who are exercising hard drink plenty of fluids. The chances are they'll keep asking for something to drink, a request that can get irritating after a while, but one that reflects a real need. Children don't develop their full ability to sweat until their teenage years and are therefore more susceptible to overheating. If you're exercising in a very hot climate, add some salt to your cooking to replace that lost through sweating.

Protection From Disease

Immunizations

With immunizations a controversial subject these days, how much or how little you choose to immunize your family is up to the individual. For ourselves, we recommend children at least be inoculated against diptheria, tetanus, and polio if you plan any foreign travel. Check with your doctor or local health clinic about what immunizations might be required for a given area. Possible diseases that require immunization are Yellow Fever, Plague, Cholera and Typhus. Immunization against Typhoid is optional. As with Hepatitis, Typhoid is transmitted through contaminated food and water and can be avoided by being careful in areas where this is a possibility, particularly places where rats abound. Typhoid can also be contracted by swimming in areas with raw sewage present. Cholera can also normally be avoided through normal hygienic practices and by avoiding infected areas.

Don't let the thought of possible diseases dissuade you from going somewhere, nor make you unduly nervous while you're there. Children have healthy systems and should be able to safely travel anywhere adults can.

Hepatitis

Hepatitis is transmitted by food or water that has come in contact with an infected person. By preparing your own food and following the general rules of thumb outlined under Food & Water, this shouldn't be a problem, even in very poor areas of the world. When eating out choose places that look clean, not makeshift food stalls alongside the street. These can lack washing facilities of any kind.

Malaria

Malaria is transmitted by mosquitoes and prevalent in a number of places throughout the world. Although applying bug repellant and using mosquito netting is sufficient for most circumstances, taking a prophylactic drug while camping or hiking in high-risk areas is a must. Various prescription drugs are available. The dosage for children varies with age so be sure you have the necessary information before starting treatment. If possible, begin treatment two weeks before visiting the area.

Tuberculosis

Tuberculosis can be contracted from the milk of contaminated cows. When adventuring abroad, drink only fresh milk that has been pasteurized or boiled. Many foreign countries sell tinned, powdered or sterilized milk, all of which are safe.

Food And Water

Most modern countries have bacteria-free food and drinking water; developing countries often do not. If you're unsure about the water, ask at the tourist bureau when you first arrive. Some countries have areas that are safe and others that aren't. In Morocco, for instance, we were told that drinking the tap water in northern cities was fine, but not elsewhere. If you notice local people drinking out of plastic bottles, the chances are the water is unsafe. Bottled water is now widely available. Taking along some water-purifying tablets or a small portable water filter is also a good idea if you plan to visit out-of-the-way places or do some back woods hiking and camping. Both are available through camping stores and catalogs. Boiling the water also works, although this can be tedious. One minute of boiling will destroy almost all types of bacteria, but a few require up to twenty minutes. Tap water is usually safe to use for cooking and hot drinks.

If you're still in doubt about the water, ask someone—a fellow camper, the proprietor of your hotel, or a local health official if there is one. The decision whether or not to drink the water is sometimes nothing more than a matter of taste or one's degree of acclimatization rather than that of possible contamination. In Turkey we were told most definitely that all water was safe to drink, yet many people chose to drink bottled water instead. While visiting there we camped for a while near a spigot where we noticed people filling their water jugs. When we asked about it we learned the water came from an underground spring and was especially good. After that we used it too. In all our travels we have only been a few places where the tap water was undrinkable, in which case bottled water was always available.

The rule of thumb for fresh food in areas where bacteria can be a problem is to only eat what is cooked or can be washed and peeled. Lettuce, for instance, should not be eaten in places where hepatitis, typhoid, or other bacterial infections are a distinct possibility. Don't be afraid to buy food from local markets, but take it home to wash, peel or cook before eating.

Despite what might sound like an ominous list of diseases, precautions and restrictions, adventuring in other cultures and eating local foods is not a high risk situation. Adventure travel is about the safest way to travel to some parts of the world because it guarantees you control over what you eat and drink. Instead of wondering just how clean the dishes are in a restaurant, how fresh the meat is, whether things were washed or refrigerated or where they got the ice for your drink, you know that everything has been handled properly from the moment it was bought to when it was served.

Common Childhood Ailments

The following are the more common ailments of children and how to treat them in the absence of a doctor. Most can be either prevented or treated successfully on your own with the proper medication, although a visit to a doctor should be done at the first opportunity. Included are preventative measures for avoiding serious illness in children in the first place.

Chicken Pox

There's not much you can do about this childhood disease except get through it. As chicken pox carries no great risk to the average child, medication is usually not prescribed. How much discomfort the child suffers varies widely, with some children running a fever and itching like mad and others hardly aware they have the disease at all. My twins fell under the first category and at age three had quite a case while we were traveling on a sailboat.

To relieve the itching, give the child frequent showers or baths with baking soda. Apply witch hazel and corn starch to the skin afterwards. Distraction is the best medicine, so do things that take his mind off his discomfort. Nighttime, of course, is the worst, especially if the child has a fever. Try anything that works. For us it was putting our children in bed with us for a few nights.

German Measles

This can be a hard disease to diagnose because most cases are so mild. We hardly knew our children had it on one trip except that they were covered with the telltale rash, small pink spots that covered their bodies. Make sure a sick child stays away from any pregnant woman, as this can cause birth defects. Otherwise, there's nothing you need to do in the way of treatment in most cases.

Ear Infection

Ear infections are caused by congestion in the ear, usually a side-effect of the common cold. Some children are more prone to infection than others. We've had more ear infections than I care to recall, including twice while adventuring—once in England and again in Turkey. If it's beginning to sound like we've had just about every possible childhood ailment while abroad, that's almost true, largely because our children have spent much of their youth adventure traveling. Knowing then about basic prevention methods we use today would have helped us avoid all those infections, but dealing with them at the time gave us confidence in our ability to cope and in foreign medical facilities.

If infection does develop in a child's ear he will complain of pain. You might also notice some fluid around the opening of the ear, a sign that the ear drum has popped under pressure from the infection. Many children never notice a thing until this happens and the infection is well established. The standard treatment is a ten-day course of an antibiotic like amoxycillin. This is generally effective, although children suffering from frequent infections can build up resistance to reoccurring uses of any antibiotic.

If you do have a child prone to ear infections, following the preventative measures outlined in the next section should prevent any reoccurrences. In any event, ears that have been infected should be checked by a doctor two weeks after completing the course of medication to ensure the infection is completely gone.

Respiratory Infections

These include the common cold, bronchitis and pneumonia and are all caused by congestion in one part of the body or another. Colds, of course, are the most common and least serious. Their greatest threat lies in that they are usually the precursor to more serious infection. The trick, therefore, is to prevent them from building up congestion—in the lungs, bronchial tubes or ears. If infection does occur, the standard treatment again is a ten-day course of antibiotics, an increasingly controversial solution at best, due to overuse and eventual ineffectiveness.

Swimmer's Ear

If your children are swimming underwater a lot or prone to ear infections, dry their ears with cotton wool after swimming. A drop of rubbing alcohol or vinegar can also be administered to each ear to aid the drying process and prevent ear fungus from developing.

Lice and Worms

Many home medical books don't even mention this prevalent problem among children, one that sooner or later your children have a good chance of picking up at some point in your adventures. Both are something that children can pick up just as easily at home as when traveling, but rarely do because of more attention to cleanliness. Knowing what to look for and how to treat it makes the whole thing seem less unsavory. Head lice should be checked for periodically and the children's hair kept as clean as possible. If they do get infected, use a shampoo that's specially made for this problem. Unfortunately, these contain a toxic pesticide that should be used sparingly, so try to avoid the problem in the first place. Threadworm, or pinworm, the type children most commonly get, comes from handling dirt. Prevention is simply a matter of washing hands before eating, something most children have a real mind-block against. Always carry soap for hand washing wherever you go—on a hike, in a canoe, on a bus—for any day outing. A liquid soap such as Dr. Bronner's is easier to carry and less messy.

If infected, a child will complain of an itching or tickling sensation in his bottom at bedtime, the time when the worms are active. To be absolutely sure before administering medication, check the child's bottom at bedtime or inspect a bowel movement. The tiny white threadworm will be evident. A prescription drug like Vermox is administered, either in liquid or chewable tablet form, and taken once, then again ten days later. As both lice and worms are highly contagious, the whole family should be treated if an outbreak occurs. Another less toxic treatment is grapefruit seed extract, available from natural food stores. To prevent picking up other types of worms, have children wear sandals when playing or walking in the dirt in hot countries. If you do forget to carry some medication on a trip, Vermox is an easy drug to find in other parts of the world, evidence of just how prevalent infection is.

Prevention Of Serious Infection

As the common cold is the usual cause of congestion leading to serious infection, controlling it is an almost guaranteed way to avoid complications. Since learning about this simple 3-day regimen, our children have never had another ear infection. The following should be done at the onset of any cold to keep most from developing beyond a few days of the sniffles. All dosages are intended for children. Here's a sample dietary schedule:

- one teaspoon of vinegar in a glass of water or apple juice before each meal
- ten drops of Echinacea extract in warm water before each meal
- fluids to drink every hour
- one half a vitamin C pill before each meal
- no sweetened foods or drinks
- no milk or citrus
- eat high protein foods: meat, fish, dairy products, ricecakes, peanut butter, dried beans.
- stress any apple products that aren't sweetened
- keep body warm, especially infected areas (chest, head, throat)
- for a sore throat: gargle with vinegar and apple juice before swallowing
- for chest congestion: apply heat to chest area with a hot water bottle or apply Vick's Vapo-Rub at bed time.

The purpose of all this is to combat infection by putting the body in as strong a position as possible. As both milk and citrus are mucus-producing, these are avoided. Because infection thrives in an alkaline, cold environment, heat and acid-producing foods like vinegar and apple products are stressed and sugared things avoided. Protein is also stressed because the body uses this to combat infection.

If you don't believe this works, try it. The vinegar is very important and not terribly popular, but apple juice masks the flavor well. If you're traveling in a place where apple juice is the last thing you can find, mix the vinegar with honey and just enough water so the child can drink it. Have some special food ready to eat the minute he's finished. Don't sweeten the drink with sugar or you will undo all its good. Honey-sweetened foods are fine.

Basic First Aid Kit

This is intended for lightweight adventure travel. For either ocean sailing or wilderness camping, a slightly more comprehensive kit would be necessary.

- Adhesive tape
- Adolph's Meat Tenderizer
- Ace bandage
- Aloe Vera gel
- Bacitracin ointment (first aid cream)
- Band-aids (assorted sizes)
- Cotton
- Echinacea extract
- Eye cup
- Gauze dressings, individually wrapped
- Gauze vaseline dressing
- Herbal tea (for headaches)
- Hydrogen peroxide
- Ipecac
- Pepto-Bismol (chewable tablets)
- Rubbing alcohol

- Sunscreen (rated #15 or higher)
- Thermometer
- Tweezers
- Tylenol (children's)
- Vermox or grapefruit seed extract
- Vinegar
- Vitamin C
- Water-purifying tablets

Periodically check all medications' expiration dates as some have a limited shelf-life.

Health Services Abroad

Visiting a doctor, hospital or health clinic abroad can seem daunting at first. The language is foreign and the facilities often unfamiliar or old-fashioned. Under that often archaic facade, however, usually lie capable medical services, ones every bit as effective as those at home for treating the average family ailment.

If the need arises, the best place to inquire about medical facilities is the local tourist bureau or a large hotel. They can recommend doctors who speak English and direct you to reliable services and pharmacies. Find out what's available before plunging into a foreign hospital or doctor's office. We've found they vary tremendously, even in the same country. A hospital on one Greek island, for instance, looked like the set for a Civil War film while another on a neighboring island was worthy of Boston's best. Where hospitals are primitive, private practises are often available with a higher level of medical expertise. Wherever you go, don't be immediately put off by appearances. Just because the equipment looks antiquated and the facilities dingy doesn't mean the doctor doesn't know his profession or that you won't get cured. Our experience with overseas doctors has always been good. Most did their training in European or American medical schools and spoke either English, Spanish or German (the languages of many medical books).

Despite carrying first aid equipment, we've been caught short a few times and needed something from the pharmacy, usually because I forgot to bring it on the trip. This is when the language gap can really play a role. If communication is difficult, see if they have a medical language dictionary (they often do), one that gives all the medical terms in their language and English. Then you can look the word up that describes your problem and show the pharmacist. Next, make sure you know how much and how often to take the prescribed medication. This can take a while, but don't leave until you're absolutely sure you know what the dosage is; otherwise, you might find yourself like us, camped in the middle of nowhere with no idea who's supposed to take how much. If communication is really at a low ebb, the chances are by now you'll have a large gathering of the local population in the pharmacy with you, hanging on every word, offering unintelligible advice, and thrusting forward anyone with a smattering of English. With practically the whole town pitching in, you'll eventually get things sorted out, even if it is at the cost of everyone knowing what your problem is. Now you see why it's easier to bring along your own medical supplies on an adventure!

No matter where you want to travel, worrying about your children's health and what type of medical services are available shouldn't keep you home. Apart from our own experience, we've met other families traveling, often with very young children. All experienced the same thing, robust health in their children and good results if they did need a doctor or medication. Adventure travel is a healthy, outdoor pursuit, one that gives rise to few medical problems. If a child does get sick, it's usually short-lived and easy to deal with, especially in warm climates. The odds are more likely that the whole family will be more physically fit and healthy than you were back home, with little or no need for all that first aid equipment you brought along.

Chapter
13
Social Needs

One day my mother voiced her usual concern over Tristan and Colin's social life while traveling. What they needed was a pen pal, she advised, to keep them in contact with another child while away. I laughed at the mere idea of the children being socially deprived during our travels. On one trip alone there had been Jennifer and Ingrid on a neighboring boat, a street baseball team of young boys, and friendly Luiz, all in the Dominican Republic. Then came Ben the Australian boy, numerous children in Puerto Rico, Carmen the multilingual boat child, and a marathon friendship with Brad on the island of Culebra. Interspersed among these were assorted toddlers and adults, letters from cousins back home, plus all the social benefits of being together as a family.

"In fact," I told my mother after an assessment of the situation, "Tristan and Colin's social life actually picks up when we're traveling."

Traveling children are usually social butterflies. Comfortable with both sexes and all ages, they cultivate friendships wherever they go. One of the first things a traveling child learns is to broaden his social criteria. The more he travels the less concerned he is with who he plays with. Once separated from the dominant factor of peer groups, traveling children develop a social versatility to match any high-ranked diplomat's. Social needs become less a matter of deprivation than of decision-making. Who do they want to play with that day - each other, their parents, fellow travelers or local children? Someone is always available.

Family Togetherness

Adventuring families are like temporary pioneer families. Separated from their familiar environment, they are bound together in their desire to achieve a common goal. Instead of heading west to settle new land, the goal is hiking a trail or canoeing a lake, bicycling some road or exploring a foreign country. Like the pioneers that came before, all this family togetherness is bound to have an effect on many things: your relationship with each other, your role as parents, your level of privacy, the quality of your parenting, and your means of entertainment. One of the nicest things about adventuring together as a family is that it shares all the benefits and none of the drawbacks of family togetherness. First of all, it's exciting for the children as well as the parents. Children can have as much interest and play as large a role in adventure travel as adults. This is different from the standard resort holiday where children and adults are provided with separate activities. In adventure travel, the goal is a shared one. Second, being together in an adventurous way means the whole family depends on each other. As the Outward Bound School has been teaching for years, dependence on one another cultivates awareness, respect, and liking for the other person.

Family togetherness needn't mean a loss of privacy. This is something that keeps a number of parents home - the thought of sharing every waking hour with their children in close quarters. As adventure travel has an outdoor focus, children have, if anything, more area to explore and play in than at home. The whole outdoors, in effect, becomes their yard. For those times like early morning, evening, and meals when parents might need a break from parenting, imposing a few rules can get you the privacy you need. Designate first thing in the morning and the half hour before bedtime as "quiet time". Quiet time is a luxury every parent should enjoy, whether adventuring or at home. Beginning as early as a year old, children can be trained to occupy themselves quietly during certain times of day. Give young children some toys, books, and nibble food to keep them happy and quiet in bed for about an hour in the morning. Older children are fine with just books. The same can be done in the evening after the children are

Traveling children soon acquire the ability to socialize with children of any age. This brother and sister paid daily visits to our campsite to play with infants Tristan and Colin.

ready for bed. This gives them an opportunity to unwind before bedtime and you parents some time to talk privately, have a drink, or eat dinner alone. Even if you're all sharing a tent, it won't take more than a few days before children are trained to quiet play or reading in the morning, and to going to sleep with a light on. At mealtimes, let older children read. This gives you parents a golden opportunity to talk without interruption from interested listeners.

Children who adventure with their parents become very family-oriented. If children running in and out the door to and from their friends' houses is what you're used to, expect quite a change during adventure travel. Because the shared trip is an exciting one, children unconsciously view their parents in a new way. Your hitherto unexciting role as breadwinner, cook, house-cleaner, laundress or designator of chores is suddenly transformed into the guise of competent adventurer. Impressed with your prowess at pitching tents, building fires, canoeing or sailing, they soon begin hanging on your every word. This new level of communication extends into all aspects of your family relationship:

helping each other, talking together, sharing a sense of humor, acquiring outdoor expertise, expressing opinions. All of which means that you should prepare yourself for children who think every conversation their parents have is teeming with interest. Set a few rules that work for you, stick to them, then sit back and be amazed that those same children who once turned a deaf ear when you spoke are now all too attentive.

Interaction With Siblings

A friend told me one day that she had canceled her planned trip to Washington D.C. with her three children. They had fought so badly in the car on her recent one-day excursion to Boston, she'd decided she couldn't handle a longer trip. Instead of being atypical, her experience is increasingly the norm. Yet here we are expounding on the virtues of family adventuring, telling people they'll have the time of their lives, and now saying the children will all have fun together. If so, where does the transition take place?

Where Many Families Go Wrong

Adventuring children do have fun together, not by accident or coincidence, but by design. In order for your children to enjoy each other you must first establish why, these days, siblings so often don't. The average child in North America now grows up in a neighborhood with a wealth of children to play with outside his own family. Unlike the old days when communities were small, children of a certain age were few, and families often lived in relative isolation, children today grow up surrounded by others their age. Beginning with play groups, children are oriented to limit their exposure and interest to their peers. Playing with siblings or children of another age isn't expected of them. Boys aren't expected to like girls, and none of them are expected to like grown-ups. Siblings have separate bedrooms, play areas are separated from living areas, and older children are channeled into a variety of activities that reduce their time with siblings to almost nothing. The stage is now set for children to function within a limited social structure, that of their peer group.

How Parents Can Help

Adventure travel supplies no peer group. The only playmates it guarantees are parents and siblings. If a good relationship between family children has already been nurtured at home, they will have no readjustment period from friends to brothers and sisters when they go traveling. By encouraging your children to play with each other, regardless of age, sex and family relationship, you can help prepare them for the close proximity of family adventuring. Give them time at home alone without the entertainment devices that so dominate children's free time these days: television, video games, organized sports, formal lessons. Even if neighborhood children come over, have all your children included in whatever game is being played. A strong bond between siblings is irreplaceable and something that will enrich their travel experience, teach them to regard all ages as potential playmates, and give them the confidence to approach other children met along the way.

Expect Some Friction Between Siblings

A certain amount of friction between siblings is, of course, inevitable and something no amount of family cohesion can completely eradicate. Some discord can be left for the children to work out themselves. Some may not even qualify as friction in their eyes, as my children informed me when I asked them to stop fighting one day. "We're not *fighting*," they replied, "we're just *discussing* things."

Some friction will take parental prodding to bring to a halt. As pin-pointing the blame is a futile exercise and punishment often has a way of perpetuating the problem, diversionary tactics can work best by appealing to their sense of fun as well as putting things in a perspective they can understand. Even with twins, I've had my moments of listening to altogether too much sibling bickering. One day while doing a hand-laundry in a campground in Portugal, I finally tired of hearing the children embroiled in some endless abusive verbal exchange.

"Okay, you guys," I announced, "you've got three choices. You can help me with the laundry, do school, or work things out immediately." A moment's silence greeted me as both children paused and looked up. "Well," said Colin, ever the witty one, "I think I'll do school."

Interaction With Other Children

Meeting and playing with other children is a benefit of family travel that few people are aware of. The assumption is usually that travel means an absence of playmates outside the family. Adventure travel provides many opportunities for meeting other children, both fellow travelers and local children. How much you utilize this social potential is up to you. Children new to travel will need some encouragement to overcome shyness at approaching strangers. The longer your trip, the more confidence they will develop in meeting other children.

Meeting Other Traveling Children

Other traveling children are usually the easiest to meet initially. Some will be very outgoing and approach your children almost immediately, generally a sign that they are experienced travelers and on the look-out for playmates. Bilingual and multilingual children are also very outgoing and possessed of little shyness when it comes to playing with foreigners. Other times, your children (perhaps with some parental urging) will need to make the first move. If children are interested in playing, the first sign will be a lot of interested watching of each other. That's the time to offer some encouragement.

Once children are old enough to formulate their own opinions, let them decide who they want to play with. By age nine Tristan and Colin recognized that a similarity in life-style and recreational pursuits was indicative of common interests, making other adventuring children the ideal playmates. They know that children who adventure like the outdoors, are imaginative and independent, and usually have a good relationship with their family. This isn't to say they weren't willing to play with someone totally unlike themselves, but the interest was usually short-lived.

If you travel off-season and during the school year, your chances increase of meeting other children of like minds. Al-

Giving your children the opportunity to make friends is important, even if it means a change in your itinerary. Here, Tristan and Colin play on an island off Portugal with South African children they met at our campground.

though comparatively few, there are other families adventuring with children at these times. We've met them on every trip. The added bonus of getting your children together is the opportunity it presents to meet other parents with similar experiences. This is one of the most enjoyable moments an adventuring family can have, meeting another family like themselves. When this happens, children need no urging to get together and play.

Give Children Their Own Social Time

Because friendships made while traveling have to end, it's important to give a little, if necessary, in your itinerary to allow children time together with new-found friends. If someone special comes along, it's worth spending a few extra days somewhere to let the children all play together, particularly on longer trips. Instead of feeling like they were always being dragged away from things, your children will remember the trip as a fun experience. As children have no sense of time, work out ahead with them what you plan to do. When Tristan and Colin made friends with

Francis, a South African boy we met in a campground in Portugal, we stayed an extra two days in order to go on a joint venture with his family to a nearby island. When asked, the boys said it was really important to them to stay longer and go to the island. This way, knowing that we had changed our schedule to incorporate some special social time for them, they didn't feel dragged away prematurely when we did leave. It also meant that Francis and his family left the campground the same day we did so none of the children felt like they were the only ones leaving. As children get older, this consideration becomes more important. A five-year-old doesn't care when he leaves one place or friend and goes to another, a ten-year-old does. To keep the older child enthusiastic, especially on a long trip, you're going to have to make some concessions. After all, you'd do the same for yourself.

The language barrier means little to children when a lively game is underway.

The Language Barrier

To children, language is not much of a barrier. On an overseas adventure, many of the children you meet will be foreign-speaking, a fact that needn't interfere with your own child's social life. Tristan and Colin expressed the theory one day that for them it's actually easier to approach children who don't speak English than ones that do. "That way we don't have to worry about what to say," they explained.

If your children are new to foreign travel, approaching a child without the benefit of a common language can seem intimidating at first. If one of you parents can speak the language, this is a good time to help them along to break the ice. After a while your children will become more relaxed and, eventually, welcome play with foreign-speaking children. Unlike adults, children have no inhibitions, no sense of cultural nuances and little embarrassment when dealing with foreigners, after the initial meeting. Their system of communication is quickly evolved; each child simply speaks his own language with little concern for how much is understood. If you stay a while in one country you'll notice your children picking up phrases from their playmates. They may not know exactly what they mean, but they'll know when to use them. I remember one time in Greece when Tristan and Colin were six, hearing a game of street soccer going on outside and realizing that two of the children yelling back and forth in Greek were mine!

Meeting Foreign Children

The more overseas adventuring you do, the easier the process of meeting foreign children becomes. You might notice that children used to hearing different languages, like those in Europe or any popular tourist area, are quite unaffected by language differences and therefore easiest to meet. To them speaking a foreign language is not odd or intimidating or an object of ridicule. Foreign children also begin learning other languages when very young in school and are usually eager to try them out. In one Moroccan mountain village we met a group of young boys who spoke Berber, Arabic, French, German and English, all of which

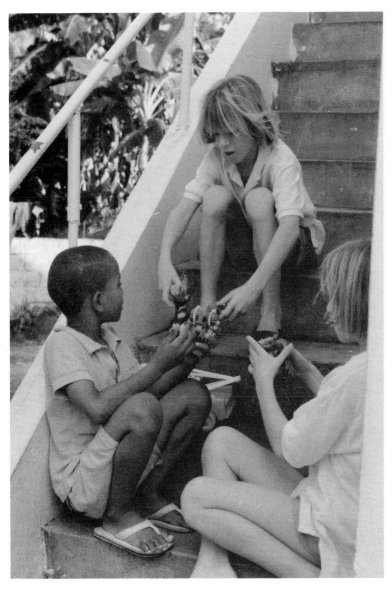

Children are the same the world over: adaptable, friendly and eager to play.

they mixed up in a delightful composite when playing with Tristan and Colin. Before you know it your own children will be doing the same, oblivious of who speaks or understands what, as long as they're all having a good time.

One thing worth remembering is that it's always easier to approach one or two children than an entire group. As with peer groups everywhere, the bigger the group, the less willing they are to incorporate outsiders. For this reason it's better to first make initial contact with just one or two children.

Social Icebreakers

Soccer Ball

Bringing along a few social icebreakers can help pave the way towards meeting other children. As far as boys are concerned, practically nothing attracts a crowd faster than the appearance of a soccer ball, or "football" as it's called throughout the rest of the world. During a five month backpacking trip we actually lugged one around with us despite its awkward size and weight. After its initial appearance in Greece, nothing would have convinced us to abandon it along the way. Without fail it acted like a magnet, precipitating quick introductions to local children wherever we went. Kevin always started things along by organizing a few pick-up games when we arrived somewhere new.

Legos & Other Toys

Legos are another useful icebreaker. This is a particularly fine toy because of its versatility, scope for creativity and undeniable appeal to boys and girls of all ages. Foreign children will find them intriguing and never turn down an opportunity to join your children for a Lego building session. Other small, imaginative toys like dolls and matchbox cars also have a universal appeal. For girls, dolls and their endless assortment of accessories can keep even a large group of children occupied as well as promote a number of imaginary games using them.

Legos have a universal appeal to children of all ages. Afternoon building sessions like this were a common occurrence at our campsite in Turkey.

Bicycles

A bicycle is another effective ice-breaker. Children are instantly attracted to the sight of a child riding one. Sometimes you'll meet children riding around campgrounds or villages on their own bikes, other times children who have never been on one at all. Do be careful about giving rides in areas where bicycles are a complete novelty. In our naivete, we wheeled some boys around on the children's bikes in a village in Morocco as a thank you for their help and generosity while we were camped there. What began as a gesture of appreciation became embroiled in something of an ordeal as more (and bigger) boys began showing up insisting on rides. Explaining our reason for limiting it to just a few children was beyond our level of communication.

Just about anything can be used to initially break the ice between your children and those living in the country you are visiting. As long as the toy or game or creative material is something they can appreciate and participate in, children will welcome the opportunity to get together and play. Choose simple items and leave the fancy, expensive toys at home. These represent too much of a contrast with the life-style of the children you will be meeting, nor are they any more creative or versatile.

The Single Child

Adventuring with a single child conjures up visions of a child completely deprived of friends his own age. While a short one or two week trip won't worry most parents, one that lasts a month or more might. Some parents of single children make a concerted effort to keep their child socially occupied at home, something they realize they won't be able to do on a trip. Single children needn't be any more difficult to keep socially fulfilled on a family adventure than any other children. The circumstances are simply different. Instead of settling sibling infractions and encouraging your children to play well together, you'll be promoting social aspects that relate to one child: a good sense of imaginative play, the confidence to approach other children, the ability to play with

The appearance of a few toys provides just the right catalyst to breaking the ice between local children and your own.

all ages. Single children can become the most outgoing of all because they have no built-in playmates, other than imaginary ones, to fall back on. We've met a number of single adventuring children during our travels, some on boats, others in campgrounds or on beaches. All struck us with their self-confidence, ability to play well, and ease with people of all ages. In a few cases the children were both younger than ours and foreign-speaking, yet they made the first move on their own to approach Tristan and Colin for play.

A single child won't feel lonely and deprived unless you make him feel that way. Encourage and help him to meet others, but don't insist on it. Imaginary friends and the ability to play alone are equally valuable.

Imaginative Play

Although imaginative play might hardly seem like a social need, on a trip it can play a large role in your children's need for

Children with a well-developed imagination never tire of dreaming up new games to play.

playmates. Keeping children occupied on a trip is an anxiety that frequently worries parents. At home the potential for entertainment is large, varied, and mostly taken for granted. Parents increasingly assume that every child needs an extensive toy collection, neighborhood playgroup and host of social activities. In their earnest pursuit to satisfy the child's entertainment needs they overlook nature's built-in baby-sitter, an imagination. Every child possesses one and given the proper environment will use it extensively. Adventure travel offers just such an opportunity. Like pioneer children of old, adventuring children are thrown upon their own resources for entertainment and socialization. Before long, imaginary friends and games supplant those at home and a piece of wood, length of rope or special stick become more favored toys than those left behind. Little is needed in the way of paraphernalia and playmates, as children learn to regard the whole outdoors and everything in it as a wealth of potential play things.

Developing Imaginative Play

If your children are unused to relying on their imagination to spark activities, some guidance might be needed at first. One friend of mine, a mother of three young children, reported that her children were bored a good portion of the time on their first trip. She was full of questions about what types of games Tristan and Colin play and how to get her own to do the same.

On a trip, the two main sources of imaginative play are the environment you're in and the books the children read or have read to them. Any adventure travel is going to provide plenty of scope for imaginative games - pioneers and Indians if you're camping, fishermen and ferries if you're on a boat or by the ocean, woodland animals, elves, and lost children if you're hiking. Toddlers' games are often an imitation of what they see around them, while older children gear much of their activities to books. Select books for both ages that work into the context of sparking the imagination. Old-fashioned books, for instance, are wonderful choices for older children because they're about children living in the pre-television era and thrown largely upon their own devices

Even when confined to a boat with few toys, little children can find things to fashion into make-believe games.

for entertainment. The books themselves are full of the types of activities children did back then: putting on plays, making forts, setting up stores, doing puppet shows, playing orphans, being pirates. This isn't to say that imaginative games aren't sparked by television as well, but the nature of TV's visibility acts as an inhibitor to the imagination because it doesn't require children to rely on themselves to "see" something, a vital ingredient to successful imaginative play. For suggested books conducive to imaginative play, refer to the reading list in Chapter Eleven.

If, at first, your children seem bored when you arrive somewhere, send them off on a search to find things. Suggest they collect sticks to fashion lean-tos or tepees or make into spears. Pieces of wood can be a raft or fort. Have them set up a store with anything they can find to buy and sell from each other (and you). Find out what books they're reading and suggest games built around them.

Make-Believe Games

The following are some of the make-believe games that are popular with our children. Many evolved from books that Tristan and Colin read before or during our trips. All of the games can be played anywhere with things gleaned from the surroundings or easily provided by you. With all make-believe games, clothes are important for adopting various guises. Even the most lightweight trip should supply plenty of selections. With a little scavenging children can also add some interesting accessories: bits of material for bandanas, rope for belts, bandoliers or lassos, sharp sticks for knives, pieces of string for tying things together, long sticks for spears, fishing rods, guns or farm tools. Hats are of particular importance when it comes to adopting various roles. As these are easy to pack, it's worth taking along a few extras to provide impetus to some imaginary games. Although a number of these games reflect the fact that they were thought up by boys, they've proved equally popular with girls met along the way—as well as their younger sister!

A sampling of make-believe games:

—Indians: use sticks for spears, make camps from things collected in the woods or at the beach. Wear headbands, beads, shirts or cloth diapers tied around the waist for loincloths.

—Pioneers: the emphasis is on moving from place to place, always beset by exciting events: a flood, Indian attack, buffalo stampede, pack of wolves. Children load up clothes, cooking gear, food and set up various camps.

—Peddlers: put an assortment of items in backpacks, tie a bundle of clothes to a stick, wear old-looking clothes and caps. Children then sell each other (and you) "bargains".

—Stores: set up shop anywhere: in the tent or camper, on a picnic table, on some rocks, in the cockpit of a boat. Use kitchen utensils, books, food, clothes and any interesting items the children have for wares. Children can get very creative with how they arrange their display of items. Have them make shop signs, advertise bargains, set up a pretend cash register. Then everyone goes shopping, using make-believe money (pebbles work well). Very amusing to see how the children price items.

—Elves: this is such a popular game with our children that I had to make them special elf hats to go with us on trips. Children

Playing peddlers—one of the many make-believe games children think up.

Who needs beach toys where driftwood like this can be found? Children learn to create toys with what's on hand.

like to wear tights and a long shirt (preferably a parent's) belted in at the waist with some string. They have special elf names, shy personalities, and sneak around doing mysterious things without being seen.

—Farmers: children wear "farmer" clothes (straw hats, overalls, aprons), work in pretend fields, herd animals, sell vegetables and endure the usual crises that liven up their games.

—Cafes: set up a cafe/restaurant with whatever dishes and food you have. Children become waiters, proprietors, cashiers, cooks. Our children especially enjoy serving difficult, fussy customers.

—Pirates: bandanas and stick knives, swords and eye patches. A log or big rock for a ship. This is an easy one to develop. Expect to be periodically attacked.

—Rich Man or Woman: a favorite with Tristan and Colin. One is the fancy man and the other his servant. The rich man, of course, is old, loud, walks with a cane and is hard to please.

—Fishermen: played from a dinghy, boat, canoe or along the shore. Long sticks for fishing rods, a length of rope for a casting

Preparing a palm-tree cannon at this seaside fort.

net. Lots of excitement - storms, sharks, rapids, thieves.

—Spies: very popular; involves nothing more complicated than spying on grown-ups, an endless source of entertainment for children. They carry binoculars, wear what they think look like spy clothes and write details of what they see and hear down on pieces of paper.

Collecting Things For Imaginative Play

Children can develop a real talent for collecting things to use in imaginative play. Just about anything the children find can be useful: bits of paper or cloth, rocks, sticks, shells, leaves, moss, whatever the area offers. All will be put to use making forts or bases for action figures, homes for little dolls, or elaborate road systems for matchbox cars.

Other Activities

Other imaginative activities for children besides make-believe are special events like puppet shows, plays or a circus. The children can make signs and programs, think up acts and perform for that most appreciative of audiences, their parents. I can still remember Tristan and Colin putting on a puppet show in Spain while we were free-camping behind a bar, with a mound of dirt for a stage, at which they served "drinks" to the audience from empty liquor bottles they had collected.

Our neighborhood soccer team on the island of Crete.

A Word Of Warning About Trash

What looks like trash to you parents looks more like a gold mine to children. Before long you'll find them accumulating an arsenal of undesirable objects that they insist are critical to their play. Empty liquor bottles, pieces of styrofoam, bits of wire, frayed rope, aluminum cans, plastic bags and bottle caps rate high on the list of valued items. Our children had a real heyday the time we sailed into a harbor in the Caribbean where over 300 sailboats were wrecked in a hurricane the previous year. Attempts to surreptitiously dispose of things will create either mass hysteria or an indignant retort that all that stuff is still good and you, the parents, are always telling them not to waste things. The only solution is to have them carry their own treasures and decide for themselves when the situation has gotten out of hand. Trying, as an adult, to place an accurate value on something a child has found is almost impossible. No one is telling you what to take and what to leave behind, so it's fair to do the same for children.

Chapter
14
Public Transportation

Nearly all forms of family adventure travel are, sooner or later, going to involve you with public transportation. In many parts of the world, use of public transportation is a fact of life, with few people owning private vehicles. This not only makes it easier for you to travel without the high cost of a rental car, but definitely adds to your adventure as well. A trip on some local means of transportation can be an adventurous experience you'll never forget, one of those rare times you share the same conditions as the local inhabitants. As with other aspects of adventure travel, the presence of children will make a difference. Seats will be found where none previously existed, food shared, and conversation sought, particularly with your children. Many is the time you'll find yourself shrinking down in your seat as your children tell everything to your nearest neighbor in a voice loud enough to be heard by all.

Airplanes

Airplanes are easy to fly on with children. While lacking in some of the cultural and adventurous aspects of more local forms of public transportation, they are the best, if not the only, choice for covering large distances. If you're flying to a destination abroad, try to fly on whatever the national airline is of the place you're going to. Each country infuses their airline with some cultural nuances, making the flight more interesting and providing you with an early taste of the culture you will be visiting.

Sometimes even short distances are better covered with one quick flight rather than a long series of connections that will tax a family traveling with children. When we looked into the various ways of getting from the British Virgin Islands to San Juan, Puerto Rico for our flight home, we discovered that one short plane ride eliminated two days of travel on a series of ferries, buses, and taxis. Having previously traveled like that, we knew how strenuous it can be for children to be repeatedly hurried along to make that next connection. Although flying is usually the most expensive way to travel, sometimes the additional cost is minimal and well worth the added ease of travel in a given situation.

Keeping Costs Down

Check into all the possible ways to get the least expensive flight, particularly when flying overseas. Advanced Purchase Excursion Fare (APEX) offers reduced fares for many overseas flights. We've used this for all our flights to Europe and North Africa. Children between two and twelve years fly for one half to two thirds the fare on all regular flights. Charter flights are an excellent way to reduce costs, although on these children will pay the full amount. Even if you plan to stay longer than the charter allows, using only half the ticket can be cheaper than the cost of a regular flight. Charter flights also have the advantage of taking you directly to your destination without stops or changes, always a nice bonus when traveling with children.

Some flights get less expensive the longer you stay, others get more expensive. Geographical area seems to have much to do with this. When investigating flight cost one year, I discovered it would cost us twice as much to fly from New England to Central America as to North Africa, although it was just over half the distance. The reason was that flights across the Atlantic had APEX while those on the American side had no cost reduction plan for visits longer than a month. Season also plays a part in cost, with off-season rates considerably lower. Tuesday through Thursday are always the least expensive days to fly on regular flights.

Before paying for tickets, get your travel agent to tell you everything about flight costs. It's amazing what bargains they can dig up when under pressure. Some travel bureaus are more adept at this than others.

Expect The Unexpected

If you're heading somewhere that involves any overseas flight connections, allow as much time as possible to make the change. Then still expect things to happen differently. Travel bureaus at home may assure you that all is in order when booking you on a flight that originates in a foreign country, but the discrepancy between their information and what actually takes place can leave you stranded and wondering what to do next. We've missed flights and ended up going stand-by, landed in entirely the wrong place, been booked on flights that didn't exist, and found we weren't even booked at all. Although none of this can be predicted and thus avoided, by being mentally prepared the experience can seem more amusing than catastrophic. One way to prevent some mishaps when abroad is to make sure you confirm any flights booked by your travel agent back home.

Pack Light

When packing for a flight, try to keep everything within the limits of what the family can carry all at once. This might mean a backpack plus one or two pieces of hand luggage per person. As long as everything can be carried at once, you eliminate the need for porters or taxis every step of the way. Although airplanes, particularly charters, have a weight limit, this shouldn't be a problem for a family. Even if the adult packs are groaning under the weight of schooling materials and camping equipment, the children's lighter gear will allow for it.

At The Airport

Once you've reached the airport, most airlines these days have made special considerations for families traveling with children. A number of airports now provide changing rooms for babies and play areas for older children. Families are permitted to board before the other passengers and a variety of items are supplied to keep children occupied during the flight.

Keeping a child occupied in the airport is more a question of maintaining control than anything else. The prospect of flying to a child is exhilarating and as every parent knows, an excited child is a hyperactive one. Try to keep calm if they dash about the corridors, ride up and down the escalator, spill their milk, or dump tea all over your lap. On one trip, a pre-dawn charter out of Boston, ours did all the above, before we'd even boarded the plane. To say that I, as recipient of the tea-dumping episode, remained calm would be stretching things. As the children sat among the shambles, wide-eyed at the prospect of what was to come, an elderly couple at the next table, oblivious of my soaked jeans and boiling temper, turned and said, "We just had to tell you what delightful children we think you have."

On The Airplane

Night flights are the easiest on children, as they can sleep. Put the arm-rest down, give them their favorite sleepy friend, pillow, or blanket, and tell them to go to sleep. Keep their seat belt on so you won't have to wake them if the plane lands or you hit turbulence. If you're flying with a baby, ask for seats in the front row where the additional space is large enough for a baby basket or an infant to stretch out on your legs. Warmed bottles or baby food are available if you give the airline prior notice. Carry on a bag with whatever you feel you might need in the next 24 hours: books, a toy or two, drawing paper and pencils, some food and a water flask, a favorite stuffed animal, a change of underwear per child, a change of clothes if you're traveling to a different climate, and a toilet bag with tooth-brushes and toothpaste, soap and washcloth, and a hair brush. Having your luggage misplaced is always a possibility so it's nice to be prepared. Also if you have a layover between flights, this means you can wash the children up and change their clothes. It's not much fun sweltering in warm clothes if you've just flown somewhere hot like the tropics.

Flying Adventures

Although flying is usually a tame experience, it can get adventurous. Some flights, like those in and out of the mountainous island of Madeira, can leave you hanging to your seat wondering whatever induced you to chose *this* for a destination. Others, like our midnight flight out of Turkey, are an adventure from the word go. In a quest to reduce expenses, we booked on a return charter flight to England, leaving a military airport at two a.m. As the flight was a one-week charter to and from Turkey, we were technically an illegality. The charter company's attitude, however, was that we were welcome to the empty seats provided the customs officials didn't make a fuss, something we wouldn't know for sure until departure time. Our tickets, they added, would be waiting for us at the airport.

Catching a midnight bus with the other charter passengers, we arrived at the gates of the military airport an hour later. By now Kevin and I were acutely aware of our high visibility in this otherwise sedate charter group of British holiday seekers. As the only passengers with children, backpacks, American passports, and obvious tans (hardly the result of a one-week vacation), we stuck out like a sore thumb. Consequently we watched with horror as three gun-toting military police boarded the bus and began perusing passports. Shrinking down in our seats, we waited in trepidation from our place at the extreme back of the bus. The officials, having looked at everyone else's passports, approached, paused, glanced at us and turned away. To this day the only explanation we can give is that they didn't want to disturb our sleeping children.

Once at the airport, we slunk in with the packs and children and went in search of our tickets. The tickets, it seemed, were still to come with another bus group, one that for some unspecified reason was late. While everyone else checked their bags through, we sat rigid waiting to be caught. By the fourth time an official came and told us to check our bags, something we could only do with tickets, Kevin went off to guzzle cups of Turkish tea, the strongest stimulant available. Subsequently, anytime someone came by I said my husband would attend to it when he got back. By the time our tickets finally arrived, Kevin's capacity for tea and mine for telling little white lies had reached saturation point. Disposing of the conspicuous packs, we moved on through security, including a complete body check, and onto the final customs formalities. As preventative measures to keep people from doing just what we were, in fact, doing, any charter flight passenger must be booked in and out of the same place. Unfortunately, our passports stated clearly that we had entered Turkey three hundred miles away. Coupled with our American nationality, the whole affair was looking a lot shakier than the charter company had made it out to be when selling us the seats. Pulling out our last trump card, we approached the two unsmiling officials with Tristan and Colin prominently displayed up front in all their tow-headed glory. Warming at the sight, the officials smiled down at the boys, flicked open the passports, smirked at our point of entry, bestowed another benevolent look on the boys, and stamped us through. Once again, the presence of children had done the trick.

Trains

Trains are an easy means of travel for the adventuring family. Unlike airports that always seem to be located miles from anywhere at the end of some major highway and only accessible by expensive taxi, train stations are in the heart of the town or city. In countries where trains are commonly used, they'll take you almost anywhere, generally for a reasonable amount. Rail passes are often available for use by locals or tourists, as well as special prices on certain trains, days, and time schedules. Be sure to ask about all the possible money-saving deals. Children almost always ride for less money or free. One word of caution about rail passes is that while they are useful for covering large distances, they can undermine the very essence of family adventure travel by encouraging you to travel too much in order to feel you're getting your money's worth. For a successful family adventure, the pace should be relaxed, the exposure to an area intimate, and the distance covered irrelevant. Leave the large scale rail passes to the young college crowd.

Bicycles are almost always permitted on trains for a small fee. Keeping bicycle gear organized, however, takes some careful forethought.

On The Train

Trains vary as much from country to country as any cultural aspect, but do have a tendency to run more efficiently than buses in countries not known for their efficiency. In places like northern Europe where trains run with precision timing, it's helpful to work out a system ahead of time for boarding and disembarking - who carries what items, who gets on or off first, etc. Otherwise you might find yourself arriving at your destination with one child claiming he can't find some precious item, another desperate for a bathroom, the corridor clogged with departing passengers, an equal number striving to get on, and three minutes to execute your departure. It's at times like these you'll wonder why you ever thought train travel was tame. This is when you send your nimblest child out onto the platform, fling open the nearest window, and heave out all the baggage. In countries where timing is critical, you'll notice other passengers doing the same. Memorize how many pieces of luggage you have so you can take a count when regrouping. We know one family with three children who, while traveling by train through Egypt, went quite a distance one day before realizing one of the children had been left behind. Disembarking at the next station, they headed back by hired vehicle to be met by the sight of the entire village escorting their child down the road in the direction they had taken.

Coping With Baggage

While not as alarming as loosing a child, keeping baggage intact during train travel can present a few challenges. No one is more sensitive to the issue of baggage on trains than we are. Having chosen bicycles as a lightweight, reduced needs, efficient means of travel, we approached our first train with the confidence of one who knows he has everything under control. Gone was the discomfort of carrying everything on our backs, the expense of a taxi or bother of waiting for a bus. On four bicycles we carried all the equipment necessary for three months of foreign travel all neatly packed into a compact, mobile unit. Peddling through the streets of Casablanca, past cars mired in traffic, we arrived at the station feeling prepared, relaxed, and, I'm afraid, a bit smug.

Shipping bicycles on trains is rarely, if ever, a problem. Our difficulty lay in the fact that first all that neatly packed, precision loaded, specialty gear had to come off. Off it came: the panniers and handlebar packs, the sleeping bags and pads, the tent and ground cover, the daypack, spare tires and grass mats, the bicycle helmets and straw hats, even the bungies and bicycle pump. The result of all this disassembling was that the bicycles were wheeled away leaving us standing in a sea of luggage. Instead of four compact units of precision packing, we were left with exactly thirty-five individual items (not including the bungies and pump) all waiting to be carried along one platform, down a flight of stairs, through an underpass, up another flight of stairs, along another platform, and onto a train. Needless to say, all vestiges of smugness had long since vanished.

Experiencing A Culture From A Train

Thirty-five pieces of luggage aside, riding on trains is a fun family affair. If you're coming from a country with few trains, a ride on one is always an adventure and something a child will never forget. Try to incorporate at least one train ride if possible, even if it's just a day trip. Seating is usually comfortable and often private. There's plenty for the children to watch out the large windows, corridors for stretching their legs, and often spare seats to lie on. As always, carry on what food and drink you think you might need to avoid the high cost of things sold on the train.

Riding on a train can provide an enjoyable glimpse into a culture. In Austria a local train might look like a child's toy with its open sides, wooden seats and high-pitched whistle. Climbing slowly up through a series of Alpine villages, its pace matches that of hikers walking a footpath alongside the track, conversing with the passengers on their way. In England, a train ride can whisk you into London for the day or drop you in an isolated spot with nothing but the train platform and endless countryside in sight. A trip on a Moroccan train is as unpredictable as its people, as though at a cross-roads between cultures. The train might barrel along like the New York subway or stop in the middle of nowhere for no apparent reason and an unspecified length of time. Vendors climb aboard, offering hot mint tea and rolls from woven baskets. Cosmopolitan passengers sit alongside those in traditional clothes. A train ride in any country is a cultural adventure in itself, one the whole family can enjoy.

Ferries

Ferries, like trains, are an appealing, romantic form of public transportation, possessed of a mystique that harks back to an era when boat and rail travel were commonplace. Ferries have the additional appeal of taking you to places often only accessible by water, always an exciting prospect.

Ferries Around The World

Ferries come in a variety of guises from full-blown ships to miniature craft bordering on the unseaworthy. What you find depends on the country you choose to travel in and the body of water you're crossing. Anywhere with numerous inhabited islands will have a ferry system: the Greek islands, the west coast

Children are usually excited at the prospect of a ferry ride. Here, Tristan and Colin wait for the ferry from Rhodes to Turkey with fully loaded backpacks. Turkey can be glimpsed in the background.

of Norway, the Pacific Northwest, the Abaco Out islands in the Bahamas, the Canadian Maritimes and Newfoundland. Major areas separated by water are also linked by ferry: Nova Scotia to New Brunswick and Maine, England to France, North Africa to Europe, Greece to Turkey, Singapore to Java and Malaysia to Sumatra. These are ferry systems that can be researched, relied on, and incorporated into a trip. Perhaps most delightful of all are the ferries that spring on you by surprise, tiny craft carrying only a handful of passengers or a few cars that ply the many inlets, rivers, and bays of the world.

A Few Tips About Ferry Travel

—Travel deck class on large ferries if possible: This is the least expensive and most fun. Find a nice, windless spot and make a family base. Even if children roam the boat, they'll know where to find you. Meeting fellow passengers, both local inhabitants and low-budget travelers like yourselves, is easy when you're all sharing deck accommodations with each other.

—**Night Travel**: If you're traveling at night, roll out the pads and sleeping bags, even if it's only for a few hours. Children will sleep through almost anything and the whole family will arrive feeling much more rested. If you arrive somewhere in the middle of the night (Greek ferries are a great one for this), find the nearest park, plaza, or whatever and go back to sleep. No one will care, particularly when you have children. If you wake before the cafes have opened, brew up some tea, coffee, or hot chocolate with your camp stove. This way nighttime ferry travel is less disruptive than it sounds. I can remember one trip in Greece when the children's night was like a progressive sleepover—on a mound of luggage at the ferry dock before departure, in sleeping bags on the ferry deck, and in a park after arrival.

—**Safety Harnesses**: Harness a toddler to keep him happily active yet safe from falling overboard. Harnesses have gone out of fashion in this lenient age, but aren't the inhibitive, cruel imple-

Ferries cross all types of waterways, from the open sea to river estuaries like this one in Nova Scotia.

ment parents seem to think them. On the contrary, a harnessed child can be allowed far more freedom than one that's forced to sit or be held the whole time.

—**Rough weather**: If the body of water is rough, give your children half a seasickness pill before departure. Sitting outside on the ferry is always better for a queasy stomach than indoors, and going to sleep is the best of all, something children often do with the motion. If the ferry is small, the outside seats high, and the waves steep, hang onto your sleeping child. Some ferries really know how to roll.

—**Bicycles**: Bicycles can always be accommodated on ferries, sometimes at no cost. We've even been on one where anyone riding bicycles went for free as well. Find out whether it's all right to leave gear on the bikes. It usually is, even on large ferries where all vehicles are down in the hold. Take your handlebar packs with you and leave everything else strapped to the bikes. Lay them over, away from the derailleur side, if rough seas are a possibility. It's a thrill to bicycle on and off a ferry in front of all those cars.

—**Safety**: A word of caution concerning ferries in some parts of the world: A number of underdeveloped countries have virtually no safety laws concerning boat travel. Boats can be unseaworthy, dangerously overloaded, and unequipped with lifejackets. We've seen fifty passengers disembark from a vessel the Coast Guard wouldn't allow twenty on. When traveling with children, these things should be taken into consideration before boarding. When in doubt, check out the ferry beforehand to decide whether it's something you want to go on.

Buses

Buses are the most common type of public transportation. Less thrilling than trains or ferries, their main appeal for families lies in their ability to get you almost anywhere for usually less money than any other mode of travel. Like cars, they are confining to children and therefore not terribly popular, but when it comes to adventure and insight into a foreign culture, very little can beat a bus ride in some parts of the world. The key to bus travel when abroad is to keep your rides as short and infrequent as possible.

Other than that, remember that some of your funniest moments, greatest adventures, and best stories will come from bus rides.

Bus Types Around The World

Buses are much the same the world over. What varies is when they run, how well they run, how many people they carry, and how frequently they stop. It's extraordinary the diversity that exists in such a basic procedure as public bus operation. Outside of modern countries with timetables and vehicles that perform like precision watches, a bus ride can be as entertaining as a three-ring circus. In developing countries where buses are the accepted means of travel, overcrowding, wasted time, and futile expenditures of energy are to be expected. This is all part of the experience and as culturally enlightening as a trip to a museum. In Indonesia, buses require a marked degree of agility, with their wooden seats, no aisles and fares that vary according to how much space your bottom takes up. Guatemalan buses are frequently recycled school buses, with seats built to the proportions of an average-size school child. Despite this obvious limitation, sitting six to a seat is standard practice, while proceeding uphill frequently requires that all passengers get out and walk. On Greek buses, one might offer cushioned comfort and precision timing, another hard-backed seats and a whimsical disposition toward schedules. Some stop while passengers shop, others almost fail to stop altogether. Destinations affixed to the front mean little and fares vary according to driver inclination. In Morocco, baggage is carried on the roof under a net, while livestock (both dead and alive) travel in the hold. Departure is signaled by a parade of itinerant salesmen selling everything from jewelry to glasses, followed by a blind beggar blessing the bus. How fast you travel is anyone's guess, with some buses executing an admirable Grand Prix reenactment and others branching off on dirt track tangents that defy imagination. Despite everything, the bus, passengers, and luggage always seem to arrive intact.

A Few Tips About Bus Travel

—**Organize a carry-on bag beforehand**. There's nothing worse than finding yourself landed for an hour on a bus with a thirsty, hungry, bored brood of children when everything to eat, drink, and play with is strapped to the roof.

—**Expect children to ride for half price or free**. In countries where buses are owned by the drivers, children's fees can vary according to the driver's temperament. Observe what the local children pay and act accordingly. Knowing what to pay ahead of time and handing over the money unasked for helps eliminate being taken advantage of as a tourist.

—**Avoid pre-school hours** in countries where public buses double as school buses. Otherwise you may find yourself wedged in among a busload of rambunctious youths for half your trip.

—**When in doubt** as to where to go, when a bus is due, when to board, ask as many times as necessary. Bus stations as we know them don't usually exist and each place has its own system. Just because one bus let you off at a certain spot doesn't mean the next one will pick you up there. In some countries buses will stop anywhere, in others only at specific points. Some buses arrive full, leaving you wondering what to do next, some have a system of reserving seats that's a mystery to the uninitiated. Fortunately for families, people are accommodating when it comes to keeping a family together and will do any amount of seat juggling.

Taxis

Any public vehicle smaller than a bus comes under the loose category of taxis. Unlike their expensive North American or European counterpart, taxis provide inexpensive, locally based transportation in countries where few people have cars. Known as "guaguas", "publicos", "dolmuses", and a host of other local terms, foreign taxis run the full gamut of vans, jeeps, cars, horse-drawn carriages, and motorized rickshaws. Riding on one can be well worth the small fee, especially at the end of a strenuous day of hiking or when loaded down with shopping from the open-air market. For tired children, a ride in a taxi, particularly some of the more intriguing types, can mean the difference between arriving home miserable or exuberant.

As with buses, taxi rides can provide some moments of entertainment hard to beat. In Turkey, a jeep-like vehicle called a

When public transportation ceases to exist, don't be afraid to enlist the help of locals to get you where you need to go. Settle on a reasonable price ahead of time.

Small local transports like this motorized rickshaw are common in developing countries where few people have cars.

dolmus is driven with a paradoxical flair of joie de vivre and suicidal disdain. The object is to squeeze as many passengers aboard as possible. Most drivers' sights seem set at 12, a number that leaves the last two arrivals hanging off the back door and someone seated on the driver's lap. As children are neither charged nor considered, when we traveled with Tristan and Colin the occupancy peaked at 14. This passion to fill a taxi beyond capacity is to be expected. Some won't even leave until the vehicle is full. One way around this, if you're feeling in the need for a little breathing room, is to pay for more seats than you need.

Because taxi rides are usually short, nothing is needed to ease the trip with children. Not that there won't be some exceptions. In the absence of a bus, we once traveled 50 miles down the coast of a Caribbean island in a so-called taxi, a derelict car of dubious vintage with a leaky front tire, three broken windows, one missing door handle, and an exhaust system that vented into the back seat. When we ran into torrential rain showers, the children and I, seated in the back, fluctuated between a desire to keep dry and our need for fresh air.

By now you may have decided that all this talk of public transportation sounds interesting and amusing, but not for you. Obviously it's easier to travel by car and maybe that's what you will decide to do, especially if your children are very young. But using public transportation can keep costs down and get you where you want to be almost as efficiently as a car. Modern countries where public transportation is widely used offer efficient, comfortable services. Even less developed countries, ones with an element of idiosyncrasy to their public transportation system, often only require a little practise before mastering the art of traveling comfortably. It's worth trying out a bus or train or two before deciding one way or another. Afterwards, if a car seems the preferred choice, get one and figure it's well worth the extra cost. No matter how you travel, the most important thing is to keep hours on the road to a minimum to ensure the maximum enjoyment for your children.

PART V
MAKING IT WORK

Chapter
15
Putting It All Together

What makes an adventure work is an accumulation of so many things. It's those moment of sheer joy and just feeling alive that only come after moments of discomfort or hardship. It's knowing your family just accomplished something you never thought you would, reaching a new pinnacle of achievement. It's the rapport and tight bond that is forged between family members thrown together on an adventure. Most of all it's an attitude, a belief that your family adventure is going to succeed.

Despite the best intentions, a few key issues can occur again and again, things that are typical of adventuring with children that can make or break a trip. In this chapter we've dealt with a number of them, plus some general budget tips for traveling with children. Knowing what to expect ahead of time and being prepared can all help contribute towards making a family adventure work.

The First 24 Hours

Nothing makes a bigger impression on a family embarking on an adventure than the first 24 hours, and nothing is more atypical to what the rest of the trip will be like. By some sort of twist of fate, we've discovered that one can almost assume that first day will be anything except fun. If we're bicycling, it always rains, even in places where rain happens about twice a year. If we're going somewhere hot, it's cold when we get there. The year we went to Greece we missed a connecting flight, went stand-by with about 100 shouting Greeks, landed in the wrong place and arrived in the middle of the night. In Madeira we spent the night in what must be the most abysmal pension ever in operation. There was laundry in the tub, cigarette burns in the carpet, holes in the bedding and a clientele that never, as far as we could ascertain, went to sleep. Despite the fact it was June, when we arrived in England it did everything except snow on us, while our first night in the Dominican Republic landed us in a hotel that turned out to be the local brothel.

In all our travels, only our trip to Guatemala broke the mold. Discovering upon arrival that our bicycles were still back in Miami, we found ourselves whisked off in a taxi, booked into the Conquistador Sheraton, and treated to dinner, breakfast and an elegant room, all courtesy of the airlines.

In terms of adventure travel, coping with the first 24 hours is an art form. The following is a list of guidelines for getting you through what can be the roughest stage of your trip. Short of going on an organized tour, this is an unavoidable situation so the best thing is to be as prepared as possible.

Prepare for bad weather—Even if you're heading for the tropics and the weather predictions are 90 degree temperatures with clear skies, have your rain jackets ready. Mother Nature likes to spring surprises, especially on newly arrived tourists.

Be prepared to pay—The first 24 hours are always the most expensive. You're new to a place and have no idea how the system works. Locals know this and act accordingly. Don't worry about it or think things will always cost this much. There will be plenty of time for economizing later.

Book your family into a nice hotel—Forget bargain-hunting the first night. If there's one time you need a splurge when adventuring, it's now while you're trying to familiarize yourself with an area. Don't bother trying to book your first night ahead unless you are absolutely sure of a place. Except for luxury accommodations, this is difficult to do despite the conveniences of phones, faxes and the assurances of a travel agent. Until you see a place, it's difficult to know what it will be like, or in some cases, even what it will cost. There are always places to stay once you

get somewhere. Our mistake in Madeira was not spending the money when we should have, after arriving in a place that was more expensive than we had expected. The experience taught us the value of paying for a first night in comfortable conditions.

Bring plenty of food—Go out somewhere nice to eat your first night, then fill in the gaps in your children's hunger with food you brought with you. It's one thing to spend $50 for a nice room and quite another to spend nearly that much just to eat. Bring along some special foods to tide your family over until you discover where to shop. Peanut butter is a good choice because even if the whole family is sick to death of it in a few days, the chances are you won't see it again until you go home. I carry peanut butter, crackers or rice cakes, trail mix, sunflower seeds and dried fruit on all our trips. We actually dined on an exclusive diet of this for three days the time we made the mistake of arriving in a country on Friday where all the shops were closed over the weekend. In the end no one cared because we never saw these foods again during five months of travel.

Bring everything you think you might need—Avoid having to go find a store in the first 24 hours. This is a time for recuperating, relaxing and getting to know a place in an enjoyable way, not rushing around trying to find shampoo or toothpaste.

Let the children play—After the rigors of traveling to wherever you are, they need a day to just have fun. Take a book along, sit in a cafe, go to a beach or a park while your children play. They'll forget whatever hardships they went through to get there and develop a positive feeling towards adventure travel.

First Impressions

First impressions are often a let-down. No matter what the brochures, books, travel agents and your friends say, don't expect to immediately grasp the appeal of a place. Places, like people, grow on you. You can't help but visualize what somewhere will be like from what you've heard or read, while the actual place is always somewhat different. In essence, if your vision is of your children frolicking on some pristine beach in the sunshine, don't expect to even find the beach or see the sun when you first arrive.

The charms of most places are subtle and less obvious than we are led to believe. I can still remember my first impression of Madeira, an island I had heard nothing but raves about over its beauty, mountains and abundance of flowers. After surviving the hair-raising landing, the exorbitant taxi ride from the airport (there was no bus), the crowded streets of Funchal and a night in a sordid pension, I was hardly in a position to notice the flowers or appreciate the mountains. In the end we stayed two months. The same thing happened when we arrived in Galini, a town on the southern coast of Crete. One glimpse of the place and I was ready to leave. There were too many hotels, too many gift shops, too many tourists and too small a beach. Within a day we had all fallen under the spell of the place and remained camped there for two blissful weeks.

Making The Best Of A Bad Destination

Some places turn out to be a mistake. Your best friend may have loved it, but it just doesn't work for your family. Despite the amount of helpful travel information, no family can really know whether they'll like a place until they go there. Most will turn out to be wonderful. A few won't. One of the reasons is that nearly all travel material is oriented to either the tourist who wants to know where to shop, where to dine and how to take a tour, or to the backpacking college crowds who are looking for nude sunbathing and where the action is. Family adventuring lies somewhere in the middle between tourist hot-spots and singles hang-outs. As travel material rarely deals with adventuring families, much of where you choose to go will be guesswork.

If you have arrived somewhere, given it a chance to grow on you and finally realized you've made a mistake, what can you do?

Look at the funny side of the situation—Nearly every bad moment in adventure travel has its humorous side. It's like taking your children to the Ice Capades. You can dread the whole experience and have a miserable time or you can laugh yourself silly. Children will simply follow your lead. If you see the funny side, they will too.

Find something fun and adventurous to do—There's always something adventurous you can do, even in the most unlikely circumstances. Try exploring the surrounding area. Few tourists venture beyond the town or city limits. We did some of our best hiking in Greece outside a village that seemed to be largely under construction, populated by unfriendly entrepreneurs and filled with young tourists ready to party. Another time we found ourselves stranded on an island in a town that turned out to be quite dreary and not at all what we were looking for. We rented two derelict one-speed bicycles for a dollar apiece, sat each chid on a backrack and biked all over the island. The whole experience was a wild adventure, culminating in a flat tire on a remote road and a hitched ride in the back of a pick-up. This is the stuff that adventuring is made of, those memorable happenings when you least expect them.

Know when to leave—Don't be afraid to leave somewhere you don't like, even at the risk of losing money. It's better to forfeit a few hundred dollars than the whole trip. This is one of the advantages of adventure travel, being able to make your own decisions and change plans when you want. There's nothing locking you into a certain place or situation except your own actions. We once traveled all the way to Central America and halfway across a country to a specific village (on the recommendation of friends) where we planned to spend a month. It didn't take one night to realize that it wasn't for us, a situation that called for some serious regrouping. Despite the extra cost, we retraced some

steps, asked around a bit, and soon found ourselves one of our best situations ever—a two-bedroom villa with beach access on one of the loveliest lakes in the world.

Inclement Weather

Everywhere has its moments of bad weather. Short trips can practically be destroyed by it and even on long ones nothing can demoralize you faster or make you more miserable than bad weather. Bad weather, for outdoor adventurers, usually means rain. Except in tropical showers where rain is actually a welcome respite, rain that lasts for more than an hour is no fun when you are outdoors, especially when camping. The first thing to realize is that rain rarely lasts more than a day. So instead of worrying about how you will survive the trip if it rains the whole time, think about just getting through the day.

Find alternative lodgings—If you're camping, find an alternative if it starts to ruin your fun. Camping in the rain can be an unpleasant experience. As bad weather doesn't last forever, it's well worth the money to find a place to stay that's warm and dry if you feel so inclined. Just about anything is going to look good if the alternative is a wet tent or a small camper, so don't feel compelled to find luxury accommodations. A simple motel room with access to an indoor pool or hot tub can seem like you just booked into Club Med. Another option is to find a place to camp with access to indoor facilities. We've done this a few times, once in the back yard of a Bed & Breakfast, another time beside a hunting lodge. In both cases we were offered use of the indoor facilities to get out of the rain.

When camping is the only option—Try to find a site near a shelter. This at least gives you somewhere to go other than your tent. If the rain is really torrential and the children desperate for exercise, send them to the rest rooms to play. The chances are no other campers will be venturing out in this weather so the children will have the whole place to themselves. Just being able to move around makes a big difference to a child and gives parents and children the break they need from each other in weather conditions like these. Tristan and Colin once spent half a day playing in the ladies room of a campground in Nova Scotia while it poured rain outside. When I checked up on them I found them mopping the floor (with a mop they had found), racing matchbox cars, floating stick "boats" in the sink and having the usual nine-year-old giggle fits. What they weren't doing was getting bored. Don't be embarrassed to make use of the bathroom this way provided your children are well behaved and not the kind to spread water or toilet paper all over the place. We've seen adults resort to the bathrooms on rainy days as well. In Spain during one major stretch of bad weather, I entered the ladies room to find a fellow camper doing her aerobics routine to music.

Playing in the rain—children like playing in the rain. Forget trying to sail or bicycle or hike, activities they won't enjoy in the rain any more than you. Instead, stay in one place and let them play outside as much as possible. Try to avoid too many wet clothes, especially if you're camping. Have them wear sandals instead of shoes to keep the shoes from getting soaked.

Walking in the rain—one outdoor activity that can still be enjoyed in the rain and help relieve the tedium of bad weather is walking. Pick somewhere to go that's interesting—through a village, down a country road, along the seashore, in a park. Try walking where you can look at houses, a fun activity for children who like to compare houses and yards and speculate which one they would live in. See if there's a coffee shop or cafe or interesting shop you can head for as a destination along the route. Before you know it you will have whiled away the rainy hours and enjoyed yourselves as well.

Treats and games—It's always nice to have a special cache of goodies, games and projects for bad weather. If you're stuck in a tent, get out some drawing paper, scissors, colored pencils and scotch tape. Children can spend a long time being creative with simple materials. A pack of cards, miniature backgammon or checkers, or a surprise paperback will keep older ones occupied as well.

The Importance Of Time

Children have no real sense of time. To them time is an endless present. What's happening now seems like it will go on forever and what's going to happen will never come. This is a basic difference between adults and children and one that should be taken into account when adventuring. Their limited concept of time means that when children are having fun, they never want to stop. If you assure them they've been playing by that stream or on that beach for an hour, they will insist they just got there. In the same way if things are tough, children feel they will never get better. Telling them that they'll be up that hill or to a certain destination in ten minutes means nothing. All they know is that they're not there yet and ten minutes is as good as saying forever. As any parent knows who has ever tried to hurry a child out the door to catch the school bus or make an appointment, children also seem to think that time can stop to accommodate them. This is where so many trips and outings go wrong, when parents feel continually held back and children continually rushed. If you don't want to find yourself harassed beyond belief when adventuring with children, some adjustments are going to have to be made to their sense of time.

Getting your children to perform within some sort of time framework is best accomplished by a series of gentle proddings. Fortunately, adventuring is free from most of the emphasis on time that dominates our lives at home. Some goals have to be met, however, if your adventure isn't to become one endless beach scene or play session. Forget telling your children they have already played for an hour or have ten minutes of uphill hiking before the next break. What they understand best is a countdown. Five more minutes to play - one more minute before we leave - finish up what you're doing now - it's time to go. After numerous warnings, a child can hardly throw a fit when you announce it really is time to stop playing. The same strategy works for bad moments. We're half way up the hill - we're two thirds - we're almost there - just one more corner - time for a break. With a steady supply of progress reports, children don't have a chance to get overwhelmed by a steep hill or long hike.

The Pace Of Travel

As with the importance of time, the pace of travel is going to be at the mercy of your children. Pace is a self-imposed structure that children want nothing to do with on a long-range basis. It's an alien concept to them and pushing it only makes them unhappy or rebellious. No child's pace is ever going to match yours, so you might as well forget the issue. Children are naturally energetic and capable of a tremendous output when it comes to outdoor activities. Your problem won't be their capabilities, but keeping them from getting distracted. Stimulated adventuring children can find a great deal to keep them interested, most of which interferes with pace setting. I can remember hikes we have had, each one's pace determined by what activity the children were involved in at the time. There was the one where they played elves and swept the trail for us the whole way with make-believe brooms. On another they built stick signs at every turn on the trail indicating which way to go. There have been times when they wanted to collect leaves of every type or look for special stones. This is a child's idea of a pace of travel, the kind that adapts to each moment.

On a larger scale, a whole trip operates this way. If they find a place they like, why move on to the next? They'd rather linger and enjoy what they've already found. Work out a compromise. Abandon your sense of a structured pace for a more sporadic one, one that keeps you moving, but allows children time to enjoy things along the way. Unless you have a bus to catch or a train to meet, be as relaxed as you can. In a world where time has come to be regarded as a vital part of daily life, adventuring is one of the few times you can ignore it. Children naturally live in the present; we could do well to emulate them. With children it's not the pace of travel that counts so much as the quality.

Improvisation

In family adventure travel, improvisation makes up much of what you do. There's no set itinerary, booked hotels or guided tours. Other than when you leave home, where you initially go and when you come back, the trip is an open opportunity. Beyond choosing an area and activities that interest you, the rest of the trip should be left to develop as you go along. You're like a pioneer family, conscious of where you are going, but not sure what will happen along the way.

Children Are Great At Improvising

If something sounds or looks promising, they pursue it with no thought for previous set plans. You won't find them complaining if you end up on the coast of Turkey when you said you'd be exploring the islands of Greece, or walking the footpaths of England instead of hiking in the Alps.

Almost any situation can be turned to advantage when adventuring, through the use of a little improvisation: bad weather, confused directions, people met along the way, a sudden inspiration, a bad destination. Each can send you off in a new direction you hadn't even thought of. An extreme example of this was the year we planned to travel by ferry up the coast of Yugoslavia, hike in Austria and fly home from England. This was also the year of the nuclear disaster at Chernobyl, thus putting an end to any exploration in the vicinity of the Alps. As our return flight to the

U.S. was from England, we took a cut-rate charter flight from Turkey and spent three weeks camping and hiking in the British Isles, something we hadn't even planned on doing that turned out to be a highlight of the trip.

Who cares if your trip takes a completely different turn from what you had intended. Eventually you will find yourself starting to sound vague when people ask what you will be doing on your next adventure. This is all part of adventuring, particularly with children when any number of unpredictable things can happen. With a little spontaneous improvisation, all can result in an added element of excitement.

Family Budget Travel Tips

The following ideas have all been used by us with great success, saving us money where we didn't feel it was necessary to spend it and adding to our experience in fun ways. People are very accommodating towards families with children, especially ones traveling in a simple, adventurous way. All the tips make use of your family status without taking advantage of the people you meet. Families sometimes have unique needs that can be accommodated just by asking.

When eating out—ask for a child's portion even if it's not on the menu, or split a dinner and drink between two children. This saves you money and the restaurant wasted food.

At a Bed & Breakfast—ask if you can get the bed without the breakfast. The food makes up a large part of what you pay for. As a place to spend the night is what you really need, you may be able to breakfast on cereal, milk and fruit in your room for a fraction of the cost.

At an inn, guesthouse, hotel, etc.—sleep the children on the floor, making beds with camping pads and sleeping bags. Most places will let the children stay for free this way.

In a pension (inexpensive hotel) when abroad—cook your meals right at the pension. Some have porches, balconies or courtyards where you can set up your campstove. Some will offer you the use of their kitchen. Expect some interest in what you're cooking, always a subject of curiosity to foreigners.

When there's no campground—try finding a B & B, guesthouse or restaurant that will let you camp out back. Settle on a small fee for the use of their bathrooms, water, refrigeration, even sometimes a washing machine. If they won't take any money, return the favor by buying a drink or food from them or giving them a picture of your family.

Don't be afraid to ask—even if you feel incredibly foolish, ask instead of assuming the answer will be no. With children it will often turn out to be yes, instead. After days of rigorous bicycling and camping in Morocco, we came on a lovely, isolated 5-Star hotel up in the mountains. As a sudden inspiration, Kevin entered its pristine portals and asked the price of a room. The proprietor looked at Kevin, our bicycles and the two children, took in our obvious aura of family-on-a-shoestring-budget and offered us a discount room at the back of the hotel with its own separate entrance. The children were soon frolicking in the outdoor pool, I cooked meals on the picnic table outside our entrance and all of us were treated like royalty by the staff. It was quite an experience, one we never would have had if Kevin hadn't asked.

Motorbike/Bicycle/Car Rental

On any family adventure, a day or two of motorbike, bicycle, or car rental can provide a real treat without breaking the budget. Keep some money in reserve for just such an occasion when the time seems right: perhaps a day spent exploring an island by bicycle or an excursion up into the mountains with motorbikes or a trip through the countryside by car. We've tried renting all three and found each lends its own element of excitement to a trip.

Motorbikes

Not surprisingly, this is the most popular with children. Infinitely more exciting than car travel and faster than bicycles, motorbikes are sure to be a success. Rentals are available all over the world, particularly in places like Europe and warm climates where this is a common mode of transportation.

If you have never ridden one, take a test drive first before carrying a child as passenger. My family will never forget the first time I ventured forth on one, terrorizing drivers and scattering pedestrians as I roared up sidewalks, careened around blind corners and drove the wrong way down one-way streets, all while trying to find the brake.

Children can ride as passengers either on the back or in front. Try sitting little ones (6 and under) up front where you can keep an eye on them and they won't fall asleep. With their hands on the handlebars alongside yours, they'll think they are the ones doing the driving, a guaranteed way to ensure they behave like models of perfection. Ask for helmets for everyone. They may be a little large on your children, but they're better than nothing.

Bicycles

A day or two of bicycle exploration is a fun way to see an area. If you've been traveling by car or bus, this will give the whole family a much needed breath of fresh air. If walking is your usual way to explore, bikes will seem revolutionary as they whisk you over distances it would take hours to cover on foot.

Any place that rents bicycles should naturally be located in an area good for bicycling - country lanes, coastal roads, islands. Drivers will be on the look-out for bikes, and facilities able to accommodate them. When it comes to the bikes themselves, don't expect to find anything too glamorous. Some places will have ten-speeds, but these aren't really necessary as you won't be carrying gear or attempting any major distances. A basic one or three-speed bike will be quite sufficient for a fun day's outing.

Ask about child-size bicycles or bicycle seats if you don't see any. These aren't always self-evident. If their supply is limited, reserve them ahead of time. On the Greek island of Cos, we inquired at three bicycle rental shops before finding one with two children's seats, both of which were in use that day. Without asking, we never would have known anyone had them. The next day, for the grand total of $8, we explored the whole coastal area, seeing far more than we ever would have on foot and enjoying a change from walking.

If there are no bicycle seats available, children 5 years and older can ride seated on a backrack. Pad the rack with a folded towel for more comfortable seating and make certain they keep their feet out of the spokes. This may sound uncomfortable, but our children claim they had the time of their lives the day they spent exploring this way. For a child used to walking, the ease of sitting and excitement of going fast will outweigh any discomfort they might feel seated this way. If car traffic is minimal infants can always be carried in a backpack, a comfortable means of transport we employed in the Bahamas when bicycling with baby Gwyneth.

Cars

Renting a car for a day or two is the best way to cover major distances if motorbikes are out of the question. The price is always comparatively high, but well worth the cost for a special occasion now and then. Pick a place to explore by car that really makes sense, an area of interest inaccessible by public transportation or somewhere you want to see at your own pace.

Shop around before choosing a rental. Avoid high-cost areas like airports and main towns frequented by tourists. The more local the clientele, the less expensive it will be in most cases. Be sure to ask about all the different rates. Bring the children and emphasize your need for the best possible deal. Try some friendly negotiating. People naturally assume that families are traveling low-budget (with good reason) and will make more of an effort to tell you their least expensive option.

Even when only renting for the day, don't overdo the driving. Children usually hate being confined to a car for hours on end and will remember the whole experience as being quite unpleasant. As any parent knows, children who aren't enjoying themselves aren't very enjoyable either. To make car rental a treat instead of a chore, choose a special destination that isn't too far away, go there and leave plenty of time for outdoor exploration after you arrive.

Celebrations

Children love celebrations. Any number of things can give rise to one—birthdays, holidays, a stretch of bad weather, a goal reached, a special place, a meeting with friends. Children hardly care what excuse you dream up for a celebration. The event is always welcome and cause for plenty of excitement. Years later they will still remember a place because it was where someone had a birthday or Carnival took place or you had an impromptu party when it rained for three days.

Let the children get involved. More than anything else, children love the preparation period. Some celebrations can be sprung as a surprise or done on the spur of the moment, but most are planned ahead and anticipated with great delight by children. Let them in on as much of the preparations as possible. Due to their enforced separation from the entertainment devices of home, adventuring children become very creative and eager to participate in activities of this type.

If you know you'll be celebrating a certain occasion while on your adventure, bring a few appropriate decorations along. Any trip should also include some basic creative materials for making decorations. The following is a list of suggested party items, all of which are lightweight and can fit in a backpack, pannier, on a boat or tucked into the corner of a car.

Suggested party items:

- Streamers
- Balloons
- Plastic colored eggs
- Cardboard cut-out hearts
- Stickers
- Paper
- Colored pencils or crayons
- Scotch tape
- Children's plastic scissors
- Colored construction paper

Balloons and streamers can be used for birthdays and other occasions. Fill plastic eggs with nuts, dried fruit or candy for Easter. Use cardboard cut-out hearts for tracing and making Valentines. Paper, pencils, scissors and tape can be made into signs, cards, pictures and invitations. One of Tristan and Colin's favorite touches for any event is cutting up pieces of colored construction paper to make confetti. This always gets swept up afterwards and recycled at the next party.

Celebrations need hardly be the costly, well-orchestrated affairs some parents make them. When children are involved with the preparation, they could care less how expensive and fancy things are. To them, nothing is more beautiful than what they themselves have created. Children don't have very discriminating taste, as any parent knows who has let their young choose something from the store. To them quality means big and bright. So be prepared for an inundation of brightly colored party decorations. Children can never have too many decorations and will continue to produce them until the event finally takes place. Store-bought items will hardly be needed other than what you brought with you plus perhaps a surprise present or two.

Things children can do:

- Make invitations
- Decorate
- Make presents
- Prepare refreshments
- Perform music
- Organize games
- Perform a puppet show
- Perform a play

Children can make presents themselves from materials at hand and things they've found along the trip. Favorite presents that surface at our celebrations are collected shells and rocks (all carefully washed), boats made from sticks and bits of cloth, homemade books, drawings, paper airplanes with messages written on them and pieces composed by the children and performed on the violin.

If celebrations are something that usually end up giving you a tension headache at home, let the children take over on a trip. Before you know it, all you'll have to do is produce refreshments and find the scotch tape. They'll have the rest under control and be enjoying themselves more than they ever did before.

Children's Travel Fears

Not all children react to travel with the enthusiasm and diplomatic aplomb of a Shirley Temple. Some are beset with fear at any slight change in their environment—fear of strangers, of sleeping in a tent, of different foods, fear of heights, of a boat's tippy motion or the close proximity of water. Even in the same family, one child might be intrepid and daring, another terror-struck at each new unknown. As travel is full of changes, helping fearful children gain confidence and learn to feel comfortable is important. Fortunately, much of this happens naturally as children travel. The more adventuring experience they have, the more relaxed they become. The thing to remember with any of these childish fears is that they are natural and quite common. Forcing a child into a situation that scares him without providing any understanding help will only perpetuate the problem. By using the following tricks, or others you devise yourselves, to make children feel comfortable, their fears will gradually disappear of their own accord. The boys remarked one day while watching families on the beach with young children:

"Why do parents always try to get their kids to go in the water? Why don't they just let them play on the beach where they're happy?" It's a lesson we parents could all learn from, allowing our children to expand their horizons at a pace they feel comfortable with.

Strangers

Hardly anyone enjoys being stared at by strangers, including children. The more unusual your destination, the more attention your young will attract. As blonds, Tristan Colin and Gwyneth have endured everything from blatant stares to ritual head-touching, culminating in the time a particularly brave Moroccan boy rushed up and kissed Colin on the mouth. For naturally shy children, all this unwanted attention can be terrifying.

If you have a baby that doesn't like being passed from lap to lap, carry him out of reach in a backpack. Let shy children stay close and cling to you during this early adjustment period. Don't be irritated by their clinging to you, or embarrassed by their apparent lack of social graces. They'll branch out on their own soon enough as they gain confidence. Experienced traveling families all agree that children who travel become outgoing, even at a very early age.

Strange Foods

For children who react with horror at the mere appearance of some new kind of food on their plate, play it safe with familiar items until their natural curiosity takes over. Just about everywhere in the world has basic ingredients like eggs, milk, bread, noodles, rice, potatoes, meat and fruit. As most types of adventuring mean you will be doing your own cooking most of the time, serving children the simple foods they are used to shouldn't be difficult. Don't bother insisting they try just one bite of something new. If their mind is already set against it, they certainly won't admit to liking something even if they do. After a while, watching you gobble down foreign foods with obvious relish will prove too much for them and they will give it a try, figuring if grown-ups like it, it must be something special.

Camping

Some children are afraid to sleep in a tent. As no parent's idea of a good time is sleeping nightly with one or two children between you, don't even think about resorting to this solution to overcome their nervousness. If possible, give children their own tent, something they can develop a feeling of proprietorship for, similar to their bedroom at home. Make it look homey with sleeping bags spread out, sleepy friends, special pillows, toys, books and their own packs and clothes. Pitch the two tents very close together with the children's directly facing yours. Spread mats out on the ground between the tents, forming a nice, cozy play area. Then have the children sleep with their heads by the door where they can easily see you through the netting. Putting them to bed early while you still have a light on in your own tent helps. For early morning wakers, have books and toys ready for quiet playtime in their tent. If you only have one tent, let the children take turns being the one who gets to sleep next to a parent. The same early morning technique works just as well in one tent as two if you are firm about not letting them wake you or make a lot of noise.

Hiking

Children are sometimes initially scared of heights when introduced to hiking. I can remember one of our first hikes when both Tristan and Colin literally crawled up parts of the trail on all fours. Trails that are above treeline are particularly alarming because children can see the long drops. Let frightened ones hold your hand and walk on the inside of the path as much as they want. A hiking stick also helps them feel more secure. Let them know that crawling up something or sliding down on their bottoms is perfectly acceptable hiking etiquette. This phase usually doesn't last long as most children have an affinity for climbing up things.

Sailing

A boat's sudden tendency to heel and bounce around takes getting used to for anyone. Some children become scared each time the boat tips, a tedious business if you are also trying to steer and handle sails. Find or make a place where they feel comfortable, a cushioned corner of the cockpit or cozy area below. Make it into a comfortable area they can snuggle down in with a book or some toys, even take a nap. Position them somewhere out of the way so they won't have to get up and move just when something tense happens. With a secure "nest" of their own, they will gradually relax about sailing and begin enjoying it.

Bicycling

Riding in a bicycle trailer might seem like a scary proposition at first, especially if the child is alone and facing backwards. Settle him with the usual arsenal of treats and toys, make the seat especially cozy with a favored blanket and pillow, then have one parent bicycle right behind the trailer where the child can see and talk to you. For children afraid of bicycling on their own, ride on the outside alongside and just slightly behind them until they feel comfortable. This will give approaching cars the room to pass you safely while still helping each child feel protected by your presence.

Canoeing

Sitting in a tippy-feeling boat inches from the water can be unsettling to a child afraid of swimming. Seat the child facing backwards within reach of the parent paddling in the stern. This allows him to see your face and easily carry on a conversation. Give him his own paddle and something to tow over the side to make him feel more comfortable about the close presence of water.

Conclusion

The Benefits Of Adventure Travel

One day, after weeks of bicycle travel through Nova Scotia, we accepted a lift in a camper with a Canadian couple we had met at the campground. The weather had been poor, delaying us a few days in our travels and leaving us in a bit of a rush to meet our ferry deadline for the return trip to the States. Piled into the camper with the bikes strapped on top and our gear heaped on bunks, we covered two days worth of bicycling in two hours. About three quarters of the way through the first hour I noticed a glazed look had settled over the children's faces. The signs were reminiscent of other car trips, a combination of latent car sickness, impending sleepiness and overwhelming boredom brought on by inactivity. In retrospect, neither chid remembered a thing about that stretch of coast except the effect of being enclosed in a vehicle.

Later they wrote an essay about it for school, expounding in the simple terms of ten-year-olds on the virtues of bicycle versus car travel. The exercise was a fruitful one because it led to the deeper question of the virtues of family adventure travel: why we do it and what its benefits are. More importantly, it allowed the children, for the most part unconscious recipients of their travel exposure, to express how they view adventure.

The benefits of a family adventure are numerous: an intimate awareness of life beyond your neighborhood boundaries, an appreciation for other cultures, a sense of family cohesion, the cultivation of self-sufficiency, independence, adaptability, tolerance. Most importantly, adventuring binds you together as a family, in adversity and pleasure, anxiety and exhilaration. Although every family will see things differently and establish its own criteria for what is beneficial in life, these are universal virtues. For some families the benefits will mean watching a previously shy child play with children from another country; for others, special moments shared together on a trail or under sail or paddling up a stillwater. All children will share the benefit of learning things about the world no text book could possibly teach. These attributes, and many more like them, are all implicit in this book, waiting for families to discover.

For children, the question is an uncomplicated one. Even at a young age, children can grasp the inherent qualities that make adventure travel beneficial. Viewed with the candor and simplicity with which they view all things, their assessment lies at the core of family adventuring.

"Adventure", our children wrote, "is fun and exciting and not like anything at home. It's looking back and knowing you can do something—because you did it."

Index

London, 7

—M—
Madeira, 58, 139
make-believe games, 248
malaria, 223
markets
    open-air, 160
math, 212-214
milk, 51
Morocco, 145
motorbikes, 284
music, 207
musical instruments, 207

—N—
Nepal & Northern India, 141
New Brunswick, 135
Newfoundland, 135
New Zealand, 142
Norway, 143
Nova Scotia, 135

—P—
paper products, 47
play, see entertainment
Portugal, 145
pregnancy, 191
Prince Edward Island, 135
public transportation, 254-269
    airplanes, 254
    buses, 265
    ferries, 262
    taxis, 267
    trains, 259
    with babies, 183

—R—
reading, 37, 205
refrigeration, 49
renting, 150
respiratory infections, 226

—S—
safety
    bicycling, 86

canoeing, 121
hiking, 67
sailing, 97
sailboats, 94
sailing, 93-115
    advantages, 93-94
    bathing, 105
    chartering, 94
    children's fears, 292
    entertainment, 111-114
    food, 104-105
    harnesses, 97
    laundry, 107
    lifejackets, 98
    multihull sailboats, 96
    owning a boat, 96
    pitfalls to avoid, 114
    safety, 97-99
    seasickness, 110
    sun protection, 109
    trailerable boats, 96
    with babies, 100
Scotland, 136
scrapbooks, 201
Sea-bands, 110
seasickness, 110
sewing kit, 31
shopping
    abroad, 154
    clothing, 157
    food, 159
    household items, 157
    open-air markets, 160
single child, 244
skin infections, 219
soccer ball, 242
social icebreakers, 242
Spain, 145
spiny urchins, 220
sports, 209
stamp collecting, 203
sun protection, 222
sunscreen, 222
swimmer's ear, 227
Switzerland, 133